Evaluating child protection

Evaluating child protection

David Thorpe

Open University Press
Buckingham · Philadelphia

Open University Press
Celtic Court
22 Ballmoor
Buckingham
MK18 1XW

and
1900 Frost Road, Suite 101
Bristol, PA 19007, USA

First published 1994

A catalogue record of this book is available from the British Library

ISBN 0 335 15752 1 (pbk)   0 335 15753 X (hbk)

Library of Congress Cataloging-in-Publication Data

Thorpe, D. H. (David H.), 1944–
    Evaluating child protection/by David Thorpe: foreword by Nigel Parton.
        p.   cm.
    Includes bibliographical references and index.
    ISBN 0–335–15753–X: $79.00 – ISBN 0–335–15752–1 (pbk.): $27.50
    1. Abused children – Services for – Evaluation.   2. Child welfare
– Evaluation.   I. Title.
    HV715.T56   1994
    362.7′68′0973 – dc20   93–50666
                                                                          CIP

Typeset by Type Study, Scarborough
Printed in Great Britain by
St Edmundsbury Press Ltd, Bury St Edmunds, Suffolk

Contents

Foreword

Nigel Parton

Since its modern (re)emergence as a social problem child abuse has been subject to considerable media, public and political interest. It has been constructed as one of *the* major social problems of modern times and perhaps *the* major priority for managers and practitioners in the child welfare agencies. For those of us who were in child welfare practice in the 1970s it was as if the discovery of the phenomenon had an enormous impact on what we did and how we did it and who we should be working with. There is no doubt that one of the consequences was that we started to 'see' practice in quite new ways and that as a result some children were helped who previously may not have been. However, even then I had concerns about what was happening. In the preface to *The Politics of Child Abuse* (1985: x) I wrote that:

> I had an uneasiness about what was happening to both clients and social workers. I was especially concerned that the nature of the new problem did not seem clear cut and straightforward as was suggested in most of the training manuals and guide-lines. Nor was I convinced that many of the new policies and procedures introduced were as humane as was assumed. They seemed to have unintended consequences which were deleterious for everyone involved.

In hindsight these comments now seem somewhat prophetic. Events over recent years have been characterized by often heated and contradictory debate about both the nature of the problems and what should be done. As a consequence those who are given responsibility for doing something about child abuse, particularly social workers, have found themselves practising in an area which is increasingly complex, ambiguous, where they have to finely balance actions and interventions which may be constructed as doing too little too late (thus putting children at risk, to the point of death), or doing too much too early (and hence be seen as undermining the rights and responsibilities of parents and interfering unwarrantably into the privacy of the family).

During the 1980s in Britain and elsewhere policy responses can be characterized by a number of interrelated dimensions: a broadening definition of what constitutes the problem to include physical abuse, neglect, emotional abuse, sexual abuse, organized abuse and, most recently, the abuse of children while in public care; increased public and professional awareness of the problem reflected in increasing referrals and workloads; increased debate about the most appropriate point and type of intervention including the need to inform and involve the parents and young people themselves in decision-making; a mushrooming of official guidance, procedures and statutory requirements in order to try and make professionals more accountable for their actions; a stringent economic context which forces managers and practitioners to coordinate and prioritize their work but in which it is unclear what these priorities should be. What is also evident, and this may be more unique to Britain, is that the context and day to day practice of the work is increasingly framed by statutory requirements and the need for 'evidence'. The role of the police and the legal profession has become increasingly central. While the emergence of the problem in the 1960s and the 1970s was dominated by the medical, disease or public health models of child abuse, increasingly the problem has been framed in socio-legal terms (Parton 1991).

It is not surprising then that those working in the field of social work feel particularly anxious about what they are doing and the way it should be done. They do not feel in control of the work for which they are given responsibility. There are perhaps three factors which underpin this situation and which help explain the anxiety and often fear which is expressed by both professionals and the young people and parents involved in child protection practices. First the policy and practice agendas have been crucially dominated by cases which have been seen to go wrong and which in Britain have been subjected to public enquiries now totalling over 40. The result is that priorities and guidance are based on the 'work scenarios' where children have died or been removed from home unwarrantably. Rather than day to day or 'typical' cases informing our work, it is what David Thorpe refers to as a 'rear-end led' system.

Second there is little agreement as to what constitutes child abuse. As Robert Dingwall has argued, the definition of the problem has undergone considerable 'diagnostic inflation' and the growth of research

> reflects the transformation of the original concerns to embrace virtually any problem which may have an adverse impact on a child and can possibly be attributed to some act of commission or omission of an adult.
>
> (Dingwall 1989: 28)

What is evident is that over the past 30 years the issue of child abuse has become symbolically and politically very powerful in arguments about the changing role of the state, the family and parenting (Parton 1985; Nelson 1986; Parton 1991). As a consequence,

> scientific research is not a neutral activity: child abuse was launched as a public issue out of a variety of private interests and its subsequent developments have continued to reflect those and other interests.
>
> (Dingwall 1989: 30)

Third therefore we should not be surprised if the knowledge base for child abuse work and decision-making itself is very limited and confusing (Hallett 1988; Parton 1989). The label of child abuse covers a wide variety of symptoms, behaviours and contexts. Child abuse cases are the products of complex processes of identification, confirmation and disposal rather than being self-evident in the child's presenting condition (Dingwall *et al.* 1983). Hence those involved in child abuse work are in desperate need of research tools to help make sense of this situation and move our thinking and approach to policy and practice forward. It is here that David Thorpe's work will be particularly valued. In many respects it reflects a new phase of research which concentrates on the mundane and the typical rather than the exceptional and the clinical which has been the focus of much empirical research to this point.

There are at least three major reasons why this book is to be welcomed. First it is concerned with describing and analysing the nature of child protection practices, decisions and outcomes on the ground in typical child welfare agencies and situations. Because the work is based on a 100 per cent sample we are not simply concerned with the many cases which drop out of the system early on. It is this concentration on the typical and mundane which helps provide an insight into the 'real' nature of child protection work and therefore the way child abuse and what we do about it is constructed in daily practice. He demonstrates that much child protection work is concerned with the observation and categorization of parenting behaviours and the moral character of parents and hence the technologies of normalization. As a consequence much of the work is concerned with the day to day problems associated with rearing children in particularly stressful situations typified by social isolation, deprivation, single parenthood, racial discrimination and the use of alcohol, and not the child who is seriously abused whether physically or sexually. Ironically and sadly priorities and resources are directed at the latter rather than the former.

Second his work is comparative. While the major focus of the book is his major research carried out in Western Australia he also draws on a similar project in a Welsh agency. While there are certain important differences, the central themes of the findings are remarkably similar. This suggests that the nature of the problems I have outlined above and which David Thorpe addresses in a detailed empirical way are of global significance. This conclusion is further substantiated when the findings are located in a historical context. In numerous ways many of the issues identified by Linda Gordon (1989) in the United States in the nineteenth century have changed very little.

Third, and this is perhaps the major significance of David Thorpe's work, he offers a practical methodology of how we can address the problems which managers and practitioners are currently experiencing. For while there is an expectation that child protection should be accountable and that rational decisions should be made as to what we should be doing and how it should be done, the tools available for doing this and the current use of information technology are at a poor level of development. In Britain *Working Together* (Department of Health 1991) requires Area Child Protection Committees to produce annual reports which should include management information which monitors and evaluates all child protection work. The methodologies which

David Thorpe outlines and discusses here and which he has developed and refined in his research are replicable elsewhere. Perhaps most crucially it allows managers and practitioners to take greater control of their work and have greater confidence in what they do and the decisions they make.

Finally, and perhaps most contentiously, he outlines his own views about how we should proceed. Crucially this depends on the need to recontextualize child protection practices and reconceptualize the work and our definitions of child abuse. He sees major problems in the way the term child abuse is used and he argues we should be much more precise and restrictive in its usage and application. In the process we should shift our attentions, priorities and resources to child welfare work rather than child protection work.

Readers will interpret and use this text in a variety of ways. It is clearly a major contribution to current debates and practices and is likely to inform and change policy significantly.

Nigel Parton
University of Huddersfield

Acknowledgements

This book owes its existence to a number of people at both ends of the world. The essential basic funding for the research was made available in 1987 to the National Committee of Social Welfare Ministers and Administrators of Australia, by the Australian branch of ISPCAN. I regard these bodies as the progenitors of the project.

My greatest personal debt of gratitude is owed to Des Semple, the then Director-General of Western Australia's Department for Community Services who volunteered his agency as the site of the pilot project. His support during 1988 and 1989, on both professional and personal levels was the one vital element on which the whole enterprise depended. It takes great courage for senior managers of social welfare agencies to open their records to independent research scrutiny especially in areas as sensitive as child protection. Not only did Des agree to host and support a study which was potentially controversial, but he also obtained permission from the Government of Western Australia for the empirical and qualitative data from the pilot project to be used in this book.

The research task itself was undertaken by Judy Anderson, Elaine Aziz and John de Jongh who patiently sifted through files, operated the computer with Helen Phelan's support and were a valuable source of good ideas and constant humour. The social workers from the Department for Community Services who participated in the initial file-reading exercises were an important resource in the project and willingly and helpfully undertook a difficult task.

Rosemary Cant and Heather D'Cruz worked on the research in Perth and on the book in Lancaster. They bridged the gap between the agency's operations and the scholarship required to produce published work. Rick Downey, consultant project leader on INTERACT ensured the possibilities of the enhanced analysis, at Lancaster, of the original research data. Jane Brazier was a continuous source of help in understanding the local, national and international context of the recent history of child protection. David Mitchie contributed considerably to my understanding of Aboriginal issues in child protection.

Andy Bilson created the original computer programme which acted as the basic research tool. He and Sue Ross enabled the research to get off to a good start. As the study developed, Andy's morning bath (at his home in the UK) was frequently interrupted by telephone calls from Perth where it was late afternoon. This I regard as an extreme example of Distance Learning.

Thanks also to Richard Harding, Professor of Law and Director of the Crime Research Centre at the University of Western Australia and Jan Carter, formerly Director of the Brotherhood of St Lawrence and now Professor of Social Work at Melbourne University. Richard gave me constant reassurance about the basic methodological validity of the research.

At Lancaster University, my colleagues Corinne Wattam, Sue Wise, Gary Denman and Linda Griffin gave valuable comments on and assistance with draft chapters. Nigel Parton of Huddersfield University agreed to write the Foreword, it has been a pleasure working with him during the past two years.

My thanks also go to Jennifer Fletcher and Susan Hubbard who typed the manuscript.

Finally I would like to acknowledge my appreciation for Suzanne's continuing support throughout the whole project. The small child in the pushchair mentioned at the beginning of Chapter 1 has since been joined by a brother and a sister. Suzanne takes small children and writing books in her stride.

1 Child protection

Introduction

This book will begin with a series of images which may appear to the reader to be disjointed and discrete. It will end with the same images and the book's major task will consist of interrogating the significance and meaning of these images for the social work profession. Some of the images are pictorial, they appear on hoardings, in newspapers and magazines, on television screens and on the front of textbooks. Other images are those which are conjured up by readings of text. They appear in case file records, within professional journals and importantly for the purpose of this analysis, on the computer screens of workers, managers and administrators in child welfare agencies.

The book describes an attempt to tackle the problem of the representation of some of the peoples and events with which social workers are involved, in ways which will hopefully enable the creative resolution of personal and structural disadvantage and tragedy. At the heart of this endeavour is the task of developing a computerized means of representing the work of child protection, with a view to creating an information system which adequately reflects and represents professional activity.

Most of the research described in this book took place in Western Australia between 1987 and 1989. More work was undertaken in a UK social services department in 1990 and 1992, most of which consisted of replicating the Australian research in order to assess the methodology's viability in a different country with different child protection legislation.

Origins of this study

In the summer and autumn of 1987, I assumed the near full-time care of a small child while my partner undertook a series of placements with commercial management consultants as part of her course in Behaviour in Organizations at Lancaster. Every time I went out of our house whether the journey was to the shops or the university, I passed a series of hoardings on the main road. Opposite the hoardings was the bus stop where I would stand and wait with the child in his pushchair for the bus. With one exception, all the posters on the hoardings were commercial advertisements. That exception was a picture of a small boy of about the same age as my son. The child on the poster was seated amongst rubble at the bottom of some concrete stairs which were part of a block of flats. The building conveyed the impression of being bleak, cheerless, damp and dirty. The walls were pitted and marked with the indecipherable scrawlings of many children. The child stared directly into the lens of the camera and his face was expressionless, with neither despair nor hope. He was small and thin, dishevelled and raggedly dressed. The dark patches on his face could have been dirt – or bruises. At the bottom of the poster was the name of a well-known national voluntary child welfare agency with the simple caption 'Needed now more than ever'.

For me, even the name of the agency carried personal overtones, my mother had trained with it as a children's nurse in the 1930s and her accounts of its work were part of my childhood memories. Much more recently, several people I had worked with on juvenile justice reform programmes during the 1980s had left local authorities to take up employment in that agency.

The contrast between the child on the poster and my son in his pushchair could not have been more marked, and the image was such that I carried it into conversations with friends and colleagues for several weeks before my return to Australia to give a paper at the International Bicentennial Congress on Corrective Services. These conversations were not concerned with the ethical issues of using children to attract funds (sadly, a painful necessity for some charities), but with empirical questions about who was responsible for the deprivation so clearly portrayed in the poster. Inevitably, as individuals with professional backgrounds in social work with children, the first question was 'Were the dark patches on the child's face bruises or dirt?' The priorities of the professional investigator of child maltreatment came to the fore: 'Is this violence or is it neglect?' The second set of questions then began to emerge; they were concerned with culpability and remedies: 'Who is responsible for this state of affairs? What should be done about it?'

Since there was no clear statement about what had *caused* this deprivation, it was not possible to formulate a set of policies and practices which could address the problems. If it was clear that the deprivation was caused by an identifiable individual or individuals, then the social work remedies could be focused and specific. On the other hand, if the dirt and squalor was a product of social and economic forces well beyond the responsibility of individual caregivers, then the focus of intervention would be on housing and income maintenance policies and practices. The poster however gave no clue as to who was culpable and what would be needed to help. So I was left with a question mark about the professional implications of the image, since the agency which was publishing the poster was an important definer of child welfare issues in the United Kingdom. If this agency was defining matters so broadly, so publicly and so ambiguously, then what sort of message was it delivering to its own staff, let alone the person in the street? The answer to the question began to emerge some 12 months later after the reading of the innumerable case files which lie at the core of this study.

A few weeks after leaving Lancaster, I was confronted with another equally emotive and ambiguous image. This time I was sitting on a bench on a railway station accompanied by the same child in the same pushchair. The location on this occasion was the inner western suburbs of Sydney. The poster was boldly titled 'Child Sexual Assault' with the sub-title 'It's often closer to home than you think'. Reflecting the multicultural policy orientation of Australian state governments, this message was repeated in 11 different languages, beginning with Italian and ending in Russian. (In between, I identified Spanish, Arabic, Greek, Vietnamese and Chinese writing; my initial reaction was to try to identify the four languages which initially were not clear to me.) The right half of the poster consisted of a picture of a child, a picture which initially I failed to notice because of the immediately compelling puzzle posed by the variety of languages. In complete contrast with the UK child, the one portrayed in the Australian poster was an exceptionally neatly and crisply dressed little girl wearing the sort of clothes normally associated with middle-class school uniforms – blouse, gymslip, long white socks and button down shoes. The girl was sitting in a modern, carpeted room in which the only furniture was her chair and a white chest of drawers. On top of the drawers were three books, the titles of two of which were visible – *Wind in the Willows* and a children's novel by Roald Dahl. The books were supported by a teddy bear wearing what appeared to be a frilly dress and a tennis racket was propped up at the back of the drawers. The girl held a dressed and beribboned doll in her arms and unlike the boy who stared into the lens in the UK poster, she hid her face in the hair of the doll. Again my mind filled with questions: 'Is this child a victim of sexual assault? What was the nature of that assault? Who was the offender? What can be done to help? Whose responsibility is it to help? What is meant by the expression "closer to home"?'

There are two different images here: one of a child living in bleak and impoverished surroundings staring into the camera, then simultaneously on the other side of the world, another child living in conspicuously affluent surroundings hiding her face in a doll's hair. Did these images represent the same or different things? Part of the answer came the next day with a knock on the door. A man left me with a large plastic sack, rolled up in a rubber band attached to which was a note saying that clothes were required for 'abused children'. I was given the vague impression that 'abused children' were somehow simultaneously the same as, but different from, 'unhappy' or 'poor' children. The term 'abuse' was not part of my training in child care social work, neither had it featured in any of the research and teaching we had undertaken at Lancaster in social work and juvenile delinquency.

Within a matter of hours of being informed of the reasons for the request for clothing, I was meeting with the Director-General of Western Australia's statutory child welfare agency, the Department for Community Services, who had accepted responsibility on behalf of the Australian Standing Committee of Social Welfare Ministers and Administrators for a research project which was intended to identify the 'patterns of child protection intervention and service provision'. At their September 1987 meeting, the Ministers and Administrators had discussed a proposal that the existing statistical collections on child abuse in state child welfare agencies should be enhanced by including data on the outcomes of the services provided by these agencies. Within a few days, I had agreed to a secondment arrangement with the University of Lancaster whereby I would remain in Australia and direct the child protection outcome study.

The immediate context of the study was provided by the International Society for Prevention of Child Abuse and Neglect (ISPCAN) which held its Sixth International Congress in Sydney in August 1986. The conference made a profit and the Australian branch of ISPCAN was approached by the Welfare Administrators with a proposal that these surplus funds be used to finance the outcome study. The negotiations between ISPCAN and the Welfare Administrators were not however concluded without a note of controversy which indicated clear differences of opinion about the nature of the research and the fundamental issue of 'child abuse'. ISPCAN took the view that the study should focus on *prevention* and in a note to the secretary of the Welfare Administrators in October 1987 the Australian ISPCAN correspondent made the following points:

6 Whilst the proposal prepared by representatives from Western Australia is a good one, it does not address the issue of prevention of child abuse and neglect. This proposal clearly addresses only intervention and management of child abuse and neglect.

7 My view is that if Australia is to begin to tackle child abuse prevention, a national incidence study is necessary to determine the best estimate of the Australian child abuse incidence. The next step would be to develop strategies for the reduction of the known incidence rate, including the establishment of Children's Trust Funds, implementation of Child Abuse Prevention Week (or month), public awareness campaigns, innovative work with the media, and working with the community to reduce the incidence of abuse and neglect of Australian children. Prevention is not only humanitarian, it is also cost effective. It is hard to ignore such features, in these times of limited resources.

Whilst some researchers are of the view that the cause of physical and emotional abuse and neglect is poverty and other social ills, many do not agree. Poverty, social isolation, poor transport facilities, and proximity to welfare and health service delivery outlets are seen by the latter group of researchers and practitioners as the trigger of abusive and neglectful actions to children rather than the cause of abuse and neglect.

8 Those who were able to hear Dr Brandt Steele present the inaugural C. Henry Kempe Memorial oration at the opening ceremony of the Sydney Congress will probably remember him saying:

> . . . we are now facing difficult decisions about where to put more time, energy and resources into primary prevention programmes. Focussing on activities in primary prevention will carry out the purpose expressed in the name of our society, i.e. the prevention of child abuse and neglect . . .'
>
> (letter from Australian branch of ISPCAN to the Welfare
> Administrators Secretariat, 6 October 1987)

This letter provides two pieces of information as a context to the study. The first indicates the belief that 'child abuse' (which remains undefined) can be 'prevented' by means of *publicity*. The second suggests that no consistent views were held across the research community about the *causes* of the phenomenon. The proceedings of the Sixth International Congress will be returned to in the next chapter along with a discussion of the editorial of the ISPCAN journal which published some of the conference's papers (Helfer 1986).

Whatever the differences between ISPCAN and the Welfare Administrators, they were resolved in the latter's favour. The Western Australian proposal was accepted and the question of prevention and publicity did not feature in the final, agreed version which formulated the *raison d'être* of the research in the following manner.

It is critical that a national data base be developed to provide information concerning the incidence of child abuse and neglect, and the patterns of intervention. This information is essential as a basis for decision making and planning and to ensure accountability to the children and families with whom States and Territories have contact as a result of child protection intervention.

National statistics will provide a means by which child protection policy and practice can be monitored, so that the degree of achievement of policy and programme objectives can be ascertained.

The monitoring process will assist with the improvement of case management techniques and development of the knowledge and practice base concerning assessment, investigation and intervention in child protection cases.

(Standing Committee 1987: item 6(i))

The Welfare Administrators were clearly looking to develop a child protection information system which would have the capacity routinely to monitor and evaluate child protection practices. This decision was set against a background of controversy about the very definition of the term 'child abuse', the scale of the phenomenon and the relative weighting which should be accorded to 'prevention' or 'intervention' and especially the question of publicity. First however we will turn to another context, that of the historical development of child protection services in the English-speaking world.

The development of child protection legislation and services

The nineteenth century saw three distinct phases in the development of child protection legislation and services in England, North America and Australia. These three phases were successively concerned with child employment and orphaned and destitute children; baby farming and foster care; and finally the care of children within their own families. The first wave of legislation primarily dealt with the exploitation of children by employers in the newly emergent industrialized societies. At that time, neither Australia nor Canada could be described as 'industrialized' in the way England and the United States of

America were. In pre-industrialized society children usually worked within the contexts of agricultural practices and 'cottage' industries where work depended on available hours of daylight and a child's physical capacities. Normally this took place under the supervision of parents, relatives or someone associated with the kin network.

Industrialization dramatically changed these customary practices. For the first time in history, children were employed for wages in settings where there was little or no possibility of supervision by a parent, relative or friend even though they might normally be domiciled within a kin network. From the late eighteenth century onwards, children were put to work for wages in factories, workshops and mines. These sites of labour were far more hazardous than the agricultural and domestic work which preceded the Industrial Revolution. Factories were badly lit, unventilated and contained unprotected machinery, while coal mines were frequent sites of serious and fatal injury. Moreover the factory and mine owners and apprentice masters could pay children much lower wages than they could adults. This exploitation received widespread publicity in the middle years of the nineteenth century which led to the Westminster Parliament passing a range of legislation during that period. Heywood comments that:

> Lord Althorp's Factory Act of 1833 limited the working hours of children and young persons in textile mills and appointed factory inspectors with right of entry. The factory child was to attend school for two hours a day. This, with Shaftsbury's factory legislation of 1844–7 provided the soil from which all our modern factory legislation has grown, and in 1875 the legislation finally brought to an end the employment of little boys as chimney sweeps. In 1842 Shaftsbury's Mines Act prohibited the underground employment of women and children under ten and paved the way for the Mines Inspectorate of 1850 and gradual intervention by the State in securing the safety and better conditions of mines
>
> (Heywood 1970: 26)

Victorian philanthropists were also very concerned about the orphaned, destitute and vagrant children who formed part of the underlife of the rapidly expanding industrialized cities of Europe and North America. Unlike employed children, vagrant children had no legal source of income, no shelter, no food and only rags for clothing. It was their plight which inspired the creation of the great nineteenth-century children's charities which included secular organizations such as Dr Barnardo's and religious child welfare foundations such as the Church of England Waifs and Strays Society. The work of these bodies consisted in the provision of very basic care for children who were without homes and families.

There was a second agenda for this group which was rapidly recognized by the state. Without shelter or income, many of these children were involved in crime and prostitution as a means of survival. Victorian street children were generally the preserve of non-government child welfare agencies except for those classed as paupers, who lived in workhouses where conditions were generally held to be so unsatisfactory that Boards of Guardians tended to seek foster care or indentured apprenticeships as alternatives. The 1891 Custody of Children Act gave authority to the child welfare charities to offer legal rights of asylum to these neglected children. One of the consequences of this – a consequence which laid the foundation of child welfare agencies in Canada and Australia – was that the charities began to send children to the colonies (see for example Parr, 1980).

Thus far, none of these developments were concerned with what would now be called child *protection*. No powers existed to ensure the adequate care of children unless they were at work or on the streets. The sites for 'protection' did not yet lie within the homes in which children lived with their biological kin. The 'private' space of the family was not to become a focus for child welfare reform and legislation until the later years of the Victorian era and the early years of the twentieth century.

Interestingly enough, these early sites of investigation were not initially those where the biological parents were directly responsible for the care of children. Three examples will be given here – from North America, England and Western Australia – in which three factors were present which precipitated the passing of protective legislation. These factors were those of poverty, substitute care and neglect. In the United States, Gordon claims that 'baby farming was one of the newly discovered forms of cruelty to children that built the SPCCs [Societies for the Prevention of Cruelty to Children]' (Gordon 1989: 44). In New York in 1873, a woman was charged with 'wholesale infanticide' – allowing children boarded with her to die. In Boston, 'the bodies of 30 dead infants were found within three-quarters of a mile of a private "lying-in hospital and nursery"'. The majority of these children were illegitimate and Gordon notes that it was often the fathers and not the mothers who brought these children to the nurseries.

In nineteenth-century England, the provisions of the 1834 Poor Law Reform Act were such as to disbar the mothers of illegitimate children from receiving any income. If the women in question did not work, then they were forced to live in workhouses. If they worked, then they had to pay for substitute care provision. This so-called 'baby farming' was a widespread practice. The *Report of the Select Committee on Protection of Infant Life* (1871) gives the following account of these practices:

> According to the evidence, which seems indisputable, there are in all parts
> of London a large number of private houses, used as lying-in estab-
> lishments, where women are confined. When the infants are born, some few
> of them may be taken away by their mothers; but if they are to be 'adopted',
> as is usually the case, the owner of the establishment receives for this
> adoption a block sum of money, sometimes as little as £5, sometimes as
> much as £50 or £100, according to the means of the party who goes to be
> confined. The infant is then removed (generally immediately after birth) to
> the worst class of baby farming establishment, by which the owners of the
> baby farming houses are remunerated, either by a small round sum, which is
> totally inadequate to the permanent maintenance of the child, or by a small
> weekly payment varying from 2s6d to 7s6d, which is supposed to cover all
> expenses. In the former case, there is obviously every inducement to get rid

of the child, and, even in the latter case, unless the mother should come to look after it (which she seldom does), improper and insufficient food, opiates, drugs, crowded rooms, bad air, want of cleanliness and wilful neglect, are sure to be followed in a few months by diarrhoea, convulsions and wasting away. Where the child has not been brought from a secret lying-in establishment, the knowledge of those houses, to which other children are taken, was, until lately, acquired by advertisements in the public newspapers; but since the more respectable of these newspapers have declined any longer to insert such advertisements, it is now obtained, though with more difficulty, by private circulars, secretly distributed in various ways, through the post or otherwise.

It will be seen that nothing can be worse than this class of houses, or more reckless than the conduct of those by whom they are kept. The children born in the lying-in establishment are usually illegitimate, and so are the children taken from elsewhere to the worst class of baby farming houses. Nobody except the owners of the houses knows anything more about them; their births are not registered, nor are their deaths; some are buried as still-born children, some are secretly disposed of, many are dropped about the streets. In illustration of this, it may be noted, that the number of infants found dead in the metropolitan and city police districts during the year 1870 was 276. The returns made up on the 19th May in this year [1871] show these were 103; a large number of these infants were less than a week old.

(quoted in Heywood 1970: 96, 97).

The immediate precursor to the setting up of the Select Committee was the prosecution and execution for murder of a Mrs Waters, who ran a house for 'adopted' children from where nine children were removed, four of whom died. The Report of the Select Committee led to the passing of the Infant Life Protection Act of 1872. This Act gave powers to local authorities in respect of *private* foster care arrangements. It was aimed specifically at the exploitation by 'baby farmers' of illegitimate children.

A new Infant Life Protection Act came into being in 1897 when another private foster mother was found guilty of murder. The medical officer of health in Manchester had reported that in the early 1890s, illegitimate children were twice as likely to die before their first birthday than were children born within wedlock. The 1897 Act gave new powers of investigation, entry and compulsory removal for children privately fostered.

Ten years later, 8000 miles away in Western Australia, we see a very similar picture. As in the UK, unmarried mothers were virtually compelled to foster their children and work, or declare themselves paupers and enter institutions for the poor. The Alice Mitchell case was every bit as scandalous as that of Mrs West in London. Alice Mitchell was a private foster mother who looked after illegitimate children while their mothers worked. In 1907 the state of several children in her house was brought to the attention of the police who entered the house and found a scene every bit as pitiful as that described by the Report of the Select Committee of 1872 in the UK. The police removed the children to hospital where one died. It was at that stage that the Coroner's Office in Perth noticed that at least 38 children had died on Alice Mitchell's premises in the preceding months. It had been her practice to sell the tins of baby food given to her by the unmarried mothers of the children in her care to a local grocer. At that time, 'baby farming' establishments in Western Australia were compelled to register with the health authorities. Not all did so and even registered premises were not properly inspected.

The Western Australian public were so shocked by the Alice Mitchell case that several public figures moved to set up the Children's Protection Society as a pressure group for more legislative action. Shortly after the scandal a Children's Act was brought into being and in 1908, a State Children's Department was established under the control of the Colonial Secretary. The Children's Department was given powers to inspect premises and remove children from registered or illegally established (unregistered) private foster homes. The fullest account of the Alice Mitchell case is in Ball (1972).

There are three issues raised by these late Victorian and early Edwardian foster care scandals. The first is that they involved illegitimate children and working mothers, what are now called 'single female parent families'. Their plight was an immediate and direct consequence of inadequate and punitive state provision. The second issue is concerned with the use for the first time of state registration and inspection procedures – in this instance of private foster care facilities. The third issue is the use for the first time by governments of the term 'protection'. Even at this early stage in the development of state child welfare services, single female parents, registration and inspection and the word 'protection' can be seen to lie at the heart of child welfare operations. The difference between then and now, the 1890–1910 period and the 1970–90 period is that in former times the focus for action was the private foster home as opposed to the 'family' home. The significance of this history will be seen in later chapters.

In the UK, state child welfare services remained largely with health authorities and local government Poor Law administrators while in Australia there was variation between states, some of which established Children's Departments while others delegated the tasks of inspection to lay Boards or Councils. In Victoria for example the Society for the Prevention of Cruelty to Children, formed in 1896, was the major agency for fulfilling those child protection tasks which were assumed by the state government in Western Australia. In the UK, government powers existed to prosecute the parents of wilfully neglected children as early as 1868 but 'cruelty' was largely left to the newly formed voluntary agencies (in this case the NSPCC).

Like the phenomenon of child 'abuse', which arrived in Australia and the UK in the late 1960s and early 1970s, the question of 'cruelty' was a North American export of the 1880s and 1890s. Linda Gordon, a historian of North American child protection policies and practices has said that:

These agencies, the most typical of which were the Societies for the Prevention of Cruelty to Children (hereafter SPCCs), were begun in the

1870s in a decade of acute international alarm about child abuse. They began as punitive and moralistic 'charitable' endeavours, characteristic of nineteenth-century élite moral purity reforms, blaming the problem on the depravity, immorality and drunkenness of individuals these traits often traced to the innate inferiority of the immigrants who constituted the great bulk of the reformers' targets.

(Gordon 1986: 64)

Interestingly, Heywood in writing of the National Society for the Prevention of Cruelty to Children's (NSPCC) work in England during the same period refers to the 1894 Westminster Act (which consolidated the 'prevention of cruelty' and 'protection' measures of earlier legislation) to similar issues of parental behaviour:

In the first place it [the Act of 1894] underlined the deterrent nature of the legislation by extending the length of maximum imprisonment, but it provided new powers to deal with offenders who were habitual drunkards. Experience had shown that the majority of cases of cruelty were committed when the adult was drunk and uncontrolled and the magistrates were now given powers to send such offenders not to prison but to an inebriate's home, where constructive treatment could be given without the branding of a prison sentence.

(Heywood 1970: 104)

Gordon, writing about similar issues in the United States says that, 'Until Prohibition the MSPCC [Massachusetts Society for the Prevention of Cruelty to Children] consistently cited intemperance as the main causal factor in cruelty to children' (Gordon 1989: 47).

Here we have an expansion of child welfare concerns which goes beyond that of single female parent families and the registration and inspection of private foster care, matters covered by the term 'protection'. The voluntary sector, by means of the term 'cruelty' has shifted attention towards drunken parents. Gordon (1986) speaks of the moralizing and parent-blaming attitudes of the SPCCs which had come to characterize 'the reformers' targets'.

Neglect and cruelty remained the watchwords of child welfare workers throughout the first half of the twentieth century. It is worth noting that in the UK, the focus of social policy moved towards more general measures designed to deal with poverty in the years before 1914. The great reforming Liberal government of 1906–12 introduced school meals, health services and unemployment and sickness benefits. The provisions of the 1834 Poor Law were slowly becoming pre-empted.

New terminology in child protection

In the late 1960s, a new term appeared in the child welfare literature, a word which once more had its origins in the US. This was the word 'abuse'. A number of writers have commented at length on the wave of changes in legislation, terminology, policies and practices which swept through western child welfare agencies during the 1970s and 1980s. Prominent among them is Parton (1985) who uses sociological theories to analyse the phenomenon. Parton begins by referring the reader to those sociological theories which deal with deviance, with that which is defined as 'wrong' or 'abnormal'. He quotes Fuller and Myers at the beginning of his analysis:

> A social problem is a condition which is defined by a considerable number of persons as a deviation from some social norm which they cherish. Every social problem thus consists of an *objective condition* and a *subjective condition*. The objective condition is a verifiable situation which can be checked as to existence and magnitude (proportions) by impartial and trained observers. The subjective definition is the awareness of certain individuals that the condition is a threat to cherished values.
>
> (Fuller and Myers 1941: 320; quoted in Parton 1985: 5–6, original emphasis)

The issue of the definition of terminologies in child protection had finally become a matter for research attention. Parton suggests that a range of matters came together during the late 1960s and early 1970s which effectively created what sociologists describe as a 'moral panic'. These matters were respectively the influence of US paediatricians, particularly on child welfare workers in the voluntary agencies, public reaction to media reports of deaths and serious injuries to a handful of children and finally, fuelled by unarticulated anxieties about the consequences of social and economic change; professional and expert views and interests simultaneously fed into media, political and administrative circles.

Pfohl (1977) times the involvement of the medical profession in child protection to the research activities of US paediatricians during the late 1940s. Specifically, he cites the work of Dr John Caffey, a paediatric radiologist who identified by means of X-rays a range of healed and healing fractures in children for which there was no apparent explanation.

Discussion of this phenomenon was largely confined to paediatricians in North America. Two members of that profession (Woolley and Evans 1955) introduced explanations which included descriptions attached to parents. These descriptions talked of 'parental indifference' and 'alcoholism'. Prominent among these paediatricians was Dr Henry Kempe, inventor of the expression 'Battered Child Syndrome' in 1961 (Kempe *et al.* 1962). This expression was modified once it had crossed the Atlantic to that of 'Battered Baby Syndrome' (Griffiths and Moynihan 1963). It appeared that one group of specialist doctors had discovered a new disease.

In England, the National Society for the Prevention of Cruelty to Children (NSPCC) responded rapidly to these medical developments by setting up the Battered Child Research Unit in 1967. This Research Unit rapidly developed links with the project being directed in Denver by Henry Kempe and his colleague Dr Brandt Steele. For the first time in the history of the development of child protection services, we see here the direct involvement of what will be termed in this book 'the rear end specialists', those professionals who deal with the most severely injured, neglected and traumatized children and who appear to have had such an inordinate influence over the past 20 years on child protection policies and practices.

Chapter 3 of Parton (1985) deals in some detail with the reasons why medical practitioners became involved in child protection matters and became such significant definers of the issues with which society should be concerned (the behaviour of parents, the physical injuries inflicted on children). He also shows how the 'Battered Baby Syndrome' revived the declining fortunes of the NSPCC. The 'cruelty' era was over, it had been superseded by 'abuse', something which was medically if not legally definable. Parton, speaking of growing US interest in 'abuse' cites the development of legislation for the compulsory reporting of suspected neglect or physical assaults on children:

> By the end of 1963, thirteen states had enacted statutory reporting laws whereby professionals who suspected abuse or neglect were legally required to report this to a designated police or child care agency. Ten more were added in 1964, twenty-six in 1965, and by 1967 every state had passed some form of reporting law.

> (Parton 1985: 52)

The question of mandatory reporting proved controversial ten years later in Australia and by the time of the research described in later chapters, it had become an issue around which views on child protection were beginning to polarize, particularly in the state of Victoria.

The much-publicized death of Maria Colwell in 1973 had a dramatic impact on public and political perceptions of child protection issues in the UK. Much has been written about the role of the media in the creation of the child protection 'moral panic' of the 1970s and 1980s (see for example Wise 1989; Parton and Franklin 1991). By 1991 there had been over 40 public enquiries into the activities of child protection workers. A significant proportion of these dealt with the deaths of children whose names became household words: Maria Colwell in the 1970s, and then after 1985, Jasmine Beckford, Kimberley Carlile, Tyra Henry and finally, the 1987 events in Cleveland. Much of the publicity attached to these enquiries focused on the role of social workers as being either negligent (in those cases where children died) or over-zealous (in the child sexual 'abuse' cases).

The steady press bombardment and political comment was paralleled by a dramatic increase in the *professional* literature written and consumed by medical practitioners, psychologists, psychotherapists, counsellors and social workers. Parton (1985) informs us that the *British Medical Journal* created a separate section to deal with the 'battered baby syndrome' from its issue of May 1971 onwards. The Maria Colwell enquiry final report generated 112 paragraphs of comment in its leading articles in late 1974 and the founding of the International Society for the Prevention of Child Abuse and Neglect (ISPCAN) by Kempe and Steele ensured the creation of a journal which was dedicated entirely to professional activity in child protection, the *International Journal of Child Abuse*

and Neglect. The first edition of that journal was published in 1977 and edited by
Henry Kempe.

The interplay between the 'experts' and the media in child protection has been
described by Parton in the following way:

> On occasions after a specific deviant event the media might go to the
> 'experts' for their comment, data, definition and explanation but this hardly
> happened in the period before Maria Colwell.

deviant event → control culture as primary definer → media reproducers

> However, once the primary definitions are in play, the media is able to
> transform them into its own language, based on its assumption about its
> audience, and place it in the existing public imagery: 'This transformation
> into a public idiom then gives the item an *external public reference,* a validity in
> images and connotations already sedimented in the stock of knowledge
> which the paper and its public share'. In the process of transforming the
> issue into popular imagery the issue becomes objectified so that it appears
> far more as a real social problem which is quite independent of the experts as
> primary definers. In the process the media can take on the guise of not only
> representing 'public opinion' and can campaign on issues on that basis.
> Certainly editorials can claim to speak and campaign on behalf of the people
> – perhaps the silent majority. In this relationship the media can be seen not
> just to reproduce the definitions of primary definers but to produce
> independently the news, and in the process transform and objectify the issue
> into a real social problem.

(Parton 1985: 86, 87)

The 'expert definers' identified by Parton massed for the first time in Geneva
under the auspices of the World Health Organization at the 1976 ISPCAN
International Congress. The first edition of the *International Journal of Child
Abuse and Neglect* published 32 of the papers given at that conference. A
breakdown of the professional backgrounds and research settings of the authors
of those papers is shown in the following:

Medically Focused Papers

Medical Practitioner	10
Medical Practitioner and Nurse	1
Medical Researcher	3
Nurse	2
Medical Social Worker	2
Psychiatric Researcher	2
TOTAL	20

This list shows us that nearly two-thirds of those papers were written by
professional practitioners, practitioner researchers or researchers working in
institutional medical settings. Of these, half were medical doctors.

The remaining 12 papers were authored as follows:

Specialist Child Protection Agency	3
Lawyer	3
Clinical Psychologist/Counsellor	3
Social Worker (voluntary agency)	1
Statutory Social Welfare Agency Administrator	2
TOTAL	12

Two of the UK contributors came from the NSPCC and were closely associated with the Battered Child Research Unit. The third was an official from the (then) Department of Health and Social Security; his paper focused on 'Non-accidental injury to children'. There were three Australian contributors, Dr Kim Oates and one of his colleagues from a children's hospital in Sydney on 'The spectrum of failure to thrive and child abuse', Dorothy Gin from a voluntary child welfare agency in the same city and Jean Hamory, a medical social worker from the children's hospital in Perth, Western Australia.

The term 'child abuse' reaches Australia

'Child abuse' arrived in Australia in the late 1960s and not surprisingly most of the early professional literature was written by people working in medical settings. The December 1969 edition of the *Australian Journal of Social Work* contained a paper by Jan Carter, a Senior Social Worker in the Perth Children's Hospital and Jane Brazier of the Western Australian Child Welfare Department. Both these women were then starting what have become long and distinguished careers in Australia child welfare matters and in the 1970s Jan Carter was to make a significant contribution in the UK at the National Institute for Social Work.

In their paper, 'Co-ordination of social work services for the maltreated child in Western Australia', Carter and Brazier (1969) used the expression 'maltreated children', and gave five examples of children who initially came to official attention in the Children's Hospital. Of the five, four had fractured bones and one had bruises and was undernourished. There was a clear 'fit' between the case examples they gave and the 'battered child syndrome' although interestingly the major focus of their discussion was on interdisciplinary work. The significance of the fact that four of the five children had fractures as a result of sustained, serious assaults lies in the *location* of the work which the writers were discussing. Understandably, in that setting, they observed and worked with those children who were so severely ill-treated as to precipitate hospital admission. It is easy to understand why the general body of the social work profession saw people in their position as 'experts', published their work and later began to assume that the term 'abuse' automatically created an association with serious physical criminal assault which caused severe injury. It is a good example of how, unintentionally, certain associations can be created by those who deal primarily with serious matters. Carter's work will be referred to later in this chapter, since she was to become a leading critic of the versions of child protection (and some of the practices and activities associated with those versions) which were to emerge in the mid and late 1980s in Australia.

Western Australia hosted the first National Australian Conference on child protection in 1975. The conference was entitled 'The Battered Child' and was very much in keeping with the terminology of the time as well as the focus on physically injured children. Two papers were published as a result of the proceedings, one by Graham Zerk from Queensland's state child welfare agency, the other by Jan Carter who had by then moved to the National Institute for Social Work in London. Zerk used the term 'child abuse' in the title of his paper, but interestingly raised the question of mandatory reporting in a critical manner:

> There is a large body of opinion in favour of mandatory reporting. As of 1974 only two of the United States (North Carolina and Washington) avoided mandatory statements.
>
> The rash of legislation leading to this situation was, however, at least in part, a bandwagon type political response . . .
>
> No such groundswell of public opinion as existed in the USA at that time is discernible (by me anyway) in this country at present. But in any event, I do not see much point in pushing for legislation that is neither necessary nor enforceable.
>
> (Zerk 1975: 38, 39)

Carter's paper was one of the first considered social science critiques of child protection services hitherto published. Like her 1969 *Australian Journal of Social Work* paper it was concerned with interdisciplinary coordination. However, the paper was based around her analysis of professional ideologies in child protection, a methodology she had developed while editing a book *The Maltreated Child* published the previous year (Carter 1974). An extract from her paper serves as an example of the extent to which she had developed a more detached, critical and sociological stance from that of her previous work as practitioner.

> We professionals, whether we are trained within the ambit of the natural or the social sciences, are often considered to follow an approach which is 'objective', free from values and open to proof by scientific procedures.
>
> But, even within the natural sciences, there have been passionate arguments about their correctness of scientific knowledge and the best way to apply it. Kuhn (described by Armor) has described these under the title of 'competing paradigms'! These arguments are even greater in the be-havioural sciences, which still in their infancy have until recently borrowed without question many of the approaches of the natural sciences.
>
> (Carter 1975: 65)

Implicit in this paper is a critique of ideologies of child protection, particularly those derived from 'scientific' and 'medical' knowledge.

The late 1970s saw accelerating professional attention being focused on child protection matters in Australia and widespread adoption of the term 'child abuse'. Carter seems to have been almost alone amongst writers in developing a critical perspective particularly in respect of the *definition* of the expression (see for example Carter 1981). The second Australian Conference of 1981 was simply titled 'Second Australasian Conference on Child Abuse'; the term Australasia (as opposed to Australia) was used since delegates came from New Zealand and Papua New Guinea.

Boss (1980) details developments in each one of Australia's eight states during that time. In New South Wales, mandatory reporting of assault and neglect was introduced in 1977, the same year as a 'Child Life Protection Unit' was set up in Sydney. Mandatory reporting was introduced in Queensland in 1978, and, as in New South Wales, much of the service development occurred in children's hospitals. The Queensland Department of Children's Services also set up a register of 'at risk' cases and other cases where neglect or assault had occurred on a similar basis to those developed in the UK in 1974/5 after the Maria Colwell Enquiry. South Australian medical practitioners were prominent in the child protection area as early as 1965 when an article was written for the *Australian Paediatric Journal* on 'baby battering' (Wurfel and Maxwell 1965). Mandatory reporting was introduced in 1969 (the earliest of any Australian state). Boss makes a comment on this:

> An early provision in the original legislation was the compulsory notification of child abuse cases by medical practitioners but that requirement does not seem to have worked very well – only around twenty cases a year being reported between 1972–74.
>
> (Boss 1980: 82)

The Community Welfare Acts of 1972–77 created a structure which consisted of four regional multi-disciplinary panels. A register was created for 'at risk' cases and those where children had been injured or neglected. Tasmania's Child Protection Act of 1974 created a specialist, dedicated child protection service, the Child Protection Assessment Board, unique in Australian child welfare services. The Board employed its own social workers to investigate cases of assault.

Boss describes the situation in Victoria in the following way:

> Although not behind other states in its display of interest and concern over child abuse, Victoria has lagged in laying its plans for positive action. Prominent Victorian medical practitioners, John and Robert Birrell and Dora Bialestock, were responsible for articles in the medical press calling attention to a child abuse problem situation in Victoria in the mid-sixties.
>
> (Boss 1980: 85)

In fact the Birrells' paper did not use the expression 'child abuse'; it was called 'The Maltreatment Syndrome in children' (Birrell and Birrell 1966) and Bialestock's paper was entitled 'Neglected babies: a study of 289 babies admitted consecutively to a reception centre' (Bialestock 1966).

Underlying what Boss implies was overly slow government action was a conflict both within government and in research circles, particularly in reaction to a study undertaken at the children's hospital in Melbourne. In 1968 the government of Victoria turned its back on mandatory reporting. The conflicts in Victoria between differing ideologies of child protection continued to simmer and boil over into public view via the media and professional journals for another ten years when they formed part of the background to the research described in later chapters. Boss, then Professor of Social Work at Monash University in Victoria makes it clear whose side he was on:

> Although the Health Department (now part of the Victorian Health Commission) took an early interest in child abuse, it has little power to act, except on a preventive basis . . . On the other hand the Department of Community Welfare Services (the State's child welfare agency) had almost nothing to say about child abuse . . . [this department] is currently engaged in replacing its former image of a lustreless and unimaginative child welfare agency to which people turned or were referred when they had nowhere else to go.'

(Boss 1980: 89)

One (sympathetic) interpretation of this could be that social welfare academics rarely enjoy good relationships with government social welfare agencies which are local to their universities. It is likely that Boss was not an exception to this phenomenon!

Boss speaks warmly of Western Australia, referring specifically to the work of Brazier, Carter (whose work has been discussed) and Hamory, a social worker who had given conference papers on child protection (Hamory and Jeffery 1977). He notes however the absence of mandatory reporting laws without comment, referring rather to the views expressed by Western Australian writers that 'hospitals and other agencies are well known and respected for their non-punitive approach and that compulsory notification would only serve to disturb the fine balance, based on mutual trust, between appeal for help and response' (Boss 1980: 91).

At the time Boss was writing, both the Australian Capital Territory and the Northern Territory were governed by federal laws enacted in Canberra. Boss summarizes the position across Australia by praising Tasmania, South Australia and Western Australia while castigating Victoria. One of his major criticisms of child protection developments across the country was what he called 'the relative narrowness of the specified manifestations of abuse'. He refers to the possible existence of 'a great deal of undiscovered need' and ends his review of state by state developments implying that much more needed to be done.

The concluding paragraphs of the chapter reviewing the different state child protection programmes, raise issues around the role of specialist child protection programmes, mandatory reporting, register keeping, inter-agency work and research. It is an interesting summary of the state of child protection services as they existed in the late 1970s. Ten years later the picture was quite different in a way which Boss could not possibly have imagined: the poster which I saw on the railway station in Sydney in late 1987, controversy in newspaper articles and correspondence in Victoria and the emergence of a new ideology of child protection scarcely discernible ten years earlier.

This 'new ideology' of child protection owed its existence to the two factors mentioned earlier in reference to Parton's diagram and discussion on moral panics. In this instance, it was the interplay between the media and professional 'experts' which began to drive the child protection industry in Australia, culminating in the 1986 ISPCAN International Conference. Additionally, it will be shown that factors internal to the organization of child welfare agencies also influenced the development of new ideas about child protection and how the 'world' in which child welfare agents worked could be viewed, described and statistically represented.

In 1982, Carter undertook a research project in Western Australia on emotional abuse, sponsored by the then Department for Community Welfare. In her report, she commented that

> legislation introduced in Australia during the 1970s and the early part of the eighties suggests a new dimension to defining a child in need of care and protection. These new dimensions imply that the child both develops and reacts; that mental and emotional faculties require protection as well as the physical state. The child is seen as sentient and able to suffer and to require relationship between him or herself and a caretaker . . . These concepts are more in keeping with a revised image of childhood concentrating on children's needs . . . Under this new conception of childhood, state intervention is justified to afford the child emotional protection if he (*sic*) suffers (or is likely to suffer) mental injury.
>
> (Carter 1982: 26)

In making the statement, Carter pin-points the nature of the shift in child protection ideology. She gives examples of new laws passed in South Australia, New South Wales and the Australian Capital Territory which she claims encapsulate a

> . . . radical reorientation of the duties of parents. For some legislation lists new obligations and opens up new dimensions of potential state intrusion. For example, in New South Wales, the Bill indicates that the child would appear to have a positive claim 'to the physical, mental, spiritual and social opportunities and facilities for healthy and normal development in conditions of freedom and dignity' (Introduction Community Welfare 1981, NSW). Thus the trend is for the 'new' legislation to be less concerned about observable parental morals, or tangible environmental deficits. Nevertheless, the 'new' legislation opens up new domains of uncertainty and indeterminacy and in doing so, provides a prominent role for the psychological or emotional experts, who as Chapter 1 has suggested, are the personnel now legitimated to define the 'needs' of the child. There is also an explicit mention in legislation about the paramount criteria of decision-making being child-centred; for example there is the 'welfare of the child' (Western Australia), the 'interests of the child' (South Australia), or the 'welfare and interests of the child' (New South Wales).

For professionals working in the field of child protection, legislation provides a symbolic banner under which the normal rules against violation of family privacy and autonomy can be suspended. At all times, legislation offers an over-arching consensus, which supports these activities, discriminates between what will (and what will not) be taken to court and the kind of resulting bargains which are struck with families. However, this process is not all one way. Whilst legislation has a great impact on the activities of professionals, they in turn can influence potential legislation by constructing a general climate of opinion within the community at large and in the organisation in which they work, about what are and are not desirable parental practices, in short what is 'normal', or 'healthy', development. One of the major problems about the use of concepts of normality is to judge whether 'normal' means the same thing as 'average', or whether 'normal' in fact, means 'ideal'. The norms on 'normal' parent–child relationships in research terms do not exist, leaving the practitioner to draw from his/her own subjective experiences about the nature of the 'average'. Alternatively he/she can measure the 'normal' by reference to an arbitrary ideal, and can assess a parent–child relationship by a degree to which it falls short of the optimal. Or a third method of defining the 'normal' for a practitioner, is by reference to a workload which is not necessarily typical of the community at large. Thus all of these methods of defining normality, or similar standards such as 'Health', have drawbacks.

Professional definitions have a wider scope than legal definitions, so might be considered inclusive rather than exclusive. In an attempt to cover all possibilities, professional definitions are geared towards covering maximum possibilities. They therefore serve a different social function to legal definitions. When maximal interventions become enshrined in law one might speculate that professionals will set their sights even higher and their definitions may become more inclusive. Will today's maximal expectations become tomorrow's minimal expectations?

(Carter 1982: 26–28)

This lengthy quotation from Carter's (1982) report ends on a rhetorical ring. In a sense, it may be argued that one of the aims of the Outcome Study requested by Social Welfare Administrators in 1987 was to answer her question of five years earlier. In succeeding chapters of this book the data will be allowed to speak for itself and an attempt will be made in the final chapter to answer the question. But the evidence is there, in an obscure report of 1982 to the Department for Community Welfare in Western Australia, that Carter had identified a major shift in child protection thinking which could potentially have an unintended consequence. Carter speaks of a new 'child centredness', of 'children's rights' and of the dangers of professional workers adopting unarticulated and subjective definitions of those matters drawn into child welfare programmes.

If the potential dangers signalled by Carter in 1982 went unheeded at the time, a second set of circumstances came into being which were organizational in character and which were to have a profound influence on the culture of practice. The Welfare Review in Western Australia (Carter *et al.* 1984), published in 1984 – and ironically chaired by Carter – recommended that Western Australia's two specialist child protection services be disbanded and that the staff of these services should be relocated within the mainstream fieldwork operations of the Department for Community Welfare (subsequently renamed the Department for Community Services). These specialized units, the Child Life Protection Unit (CLPU) and the Child Sexual Assault Unit (CSAU), dealt only with identified victims of physical and sexual assaults, they were 'rear end' services which saw the most seriously traumatized children after they had been filtered out by other agencies including front-line fieldworkers in the Department for Community Welfare who routinely investigated and dealt with child welfare referrals. The specialized units and their staff were perceived as being 'isolated' and 'élitist' by fieldworkers. In a 1982 report, middle managers of fieldwork services commented that

> CLPU should get involved in cases other than confirmed physical abuse. It was the perception of some supervisors that CLPU accepted only confirmed physical abuse cases and that it was difficult to persuade them to take on anything else. The unit needs to be more visible in some divisions [front-line fieldwork operations] ... Divisions which have inexperienced staff also need more training consultation with CLPU.
>
> (Williams 1982: 54, 55)

In the event, the Welfare Review's recommendations were acted on in 1985. The 'rear end' specialized units were disbanded and their staff absorbed into fieldwork operations. One immediate effect of this was to raise considerably the profile of child protection by importing into front-line operations a new ideology of child protection based on the experiences of those whose familiarity with such matters had hitherto been confined almost entirely to the worst possible cases. The original intention of dismantling the specialist units was one of raising morale and feeding in expertise.

> Within the divisions, a speciality of 'children's protection' needs to be developed. The service should not only take on serious cases, as this experience in the Child Life Protection Unit appears to have narrowed the perspective of staff and led to exhaustion and low morale ... If the government does not decide to implement the Child Sexual Abuse Unit and the Law Report the skills developed in the CSAU need to be formally consolidated, disseminated and implemented in the Department field services.
>
> (Carter *et al.* 1984: 109)

Knowledge about child 'abuse' and child protection practices in the specialist units had been constructed around 'worst possible cases'. It was this knowledge and attendant technologies of intervention which were abruptly released into the field. A research report of 1986 which 'set out to identify the resources required for assessment and intervention in abusing families serviced by the Child Life Protection Unit' (Atkinson *et al.* 1986) took a 100 per cent sample of cases referred to that Unit in a three month period of 1984. There were in total only 43 cases, and they were all children under six years of age (the upper age limit for cases accepted by the Unit). The report recommended more training, legislative changes and the creation of new 'treatment programmes'. In late 1987, at the time the Welfare Administrators were deciding on the Outcome Study described in following chapters, an internal survey of 24 of the newly appointed 34 child protection workers made the following report:

> There was now a greater awareness and sensitivity as to what is appropri-ately a child protection matter and how services to children and their families should be provided. There was a perceived negative consequence to this greater awareness both within the Department and the community. This awareness has resulted in a larger number of allegations coming to the notice of the Department both from within and without and thus significantly increasing the workload.
>
> (Department for Community Services 1987: 14)

Apart from a recommendation for another increase in resources, the report noted a 'lack of receptiveness' to training offered by specialist child protection workers to non-specialist fieldwork staff, a problem of low morale amongst specialists and a general lack of support within the Department for their activities. It would appear that the reorganization of child protection work, and an increase in resources dedicated to that specialism had a mixed reception, suggesting that the 'new' ideology identified five years earlier by Carter was not wholly welcomed when front-line fieldworkers were exposed to it.

In New South Wales, a newspaper reported that child 'abuse' was increasing 'by 50 per cent each year' in late 1985. Vinson (1987) quotes *The Daily Mirror* of 13 December 1985 which claimed that 'Every 24 hours between 40 and 50 children are violently beaten or sexually assaulted. And those, God help them, are only the ones we know about. The real total may be twice as high'. Vinson discovered that this newspaper's claim resulted from 'dividing 16,000 notifi-cations by 365!' Like Carter, he discerned a change in the 'definition of abuse' which in his view 'blurred' the links between child protection as traditionally perceived, and poverty. The New South Wales media campaign continued on into 1986, especially after the opening of ISPCAN's Sixth International Congress in Sydney held in August of that year. Stephenson notes:

> The media reports which flowed profusely over the following weeks thus emanated from the 'fortunate conjuncture of accumulated expertise with an alleged avalanche of reported cases of abuse. Close at hand for journalists was a battery of professionals and academics who could define and interpret otherwise inexplicable episodes of violation of children within psycho-social, penal and medical discourses.
>
> (Stephenson 1987: 7)

These experts were 'predominantly American'.

Within a relatively short period of time, the media campaign fizzled out in New South Wales, but in Victoria a similar phenomenon began to emerge. Tragic cases were described in *The Age* and correspondence columns filled with letters critical of the State's child welfare agency and its child protection practices.

Superficially the debate was about the 'dual track' system of investigating allegations. In that state, the police statutorily shared some of the investigations of allegations and in doing so were perceived as failing to conform in practice to the 'new' ideology of child protection, but preferring an older, narrow and legalistic approach to the problems they encountered. The suggestion was made that those children who were exposed to serious violence by caregivers had not been investigated properly or serviced adequately.

It can be seen that since Boss completed his book about child protection in Australia in 1980, the picture had changed primarily as a result of professionals and the media, in concert, reconstructing knowledge about the problem of child 'abuse'. Underlying this reconstruction was a 'new' ideology of child welfare based on a newly emergent ideal view of parenting and a technology, a set of professional procedures and practices, and definitions which were released into mainstream routine child welfare work and which had previously been confined to isolated, specialist 'rear end' services.

This clearly marked a new phase in the evolution of child protection services. As this chapter has shown, it conforms to a historical pattern which began with concerns about child employment in the early nineteenth century and moved on to encompass baby farming, foster care and drunken parents by the end of that century. Each phase reflected changing perceptions about childhood and changing attitudes towards parenting. Carter, in her 1982 paper, had already identified the beginnings of the most recent phase as they were reflected in child welfare legislation in the early 1980s. She also suggested that there were potential dangers inherent in the new 'child centredness' and 'children's rights' rhetoric. The remainder of this book will, after a brief review of some of the 'outcome' literature, describe the research which explores the issues as they emerged in practice in Western Australia. It will attempt to analyse the extent to which social workers are affected by subjective attitudes towards child rearing and the moral character of parents and show how these affect decisions to allocate different types of service.

2 Outcomes in child welfare research

Introduction

We have seen in the previous chapter that the driving force behind the creation of the new child protection movement of the 1965–88 period was more often than not specialist paediatric, clinical and social work professionals who dealt predominantly as experts with those children who were so traumatized by physical or sexual assaults or neglect, that they required medical attention. Very skilful and extensive use was made during that period of various media representations of the 'problem' enhanced in the UK in particular by newspaper and television reports of the most tragic cases. In the main however, responsibility for responding to allegations of assaults on or the neglect of children remained with legally mandated state child welfare agencies. It was these agencies which carried the legal responsibilities for child welfare matters. The police's mandate was to investigate complaints about criminal activity and where appropriate prosecute offenders for committing *criminal offences* as defined narrowly by legal codes. The issue of the *welfare* of children remained with a separate branch of the state. In both Australia and the UK, state child welfare agencies responded to the demands of the child protection 'experts' and media, political and public opinion by expanding that area of their activities which focused on the investigation of allegations and the provision of services, including legal intervention, in appropriate cases.

In Western Australia, the newly created Department for Community Services which came out of the Welfare Review of 1984 injected a substantial resource into those aspects of its work which were concerned with child protection. After the reorganization in 1985, a total of 35 new posts were created for specialist Senior Social Workers in Child Protection. Other Australian child welfare agencies were already expanding their role in this area. However, the expansion of child protection services did not result in a decrease in pressure by the new child protection movement as attested by Vinson (1987) in New South Wales and the reporting by *The Age* in Victoria. Far from acknowledging the increase in official attention, media campaigns were stepped up. It is understandable why the Social Welfare Ministers needed some feedback about the effects and effectiveness of all the new services which were now being provided for child protection.

Professional discussions of child 'abuse':
the 1986 ISPCAN conference

Coincidentally, the very same 1986 ISPCAN conference in Sydney, whose proceeds were given to the Standing Committee of Social Welfare Ministers and
Administrators for this study, also chose 'Looking at Outcomes' as the major title
for the edition of the International Journal of Child Abuse and Neglect. The editorial was simply entitled 'Looking at Outcomes' and began by saying,

> As we considered the manner in which the Journal might give recognition to
> the Sixth International Congress of our Society, several options were
> weighed. We wanted something which not only paid tribute to this special
> event but also provided many who have devoted their time and talent to both
> the Journal and the Society, an opportunity to share with the readers some of
> the results of their research and years of experience.
>   The theme 'Outcomes' was selected. Several months ago a call went out
> to many on our Board of Editors inviting them to contribute an original
> article to the congress issue of the Journal . . .'
>   As these contributions on outcomes are read, you will recognise the wide
> interpretation given of this work. Concepts and measurements vary greatly.
> One common thread continues to appear throughout, i.e. *the basic interper-*
> *sonal skills necessary to develop and maintain a long-term relationship with those*
> *one likes the very most have been severely hampered by childhood experiences*
> *shrouded by abuse, neglect and sexual exploitation.* The manner in which these
> developmental deficits are manifested and measured vary greatly, as our
> contributors demonstrate in their respective articles.
>
>   (Helfer 1986: 277, original emphasis)

The editor perceived outcomes as achieving what he called 'a long-term relationship with those one likes the very most'. The assumption here suggests
direct causal links between something called 'abuse' and unsatisfactory relationships throughout life. Moreover, according to the editor they appear to be things
which can be objectively perceived and measured in a scientific sense. Brandt
Steele wrote a cautionary note about this matter in his summary paper, saying that

> it is obvious that we need to know a great deal about what has gone on in a
> person's early life before we can attribute features of the adult situation to
> the abusive, neglectful situations of childhood. It is difficult to say with cer-
> tainty just what specific features of the childhood experience led to what
> specific things in adult life. The growing child has many experiences both
> inside the home and outside, particularly after starting school and on
> through adolescence which profoundly influence the development of his
> (*sic*) personality and character and style of living. These are the influences
> that impinge upon all people and can create in the formerly abused and neg-
> lected child any of the neurotic or characterological states we see in the gen-
> eral population, including those who have never been abused or neglected.
>
>   (Steele 1986: 285)

Despite this caveat, Steele suggested that 'common themes' existed in the lives of adults who were childhood victims of 'abuse' and 'neglect'. He alluded to changes in family structure and even mentioned unemployment on page 284. Significantly absent from his list were those aspects of deprivation caused by discrimination, whether they were on the grounds of gender, ethnicity or social class. We shall see how these matters featured in the 'Looking at Outcomes' journal edition.

The editorial, the Presidential address and Brandt Steele's summary paper (all three men with *medical* backgrounds) was followed by 11 papers, two of which were written or part-authored by medical doctors. A further three papers were written by medical/clinical researchers, one was written by a lawyer and the remaining five papers were written by researchers and practitioners who specialized in the care or study of specific sectors of the population. A further analysis of these 'outcome' papers show that they do not all refer to the results of medical/legal/psychiatric or welfare interventions. The following listing provides a summary of the contributions on 'outcomes':

1 'Using lay volunteers to represent children in child protection court proceedings' (Outcome of legal interventions).
2 'A cost effectiveness evaluation of lay therapy treatment for child abusing and high-risk parents' (The use of low paid support for mothers).
3 'Outcomes of abuse during childhood among pregnant low income women' (A comparison of potential mothers who recalled being hit as children, with a similar group of women who didn't have such recollections).
4 'Childhood histories of women imprisoned for fatal child maltreatment' (The histories of nine women who fatally injured their children).
5 'A profile of survival' (A study of 28 children who received medical treatment in hospital as a result of physical assaults).
6 'Outcome of residential treatments for abused and high risk infants' (A study of 31 children in out-of-home care).
7 'Prognosis of children admitted to institutional care in infancy' (A study of the medical and placement histories of 176 children in institutional care).
8 'Prenatal screening for risk of major parenting problems: Further results from the Queen Mary Maternity Hospital Child Care Unit' (How to identify 'at risk' mothers. Limited outcome measures of intervention).
9 'Individual psychotherapy for the sexually abused child' (A theoretical discussion of child psychotherapy).
10 'Runaway youths and sexual victimization: Gender differences in an adolescent runaway population' (A study of some of the difficulties experienced by 149 runaway youths in one refuge).
11 'Differences in abusive, at-risk for abuse, and control mothers' descriptions of normal child behaviour' (A study of the expectations and understandings of mothers about children's behaviour).

In fact only six of the 11 papers dealt with the results of intervention and of these six, one concerned itself with *legal* interventions and two were studies of children in various types of substitute care. What is even more interesting however is the way in which the theme of *mothering* emerges. Three of the papers specifically mention mothers in their titles (papers 3, 4 and 11) while two make it clear that they deal solely with female parents. Paper 2 uses the expression 'child abusing and high-risk parents' yet in the text describes the service intervention in the following way:

> The main functions of the supportive home helpers were to provide nurturance to the abusing mothers, act as a parenting model for the mother, and teach home making skills to improve the physical functioning of the home.
>
> (Hornick and Clarke 1986: 311)

Paper 8 uses the expression 'parenting problems' in its title, but in the text describes the subjects of the research as '300 mothers'. So, nearly half of the 'outcome' papers are concerned entirely with women, while none deal exclusively with men.

Eight of the 11 papers use 'scientific' methods of analysis, that is to say statistical studies of selected groups of individuals located in specific parts of local child protection systems. There are no papers which deal with whole child protection systems and the full range of medical, legal, psychiatric and social welfare services available. This is not to dismiss the importance of some of the findings – of particular interest and relevance in this book is paper 2 which deals with support services for mothers. The authors concluded that:

> overall, this study demonstrates the effectiveness of using lay therapists in conjunction with social workers in the treatment of abusing and high risk mothers. The major benefit was that the lay therapists spent a great deal of time with the clients and, in response, the clients changed and improved even though the social workers spent less time with them. Moreover, there was considerably less attrition for the lay therapy group than for the standard treatment group. The major drawback of using paid lay therapists was the increased cost.
>
> (Hornick and Clarke 1986: 317)

The 'lay therapists' were also described as 'supportive home helpers' and the intervention was generically referred to as 'the supportive Home Helper Programme'. Why this was redefined as 'lay therapy' is not clear, but one of the authors was a paediatrician. The practical assistance given to the women in the programme could hardly be described as 'treatment' or 'therapy'. The 'outcome' measures adopted by this study were related to 'nurturance', 'parental attitude/ belief items' and 'parental behaviour rating scales'. They were all directly concerned with the practicabilities of child care and the internalization of specific unstated social identities ('parental attitude/belief items') which may be otherwise described as the values and beliefs about child rearing practices which are common to middle-class European culture. In short, what the programme was aiming to do, was to enable and encourage women to conform to a set of 'standards' of child rearing which are value loaded.

In this respect, other papers in the 'Looking at Outcomes' special edition also adopted relatively narrow outcome measures which reflect beliefs and values about child rearing practices. Lumped together in this we find women on low incomes, women in antenatal clinics (described as 'abusive' or 'at risk') and nine women who were responsible for fatally injuring children and who were serving prison sentences. The latter group may well have been reported on in a journal of forensic psychiatry or criminology. The former groups are quantitatively and qualitatively quite different.

So here we find a number of different emphases: value judgement about child rearing dressed up as medical science, a deep focus on low income mothers and one paper devoted to a very small number of women responsible for the deaths of children. None of these studies looked at rich outcome measures across the full range of situations which may be described as 'at risk' or 'abusive' since 100 per cent samples of everything referred to statutory child protection agencies are absent from the papers, along with evidence to the effect that child protection programmes actually protect 'abused' children from further harm, injury or neglect, which is the bottom line position, some would argue, of any outcome measure in such programmes.

In Australia, the Standing Committee of Social Welfare Ministers and Administrators were obviously thinking of 'outcomes' in the sense of 'policy and programme objectives'. Their requirements in many respects were quite specific.

> It is critical to know what types of intervention and service provision were provided to abused and neglected children and their families: and the effectiveness, efficiency and equity of those services.
>
> Examples of intervention patterns could include:
>
> - The number and percentage of statutory interventions by the type of harm.
> - The number and percentage of diversionary interventions by the type of harm.
> - The number of instances when statutory intervention was preceded by diversionary intervention and the nature of this intervention.
> - The number and percentage of perpetrators removed from home.
> - The number and percentage of children placed away from home by the length of time in placements.
> - The nature of alternative placements for children by length of time in each type of placement.
> - The nature of services provided to children and their families.
> - The effects of intervention on services and children and families.
>
> The items listed above are only examples, and do not comprise an exhaustive list of intervention patterns. They would be expanded and refined through consultations with other State welfare departments concerned when the pilot project is implemented.
>
> (Standing Committee 1987: 2, 3)

Very broadly speaking, the Welfare Ministers and Administrators wanted to develop an instrument which could ask the following broad range of questions and get answers in detail: 'Why do child protection cases become child protection cases?' and 'What happens in these cases as a result of specific interventions?'

By interventions, they meant legal, medical and clinical measures, the vast range of supportive child welfare services available and the ways in which substitute care services were provided. All of this was under the general heading of 'Patterns of Child Protection Intervention and Service Delivery'.

The implications for research design were twofold:

1 the study would have to be based on a 100 per cent sample of all cases referred to a statutory child protection agency, and
2 it would have to be a longitudinal study which charted the events arising out of decisions to provide or not provide services and the extent to which these services protected children.

None of the outcome studies in the International Journal published in 1986 met these requirements. Indeed, published intervention studies almost always dealt with the kinds of limited samples described by that journal. In the studies where interventions were evaluated, measures were used which attempted to demonstrate the *effects* of intervention on very specific aspects of behaviour and attitudes. This was done by means of control groups which were matched in some way to the experimental groups. The classical research designs of medical sciences were used despite the existence of value judgements about what was considered to be 'good' and 'bad' parenting.

Very early on in the design of the research described in this book, the 'scientific' method was quite specifically rejected and a separate paradigm was adopted. The reasons for this were several. First of all it was impractical to assign child protection referrals on such a large scale to experimental and control groups, since no experiment was actually involved in the study! The central requirement was that of discerning patterns. Second, the 'efficiency, effectiveness and equity' requirements were all entirely value-laden. No definition of these words was offered to the researcher although the intention was to get some idea of the effectiveness of intervention in terms of preventing further trauma in those children who had been harmed or injured. Third, the scientific paradigm neatly avoids the whole question of the way in which knowledge is constructed about both 'natural' and 'social' phenomena.

The latter point is one of great importance for the social scientist who researches welfare programmes, since as we have seen, they are of their very nature thoroughly imbued with value judgements which are products of varying cultural and ideological beliefs about what is 'good' and what is 'bad'. The scientist believes in cause–effect relationships, the social scientist looks at actions which are themselves described in value-laden terms. All vocabularies of action are underpinned by value assumptions. This is especially true of child protection where there is no clear definition of what the term 'abuse' means, a matter which will be addressed in the next chapter.

Problems with the positivist paradigm

Guba and Lincoln (1989) speak of the 'positivist' approach to research and the 'constructivist' approach. Positivism is a word which can be used to describe the scientific paradigm. Of positivists and constructivists they say

> Convinced that there exists one single, true reality, driven by natural laws, open to discovery and harnessing by the methods of science, positivists reject all relativist views, of which constructivism is one, as not only seriously in error but pernicious and repugnant. Advocates of such a view, they feel, rank but a notch above con men and snake-oil salesmen . . . on the other hand, the relativist constructivist, while not agreeing with the positivist formulation, can nevertheless accept it as one of many possible constructions. The constructivist may find the positivist view ill-informed and unsophisticated, but not *wrong* or *untrue*.
>
> (Guba and Lincoln 1989: 16)

Specifically, Guba and Lincoln make five telling criticisms of the use of the scientific or positivist paradigm in evaluative studies. Each one is of importance within the context of assessing such research in child protection. Their first criticism is concerned with 'context stripping', the subjects of research are decontexualized and objectified. The surrounding social circumstances of low-income mothers for example would suggest that low income goes along with poor housing, poor health and associated stresses. Yet these are called 'abusing' or 'at risk' mothers. It also denies the existence of very specific and local factors.

Their second criticism is aimed at the over-dependence on numerical and quantifiable data which are presented as 'scientific variables'. As they say, this obsession with the numerical leads to a situation where 'it follows that what cannot be measured cannot be real'. Quantification excludes other non-quantifiable matters.

The third criticism levelled by Guba and Lincoln relates to the non-negotiable nature of 'scientific' findings. 'Truth', as they say, is 'coercive'. All this stems from the scientific claim that it alone can 'provide us with information about the way things really are'. No one seems to have asked the low-income mothers in the journal paper what it is that they wanted. Could it have been for example that they might have seen themselves as benefiting more from a quadrupling of income rather than the presence of a 'lay therapist'?

The fourth criticism raised relates to the 'exclusiveness' of scientific truth which tends to suggest that 'alternatives must be in error'. The authority claimed by science tends to force beliefs about its findings to be taken at face value.

Finally, the claims of science to be value-free, especially in social welfare programmes which are potentially coercive, are fundamentally dishonest within the context of child protection. The very nature of a belief that children require protection (whatever the circumstances) is a value stance. The basic assumptions of positivist, scientific research in child protection are fundamentally dishonest. It is a moral enterprise.

The career heuristic

What then is the researcher left with? In this instance, the adoption of what sociologists have come to call the 'career heuristic', a method of social investigation which incorporates some quantification and measurement since it gives *scale* to social events, but it also crucially allows for an interactionist perspective to be introduced. This perspective can be used to demonstrate how client careers are constructed and investigate the contingencies which, acting together in sequence, develop specific, official welfare identities. Abercrombie *et al.* define the career concept in social science in this way:

> Careers may be viewed as the sequence of jobs performed by individuals in the course of their working lives. Careers may be structured into ordered sequences that relate to each other or unstructured; if structured, job sequences are frequently arranged as a hierarchy of increasing income and prestige.
>
> The concept of career is most often applied in the study of occupations. Manual workers, particularly if unskilled, typically have unstructured careers marked by job movement of an apparently haphazard nature, though older workers have greater job stability. Skilled workers exhibit more structured patterns. In both cases, peak earnings are usually reached by the early thirties and thereafter often decline, and careers provide little advancement through an income/social prestige hierarchy.
>
> H. S. Becker (1963) claimed that the concept was valuable 'in developing sequential models of various kinds of deviant behaviour'. For example he studied the stages by which a person becomes a regular marijuana user. These stages in the career included learning the technique, perceiving the effects and learning to enjoy the sensations. E. Goffman (1961b) used the notion of 'moral career' to describe the experience of mental patients in asylums. He suggested that a moral career had an objective dimension (the official institutional processing of the patient) and a subjective dimension (the personal experience of the patient). The concept is extensively used in symbolic interactionism.
>
> (Abercrombie *et al.* 1988: 27–8)

Goffman (1959; 1961) makes the point that the mentally ill actually consist of an extraordinarily diverse set of individuals, but the asylum provided an institutional mechanism whereby their behaviour and status came to possess a remarkable homogeneity. In his own words,

> once started on their way (as patients), they are confronted by some importantly similar circumstances and respond to these in importantly similar ways. Since these similarities do not come from mental illness, they would seem to occur in spite of it.
>
> (Goffman 1961: 121)

What Goffman is stating here is that one would normally expect the mentally ill to be that group of people who have least in common, yet the asylum succeeded in creating similar patterns of behaviour and hospital status which have nothing to do with mental illness. He suggests that patients acquire a 'common character' as a result of institutions. The acquisition of this character is what he defines as a 'moral career', those interactions between individuals and social institutions which have the capacity to confer certain specific social statuses which were not originally attributes of individuals. Again, Goffman makes this clear:

> The perspective of natural history is taken: unique outcomes are neglected in favour of such changes over time as are basic and common to the members of a social category, although occurring independently to each of them. Such a career is not a theory that can be brilliant or disappointing; it can no more be a success than a failure.
>
> (Goffman 1961: 129)

Goffman here says he is not concerned with unique individual outcomes, but those outcomes which 'are basic and common to the members of a social category, although occurring independently to each one of them'. The social categories studied by social welfare researchers are those of welfare clients and once client status has been accorded, then client type can become a second status. Client type is not an attribute of the individual but a description conferred by an agency. Client types are a result of decisions made by welfare officials in interaction with unique individuals and these decisions are in turn predicated on moral premises. The very status 'child protection case' is one created by a child protection agency. Without the agency, the status cannot be conferred.

The career concept has a long and distinguished history in the School of Sociology at the University of Chicago beginning at the turn of the century with the work of Robert Park, moving into the 1920s and 1930s with Clifford Shaw and Everett Hughes. Their basic technique was called 'the life history' in which they invited the subjects of their research to document their experiences in order to reconstruct and understand the contingencies which created certain specific social identities. In the pre-World War II research these social identities were generally those which can best be described as deviant – delinquents, prostitutes, tramps. After 1945 a new generation of Chicago-trained social researchers continued this tradition and Goffman's work is an early example of this.

Longitudinal 'life history' techniques are not unknown in child welfare research. Here it is important to make a distinction between *follow-up* studies and *career* studies. Follow-up studies consist of procedures in which the situations of ex-clients are examined when a specified period of time has elapsed after intervention has ended. MacDonald (1960) cites a follow-up study of 910 ex-foster care children in New York state in which evaluators attempted to examine the adjustments children made when they became adults. The report based on this study *How Foster Children Turn Out* by Van Senden Theis, was published in 1924. It utilized 16 specially trained researchers who were required to make judgements on the social and personal adjustments made by ex-foster care children. It can be seen that the statistical research published in the ISPCAN 'Looking at Outcomes' Journal used essentially a similar technique.

The major difficulty with follow-up studies is that they cannot identify with any degree of precision the contingencies which create particular official identities. Rather, they consist of 'before and after' snapshots.

During the 1970s and 1980s, child welfare researchers in the UK began to use the career concept as a means of arriving at detailed understandings of those factors in child welfare agencies and programmes which generate particular long-term outcomes. The Dartington Research Unit has been particularly prominent in the substitute care field. *Locking up Children* (Millham *et al.* 1978) was a study of secure accommodation for children in care in the UK using a range of data to reconstruct the care and delinquent histories of the youths they studied, and asking such questions as, 'Why did these children go into secure accommodation and what happened to them after they arrived?'

At the University of Lancaster a number of retrospective career studies were undertaken in several local authorities of youths sentenced to Section 7(7) Care Orders by Juvenile Courts. This work enabled the reconstruction of delinquent and welfare careers in parallel and showed how decisions made by child welfare officials affected the sentencing behaviour of magistrates. It was particularly the matter of welfare histories and welfare services which became the focus for the attention of juvenile justice reformers (Thorpe *et al.* 1980). The juvenile justice system studies of that period identified the decision-making points in local juvenile criminal justice systems and permitted an examination of the contingencies which were responsible, in combination and in sequence, for the creation of specific delinquent career types.

In the United States, Fanshel and Shin (1978) recorded the careers of 642 children in foster care over a five year period. While theirs was not a 100 per cent sample (they excluded children who were in foster care for less than 90 days and children over 12 years of age), nevertheless they examined both changes in individuals (personal and social adjustment) as well as the decision-making by foster parents and agency officials which created placement changes.

In the UK, the Dartington research team commenced a prospective career study of 450 children entering care in five local authorities in England and Wales in 1980. Their comment on the use of the career heuristic is revealing.

Our research into delinquency and our exploratory studies of children in care in one local authority have shown how children embark on a 'career' once they arrive in care. This echoes many studies in the sociology of education, medicine, deviance and in the psychology of organisations and mental health. Several of our previous studies have used this perspective, for example in boarding education, in efforts to reform offenders or to provide for difficult children; indeed, even in research into social work training, we have found that a longitudinal perspective has been very fruitful . . .

Children's responses to their placements, their emotional and educational progress and their ability to cope with new social roles are very much part of the care process and children's careers in care are shaped as much by their adaptations as by the resources at hand. Thus it is important to monitor their 'career'.

(Millham *et al.* 1986: 11, 12)

The Dartington team used a 100 per cent sample of children entering care and followed them up for two years, recording events and contingencies on a computer. Their expression for the study of the child care process was 'Child Care: The Movie', reflecting the use of a research method which saw career construction as a process or story rather than a singular event.

Other child care career studies of the late 1980s in the UK were Berridge and Cleaver (1987), Packman *et al.* (1986), Bilson and Thorpe (1988) and Thorpe (1988). All these were essentially process and outcome studies rather than follow-up studies, since they aimed to identify the essential features of particular types of career. Significantly too, they all used various forms of information technology to both record and analyse the phenomena they were researching.

We have seen in this chapter some of the limitations of 'scientific' outcome studies in child protection as evidenced by ISPCAN's selection of papers for their 'outcomes' special edition of 1987. Essentially these were follow-up studies of a 'before and after' nature which did not take account of social welfare agencies' organizational contingencies. We have seen too how these papers dealt with dramatically different social phenomena using the same three terms, 'at risk', 'abuse' and 'neglect'. The Social Welfare Ministers and Administrators wanted information about the effects and effectiveness of their services which could be used for the practical purposes of managing the programmes for which they were responsible. Accordingly in the next chapter we will discuss the principles and practices governing the creation of a Child Protection Information System incorporating elements of research (career studies) which identify decision-making points and career types and applying the results of that research to information system design.

3 Designing a child protection information system

The Standing Committee of Social Welfare Ministers and Administrators didn't simply want a research project which could identify outcomes in child protection programmes, they wanted research which could be applied directly to the task of enhancing existing information systems. This was made clear in the September 1987 proposal which spoke of the development of a database and a 'means by which Child Protection policy and practice can be monitored'. This chapter will deal with the theories and practices of developing an information system for a social welfare programme. These theories will be drawn from branches of ethnomethodology and systems theory underpinned by the career heuristic described in the previous chapter. The first section of this chapter will explore contemporary issues in information system design and their rationale, while the second will describe the activity in which the research team engaged in taking account of these theories leading up to the final production of a flow chart which was used as the basic blueprint on which the rest of the research was based.

The problems of technological representations of child protection work

Shortly after my arrival in Western Australia I sat in on several meetings where a child protection information system was being planned. The basis of that planning took the form of adding a set of nationally agreed definitions of child 'abuse' and neglect to a list of child protection procedures which had recently been developed in that State. 'Expert' practitioners and advisers from child protection had developed a *Guide to Case Practice* (Department for Community Services 1987), a manual of procedures in which social workers were to be trained. Essentially this was a 'painting by numbers' kit designed to improve the investigation of allegations of 'abuse' or neglect.

The basic framework for this process had originally been created by WELSTAT, a subcommittee of the Standing Committee charged with the task of creating common standards of data collection and analysis for all eight Australian states and territories. A considerable amount of work had already been done by WELSTAT in attempting to define Data Items and Data Values (Fields and Field Values) in order to collect statistics on the incidence of 'abuse' and neglect in Australia. In the introduction to WELSTAT's *Child Maltreatment Standards*, the aim of the statistical collection was set out:

> The collection of statistics according to these standards will provide a broad indication of the occurrence and nature of reported cases of child maltreatment in Australia; it will promote Australia-wide comparability of child welfare statistics and provide data to assist in the evaluation of child welfare programmes.
>
> (WELSTAT 1987a: 1)

This document defined 'child maltreatment' as

> a situation wherein a parent(s) or any other person(s) having the care of a child inflicts or allows to be inflicted on the child physical injury or deprivation which may cause or create a substantial risk of death, disfigurement, impairment of physical or emotional health or development, or create or allow to be created a substantial risk of such injury other than by accidental means. This definition includes sexual abuse or sexual exploitation of the child.
>
> (WELSTAT 1987a: 2)

Four types of 'maltreatment' are defined in this document, physical maltreatment, emotional maltreatment, sexual maltreatment and neglect. The research project accepted WELSTAT's definitions, which are incorporated into this book's appendix, since its main purpose was to enhance this existing system. For the moment however it is sufficient within the context of this chapter merely to describe them.

> *Physical maltreatment:* Any non-accidental physical injury inflicted upon a child by a person having the care of the child.

> *Emotional maltreatment:* Any act by a person having the care of a child which results in the child suffering any kind of significant emotional deprivation and/or trauma.

> *Sexual maltreatment:* Any act by a person having the care of the child, exposing a child to or involving a child in sexual processes beyond his/her understanding or contrary to accepted community standards.

> *Neglect:* Any serious omissions or commissions by a person having the care of a child which, within the bounds of cultural tradition, constitute a failure to provide conditions which are essential for the healthy physical and emotional development of a child.
>
> (WELSTAT 1987a: 4)

A further categorization of the child 'abuse' phenomenon, 'at risk', is available under the WELSTAT system and is defined as follows:

> Where following an investigation of the circumstances surrounding the report by the relevant authority, no maltreatment can be substantiated but

there are reasonable grounds to suspect the possibility of prior or future maltreatment and it is considered that continued departmental involvement is warranted.

(WELSTAT 1987a: 9)

To the lay outsider these simple definitions and categorizations would appear to be very straightforward and unambiguous. To the social scientist however they can pose serious problems.

Dingwall *et al.* (1983) in their seminal study of a child protection programme in the UK make the point that there are two components to the judgements which make up the definition of 'abuse' or in this case 'maltreatment'. They are both the objective, *physical* injuries, be they visible or experienced as pain by a child, and the subjective interpretation of their cause, the *social* meaning of the injuries which is entirely a moral judgement, an impartation of culpability on the part of the observer. It is not as simple as describing an injury or the experience of pain, it is the complex matter of assigning responsibility. For this very reason, the whole question of the definition of 'abuse' has proved highly problematic. Parton summarizes the problem:

There is no standardized definition of child abuse that has been developed by researchers and accepted by welfare professionals. More particularly the definitional boundaries of the problem have broadened. The 'battered child syndrome' first discovered by Henry Kempe in 1962 referred to a clinical condition in young children, invariably under three, who had received serious physical abuse, usually from a parent . . . By 1976 however, Henry Kempe and his colleagues had abandoned the concept of the 'battered child syndrome' in favour of a more inclusive term, 'child abuse and neglect' which referred to 'the permanent adverse effects on the development process and the child's emotional well-being'.

As Robert Dingwall (1989) has argued, the definition of the problem has undergone considerable 'diagnostic inflation' and the growth of research 'reflects the transformation of the original concepts to embrace virtually any problem which may have an adverse impact on a child and can possibly be attributed to some act of commission or omission by an adult'.

(Parton 1989: 59–60)

It is not the intention at this stage of the book to deal with the definitional problems of 'abuse' and 'maltreatment'; they will be returned to later. Rather, it is important to recognize that the WELSTAT definitions take for granted the existence of culpability in a 'take or leave it' fashion. There is either 'maltreatment' or neglect, or there is 'risk', or there is nothing. Translated into the single, simple 'yes' or 'no' categorization permitted by the computer, then the word is reduced for *official and public purposes* to a simple matter of black or white, true or false, wrong or right. Degrees of culpability are not permitted by this form of classification. Indeed, the simple binomial mechanics of the computer actually reinforce this stark version of reality. Yet it is clear that this final result of an investigation, this WELSTAT categorization comes at the end of a *process* of weighing evidence and constructing a version of reality which potentially can be separately encoded.

Representations of moral categories in social work

The Western Australian working party on the child protection information system consisted of child protection 'experts' and information technology specialists without any background, theoretical or practical, in child welfare. The 'expert' views of information were that managers would want to know whether or not workers were carrying out their jobs as they were *administratively* and *organizationally* defined. They assumed that the 'work' in child protection consisted of carrying out a set of procedures designed to establish whether or not 'abuse', neglect or 'risk' existed. In fact what this appeared to ignore was the detailed reasoning behind the question of culpability, the way in which value positions were translated into categorizations and then beyond that, what measures, if any, should be implemented in individual cases.

During the late 1970s and early 1980s I designed a computerized instrument for evaluating the effectiveness of social welfare and diversionary strategies in juvenile justice programmes which had successfully supported a range of reform measures in the UK and Australia. That system was designed around sequential decision-making in local juvenile criminal justice systems and it focused on police decision-making (to prosecute or caution) and social work decision-making (to make recommendations to the police, courts, or to provide services). Discretion by social workers in respect of their decisions was represented on the computer by the Data Item (Field) Social Inquiry Report Recommendation. This information allowed local practitioners to understand the nature of the impact of their representation to juvenile courts. It enabled the development of graduated 'welfare' responses to delinquent behaviour where previously the moral judgements predicated on the families of delinquents had been their major consideration.

In that sense, the system very crudely explored the way in which social workers constructed the social causes and meanings of individual delinquent acts and interpreted them to courts. Sentences were not then perceived as the immediate decisions of magistrates, but decisions arising out of a process involving several agencies in which social workers played a critical role (see for example Thorpe *et al.* 1980). Commercially adapted versions of this system had a marked effect on reform efforts in juvenile justice. Without the Social Inquiry Report Recommendation Data Item, interpreted in conjunction with information about the seriousness and frequency of a youth's delinquent history, the system would merely have acted as a file and retrieval information system which would only have supported the administrative 'work' of Court Sections and not the operational tactical and strategic management of local juvenile criminal justice systems. The information system was designed to monitor professional, social welfare 'work', something which established 'brand name' client information systems could not do.

Ironically, since 1986, information system designers have been turning to social scientists – specifically social anthropologists and ethnomethodologists – to assist in the design and implementation of computerized information systems which support 'work'. It has already been suggested that the 'work' in social work lies not so much in those activities involving the direct delivery of services, but the 'hidden' tasks of moral reasoning, classification, categorization and *then* a decision about service. The fact that conventional client information systems do not capture, represent or support this 'hidden work' provides one important explanation as to why these systems have visibly failed to prevent public controversy by enabling management and field-work scrutiny of decision-making in child protection.

The information technology specialists in Western Australia behaved correctly according to the maxims of their profession; they asked the child protection expert advisers and practitioners what it was that they wanted in an information system. What they were given was a set of at best ambiguous and vague definitions derived from WELSTAT and a set of procedures designed to assist the investigation process. Both of these general areas of 'information' transformed the essentially *moral* nature of the reasoning process into crude 'technical' and 'administrative' descriptions which hid important parts of child protection work from view.

This was not a deliberate act, rather a result of taking for granted that the moral reasoning underlying decision-making and classification would be transparent. It is precisely this sort of problem which social anthropologists and ethnomethodologists have been required to deal with of late, during the design phases of information systems.

Suchman (1987) dwells on the *planning* model assumed by European culture. She makes a distinction between planned action where goals can be stipulated and circumstances generalized, and *ad hoc* action which deals with the unique and unexpected by taking account of both the plan *and* the circumstances which require that plans be adjusted even if only temporarily.

> However planned, purposeful actions are inevitably *situated actions*. By situated actions I mean simply actions taken in the conduct of particular, concrete circumstances . . . As a consequence our actions, while systematic, are never planned in the strong sense that cognitive science would have it. Rather, plans are best viewed as a weak resource for what is primarily *ad hoc* activity. It is only when we are pressed to account for the rationality of our actions, given the biases of European culture, that we invoke the guidance of a plan. Stated in advance, plans are necessarily vague, insofar as they must accommodate the unforeseeable contingencies of particular situations. Reconstructed in retrospect, plans systematically filter out the particularity of detail that characterises situated actions, in favour of those aspects of the actions that can be seen to accord with the plan.
>
> (Suchman 1987: ix, original emphasis)

If the plan in the child protection instance is to investigate an allegation of 'child abuse' or neglect according to a fixed definition, which presupposes and assumes an unstated degree of culpability by caregivers, then what would be required of an information system designed to monitor child protection activities is that it could give the detail of 'particular situations' as described by the categorizer. Suchman's work is concerned primarily with exploring the unstated, seemingly *ad hoc* rules which permit the accomplishment of specific 'work' tasks. Her criticism of the design of computerized information systems centres around the fact that they do not display this hidden, cognitive activity. They do not represent the 'work' which is taken for granted.

At the heart of the matter of information system design in child protection lies two questions: 'What is the "work" of child protection workers?' and 'What is the "work" of child protection system managers?' The answers to these questions can be gleaned from a number of sources provided that the designer sets aside *administrative* 'work' and requirements. It is important here to make a distinction between the three types of 'work' in child protection programmes. The immediate and most obvious 'work' is that of the administrative tasks of the worker and administrative accounting methods. This 'work' can be represented by the electronic (as opposed to card or paper) reproduction of names, addresses, dates of birth and those matters which can briefly be described as 'case details'. The tasks which are accomplished by this work are connected with the speedy and accurate identification of individuals and very limited attributes of individuals – names, addresses, dates of birth, category of case, area office and the services and workers involved. The computer can display these fields and bring them to hand much more speedily than a manual search of a card index box or a filing cabinet. This is the essence of the 'file and retrieval' client information system. It represents the administration aspects of 'work' by making it easier to keep track of people.

The second aspect of 'work' is, however, absent from the administrative one. Virtually all welfare information system designers see 'work' as being administration or face-to-face service. It is not, since the three are connected by the 'work' of categorization and the moral reasoning underlying this. It is this moral reasoning which provides the contingencies which sequentially construct the client career discussed in the previous chapter. Interestingly Suchman uses the word 'contingency' to define matters surrounding 'particular situations'. If the information system cannot account for and represent moral reasoning and the contingencies which crystallize client careers then it cannot represent a significant aspect of the 'work' in child protection. *A Guide to Case Practice* (Department for Community Services 1987) as it was being translated into computer language merely listed and itemized plans concerned with the investigation of allegations.

The third type of 'work' in child protection is located within the domain of programme supervision and management. The types of question to be asked of an information system might be 'what are current child protection practices, are they effective, what are their unintended consequences?'.

If the 'work' of the child protection worker cannot, however, be represented or supported by conventional 'file and retrieval' client information systems, then important aspects of the 'work' of the system manager are rendered impossible. There are two difficulties here, concerned with

1 how managers currently manage child protection programmes and
2 what tasks they ought to be doing.

Neither of these difficulties is easily surmountable. In the first case, they may rightly claim that their task is to offer support and supervision to the fieldworker in respect of those individual cases *which are brought to their attention*. If one were then to speak of managing a programme (which consisted of investigating allegations and providing appropriate services and consultations), then the manager might describe his or her responsibilities as being to ensure that all allegations were recorded and investigated. In accounting for this work to the agency as a whole, the manager would then simply supply a list or table of allegations made and their nature, along with the results of investigations, in short, an aggregation of the administrative information available.

In the second case, the question of what it is that managers *ought* to be doing would depend almost entirely on interpretations of the results of research or other investigations into what went on in child protection programmes. Sadly, with some notable exceptions – especially Dingwall *et al.* (1983) and Parton (1991) – this type of research has either not been done, or if it has, it has not been published. The sequence of questions to be asked by the manager and the answers to them which would enable productive programme management are generally absent from the literature. The types of question to be asked and the way in which information can be presented in order to answer these questions will be addressed at the end of the next chapter on early results. For the time being however it is sufficient to note that in its review of public inquiries into child abuse and neglect between 1973 and 1981, the Department of Health and Social Security (DHSS) (1982) summarized its findings by asking management to pay attention to interagency matters, communications, record-keeping, clear plans of action and the need for specialized training. Without doubt these recommendations dealt with some of the issues raised by the inquiries which examined cases where there were tragic consequences for children. The nearest the paper came to being specific about the management task in respect of *system* management was where the matter of supervision and resource deployment was raised.

> Poor practice may arise from inadequate supervision and effective supervision is crucial to supporting and monitoring staff, ensuring the regular and objective review of cases, and securing the best deployment of resources and staff.
>
> (DHSS 1982: 70)

No attempt was made to define the nature of the tasks summarized under the headings of 'supervision', 'objective review' and the 'deployment of resources and staff'.

One of the most interesting pieces of research published in recent years was Pithouse's study of a child care social work team which speaks of social work as an

> 'invisible' trade that cannot be 'seen' without engaging in the workers' own routines for understanding their complex occupational terrain. Social work

is invisible in three particular ways. First, social workers who visit people in the privacy of their own homes or see them in the office usually do so free from observation and interference by their colleagues, who likewise pursue a similar form of intervention. Secondly, social work is invisible to the extent that the outcomes of intervention are uncertain and ambiguous . . . Thirdly, social work is invisible insofar as practitioners do not typically retrieve and analyse the occupational processes that surround their endeavours. Like most of us they rely upon rarely stated motives and taken for granted assumptions.

(Pithouse 1987: 2)

Pithouse proceeds in his book to examine those circumstances under which the invisible 'work' of social work is made visible and accountable to the supervisor and agency. The phenomena of supervision, discussion with colleagues and case description ('Telling the Case') are analysed in some detail. He makes the comment that the realities of 'work' with clients are so greatly at variance with 'official institutional criteria' that these criteria are either ignored or discredited. Rather, the worker turns to colleagues for direction. He identifies this as one factor in accounting for the way in which the culture of local teams serves to create a distance from 'official' headquarter's demands and directions. He comments:

It would seem that case categories and formal procedures have limited relevance for the way that work is carried out and do not indicate the amount or the style and quality of work that is applied.

(Pithouse 1987: 28)

One of the zones where the 'work' is made visible is the case file, the written record of events which makes visible *some* aspects of social work practice and Pithouse notes that written records 'are a universal feature of contemporary organisations'. In social work they contain that which is visible and accountable to the agency.

File reading

It was to the written records of child protection social work that the research described in this book directed itself in order to lay bare the careers and attendant situated moral reasoning which are the products of the 'work'. The choice of this particular method of data collection was made for a number of reasons.

First, it was necessary to obtain a 100 per cent sample of child protection cases with which the agency was involved and which were formally and officially designated as such. In other words the study of child protection had to take account of everything which was deemed to come under that heading, since it is these matters which construct the basic 'referral' or 'allegation' statistics which the agency formally acknowledges and takes account of. Cases not accorded that status either because they were not recorded at all or because they were classified as something else were discounted since originally they were not subject to *accountable* child protection measures.

Undoubtedly, many cases might have been missed, just as many cases were included which arguably should not have belonged under that heading. The point here is that the very act of categorization 'child protection case' or 'not child protection case' represents 'work' at the initial stage of referral where the duty worker decides to make a case a case and accords it an organizational status. While it is not the purpose of this book to discuss the 'work' of *initial* categorization and the situated moral reasoning underpinning it, nevertheless a later examination of categorizations following investigation will give some indication how that 'work' was accomplished in that agency. The only record the agency possessed of child protection cases were the case files which were a necessary source of data.

Second, as part of the process of identifying patterns of intervention over time, it was necessary to develop a *longitudinal* dimension in the analysis. Case files usually contain documents and materials which cover a number of events from the time when the case opens to the time when it is formally closed. The longitudinal dimension exists in the record. An added advantage of this method is that cut-off points can be identified which permits the identification of career types over specific periods of time. For example if a researcher was interested in six-month careers, then data would be extracted from files which referred only to the first 26 weeks for which they were open. If one-year careers were the preferred time period, then the cut-off point would be 52 weeks. The length of time to the cut-off point is a critical issue in longitudinal studies and constitutes an important limitation of the methodology since doubling or even quadrupling the length of time for which careers are allowed to develop could also theoretically double or quadruple the possibilities of different types of outcomes emerging.

The third reason for collecting data from case files is that at least it provides an *account*, albeit not necessarily coherent or even complete, of the 'life' of a case as it is made officially available for scrutiny. Quite rightly, the intelligent and informed critic would claim that the case file is an incomplete record of events; it generally only includes those events and matters which the organization stipulates as a minimum record of 'work'. In that sense, it constitutes what may best be defined as official narrative rather than the verbal narratives of workers or clients who may well choose to describe their experiences differently to an independent researcher. Interviews with those subjects involved in the events chronicled by case files or even 'before and after' psychological testing of principal actors might produce very different accounts of phenomena. They would have the advantage of having a *direct* relationship with these events rather than having them presented indirectly and filtered through how the worker(s) who construct files might perceive the rules and purposes of recording. Pithouse says that:

> In this sense records cannot simply be treated as accounts about 'work', they are also part of work itself. Writing records *is* work and one of the many skilled crafts that occur in the office. Like other workers (Goldberg and

Fruin 1976: 12) the child care workers are largely unenthusiastic about this task and scarcely see it as a cherished mark of professional identity. In the Area Office records are rarely read by anyone apart from the practitioner, who typically does not view them as a relevant source of information about her (*sic*) own skills and practices. Instead, the records stand as a potential resource for indicating practices in specific circumstances and do not routinely contribute to the assessment of unobserved intervention in the lives of consumers by the workers

(Pithouse 1987: 33–34)

So here we have a resource, a source of data which tells a story, delivers a chronicle, whose major task is to justify and indicate 'practices in specific circumstances'. These files all relate to individuals, not in an abstracted and isolated sense, but within the terms and conditions which the agency (not usually articulated) 'sees' its role. Garfinkel (1974) in describing clinic records suggests that they represent a kind of 'contract' which does not describe either what should have happened (and didn't happen) but what is written in accordance with the unspoken notion of what the clinic could and could not do and what the patient could or could not do.

Folder contents are assembled against the contingent need, by some clinic member, to construct a potential or a past course of transactions between the clinic and the patient as a 'case', and thereby as an instance of a therapeutic contract, frequently in the interests of justifying an actual or potential course of actions between clinic persons and patients. Hence, whatever their diversity, a folder's contents can be read without incongruity by a clinic member if, in much the same way as a lawyer 'makes the brief', the clinic member 'makes a case' from the fragmented remains *in the course* of having to read into documents their relevance for each other as an account of legitimate clinic activity.

(Garfinkel 1974: 123, original emphasis)

Many social work practitioners will smile at the title of Garfinkel's paper quoted above ('"Good" organisational reasons for "bad" clinic records'). The point of the paper is that no matter what the brevity or shortcomings of the record, the member–reader can 'make' a case, and the case is made by understanding what the outsider, the non-member cannot see, namely, the situated moral reasoning. Take for example the reasons given for closing cases. If the statement in a case record was 'there is nothing more to be done' it could mean one of several things:

1 The agency has fulfilled *all* of its unstated contractual obligations.
2 The 'problems' exhibited by the case lie outside the remit of the agency.
3 The client refuses service.
4 The client wants service, but cannot be given it.
5 The client disappears.

With the exception of the last reason on the list, all the other reasons, whether alone or in combination with others, can be gleaned from surrounding contextual information – a letter, a note from an interview, a telephone call or a memorandum. The task of 'making a case' is accomplished by the researcher who reads the file as a chronicle, an 'official narrative' as if he or she were a member of the organization. Case records are a vast source of untapped data for the social work researcher.

In Western Australia, two types of file reading took place, each one of which was used to serve a different purpose. The first file reading was done solely to obtain information about child protection case careers and the contingencies which created them. The second was to apply the findings from this pilot study to a 100 per cent sample of cases drawn from across the state.

The pilot 'career' study was located in three of Western Australia's Department for Community Services Area offices and it commenced in March 1988. Workers in each of these offices were asked to identify *all new* child protection cases which came into the office between 1 January and 31 March 1987, that is, cases which theoretically could have been open or opened and closed or opened, closed and reopened over a 52 week period. All the case records were then collected together in one room and read by myself and a research officer. In the first office, a lengthy list of relevant Data Items and Data Values (Fields and Field Values) were drawn up incorporating both the WELSTAT Data Items (see Appendix) and then the decisions which were made by workers in respect of ceasing, allocating, increasing or reducing services. In addition a separate list was drawn up about the types of service supplied, including those where the agency took legal action. The first round of file reading in the first office (50 records) produced a diagram (Figure 4.1) which included six separate areas which, while not necessarily common to *all* cases, gave some indication of the zones of activity in sequence. The sequence of events was:

1 an allegation;
2 an investigation;
3 the reported result of an investigation;
4 a decision to allocate services to some cases and not to others;
5 a decision to close a case;
6 events which occurred at any time between 1 and 4 above (e.g. the use of legal powers, police involvement, further harm or injury etc.).

In the second area office, a further 50 records were read and an attempt was made to fit them into the zones of activity and sequences of events listed above. Modifications were made to the list and a flow chart was created which diagrammatically illustrated the child protection process. The modifications were threefold and related to details about the reported results of investigations and the variety of services. The second list had the same six events, but more details with regard to three of them:

1 an allegation;
2 an investigation;

3 the reported result of an investigation;
   – harms or injuries sustained by children;
   – actions believed to be responsible for those harms or injuries;
   – person believed responsible;
   – person believed responsible's relationship to the child;
4 a decision to allocate services to some cases and not to others;
   – the child enters care during or very shortly after the investigation;
   – the child receives home-based services;
   – the child receives home-based services but a crisis occurs during the 52 week period which results in admission to care;
5 a decision to close a case;
6 events which occurred at any time between 1 and 4 above (e.g. the use of legal powers, police involvement) including the possibility of Registration in other Australian States, further harm or injury, further child protection episodes etc.).

The changes to three of the zones were made for different reasons. In the reported results of an investigation zone it was decided very early on to incorporate 'the principle of specificity' and break down the expressions 'abuse' and 'neglect' into very specific harms or injuries and the specific action that caused them. This was done partly to guard against what Dingwall (1989) has called 'diagnostic inflation', since from the file readings it was clear by then that the term 'abuse' covered an enormous range of mishaps and more actually or potentially dangerous events. Similarly, the term 'neglect' was used (as a classificatory device) to describe what appears to be relatively minor caregivers' shortcomings.

The term 'perpetrator' was dropped at the suggestion of the Research Officer. He had been an 'expert' who had worked in a specialized 'child sexual abuse' facility and had extensive experience of dealing with children who had been severely traumatized as a result of sexual assaults. His assumption initially was that all child protection matters were equally serious and had been expecting to read records filled with accounts of desperately unhappy children and wilfully violent or exploitative adults. He had been happy enough originally to bandy the word 'perpetrator' around, but the realities represented by the cases he and I read pointed to completely different situations in most cases. It was at his suggestion that the expression 'person believed responsible' was adopted.

The 'principle of specificity' was incorporated as a result of the experience of past research in juvenile justice (see for example Thorpe, 1982). During one era of moral panic about delinquency in the UK, many social workers had assumed that all 'delinquents' constituted serious and dangerous threats to members of the public and made decisions to recommend care or custodial sentences based on that assumption. Subsequent research which detailed the delinquent activities in which these youths were involved revealed that less than 20 per cent of those sentenced to care could have been potentially dangerous and that the bulk of offending was primarily minor theft or damage to property (Thorpe *et al.* 1980).

This research had been of considerable significance in changing the responses of social workers to juvenile offenders.

Zone 6, which dealt with 'other events', was to be used for the purposes of legal and administrative matters. This was important for three reasons. First, a range of events could occur at any time between the beginning and end of a child protection episode. This included the work of other agencies involved in child protection – medical services, the police and courts to name but three. Second, there are eight varieties of child protection legislation in Australia, each state has a range of different statutes, procedures and cooperative arrangements. In Western Australia for example there was and still is no system of registration. In other states and the UK however, the register often forms the basic source of local and national knowledge about child protection. Registration can occur at any time during the life of a case, as can the use of any legal powers. Third, significant outcome measures such as further harm, injury or neglect could occur at any time during an episode.

The final pilot file reading took place in the third area office where another 100 per cent sample of child protection cases was looked at in detail in order to ensure that the career flow chart under development matched the range and variety of existing cases. This final reading resulted in some very minor changes under each zone. A systems analyst then joined the research team to refine the flow chart and simplify it so it could become a tool around which to build the main research.

The flow chart was a blueprint which guided the design of the survey form to be completed by file readers during the main study and provided a structure round which the computer programme could be built. Essentially, it provided a means by which cases could be classified into career types and details of the contingencies surrounding career development could be recorded and linked to other matters such as ethnicity and gender. In effect, it was a 'heuristic device', a means by which relationships could be traced and discovered outside the textual record. It was a very basic and essential requirement of the overall research strategy which was to develop a means by which the outcomes of child protection services could be routinely monitored and evaluated. After the flow chart was drawn up and tested, the project was ready to move on to the next, substantive phase, namely the collection of data from a 100 per cent sample of cases and the preliminary analysis of the data, which will be the subject of the next chapter.

4 Early results

Once the flow chart had been created and tested in the pilot phase of the study, a survey sheet was designed which incorporated its major features. This chapter will begin with an outline of the flow chart and then describe the tasks of data collection and analysis, including some of the early results from Western Australia compared with those of a Welsh local authority where a very similar methodology was used.

Charting outcomes

Figure 4.1 is a basic career flow chart which contains all the very basic essentials of child protection careers. It is capable of a considerable amount of expansion depending on the nature of the research or monitoring exercise required of it. Fundamentally it allows for five basic career types, each one of which can be elaborated, since they can be further divided into a range of subcareers. The five career types are:

1 Not substantiated after investigation.
2 Substantiated or 'at risk', case closed without service and with no further action.
3 Child/family receives home-based services.
4 Child/family begins with home-based services but admission to care becomes necessary.
5 Child enters care either during the investigation or very shortly afterwards.

These constitute the fundamental outcomes of the child protection service, since they represent single, exclusive career types. The third set of pilot file reading showed that it was possible to fit every case into one of these categories. The flow chart also fits the INPUT–PROCESS–OUTCOME sequence used by systems analysts to represent the ways in which organizational products are constructed (see for example Thorpe and Thorpe 1992). In the social welfare sphere, these products are (as has been noted before) client careers.

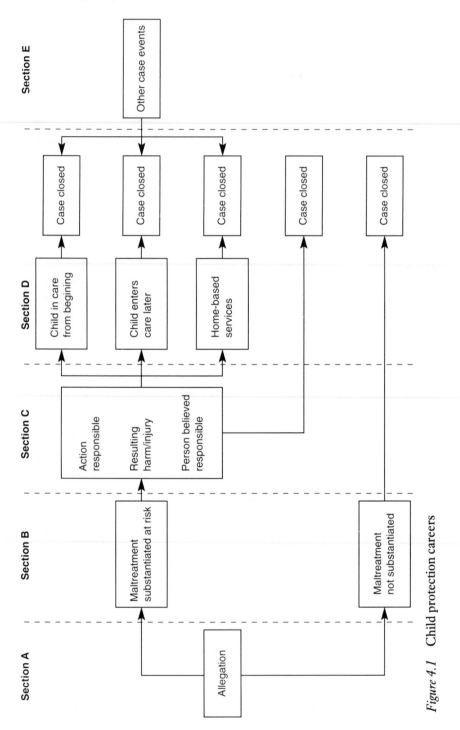

Figure 4.1 Child protection careers

INPUTS in Section A are the allegation/s from a particular source about a particular child, living in particular circumstances, having an age, gender and ethnicity.

PROCESSES are the services of investigation, categorization (situated moral reasoning) and the decisions to provide service or close cases (Sections B–D and some of E).

OUTCOMES are the five client careers and some of the events listed in Section E such as further harm or injury, the use of legal powers, medical services and police activity. These are rich and varied outcome measures which can potentially be expanded to include for example the effects and effectiveness of specific therapeutic interventions in specific cases.

The important thing to bear in mind when considering outcomes is that both qualitative and/or quantitative measures can be applied depending on the nature of the research. Not only that, but just as importantly, it becomes possible to compare 'like with like' within the context of the career dimension. Children receiving or not receiving services, of similar ages who have been victims of similar acts of 'abuse' or neglect can be compared with each other in a number of ways.

Figure 4.1 is a diagram of *one* complete child protection episode (from case opening to case closing). Section A provides information about the source and nature of allegations and gives details of the child concerned, the context in which the allegation was made and the situation in which the child was living.

Section B widely classifies the result of the investigation into substantiation type. This includes the 'at risk' categorization as well as substantiated neglect and emotional, physical or sexual 'abuse'. Cases not substantiated are categorized here along with those where no investigation was possible. This section supplies what Suchman (1987) refers to as a 'weak resource' in describing *ad hoc* and complex unique events and situations. It permits an early, crude categorization primarily as an aid to analysis rather than as a way of describing the world.

Section C supplies the detail absent from Section B about the results of investigations where 'abuse' or neglect has been substantiated. It incorporates the principle of specificity as outlined earlier about the nature of harms or injuries and the actions or inactions which caused them, as well as details about the persons believed responsible when they were known.

Section D describes the services which were made available by government or non-government child welfare services. It charts aspects of 'service' careers. This section also deals with the reasons for closing cases (if they closed during the 52 week time period).

Section E details those events which may or may not have occurred during the episode at any time from beginning to end. This includes the use of legal powers, the nature of police involvement, medical services and further harm or injury. It was also used to indicate whether or not, subsequent to case closure, there were more child protection episodes during the succeeding 52 weeks of the study.

Construction of the study: surveys and software

After the pilot file readings and the construction of the career flow chart, a survey form was drawn up which was the instrument to be applied to the main study. The aim was to enter all the details where possible of every child protection case in the state on a form after reading the file. The procedure was as follows:

1 Read the file.
2 Record information from the file on the survey form which captured all the information required in the career flow chart (Figure 4.1).
3 Enter every case onto a computer.

The Data Items, Data Values and their definitions used in the survey form were modified and are contained in the Appendix.

The selection of software for this research presented few problems. Most research of this nature would normally use the Statistical Package for Social Scientists (SPSS), but in the circumstances of the study it was decided not to use it for a number of reasons. First, SPSS was not then user friendly; the frequency and cross-tabulation routines required a lot of familiarity with computers and there was no time to teach the research team – who were social workers – the necessary skills.

Second, for the purposes of developing an information system as a practical tool to be used by area, regional and headquarters managers, it was out of the question. Over the years I have seen many social welfare agency managers delegating all tasks connected with information systems to information technology specialists or research staff. This has usually had two consequences. The first was that managers distanced themselves from data, they either rarely asked questions or asked the wrong questions. The information technology specialists then produced volumes of tables which occupied shelf space and served an entirely symbolic function – they supported the illusion of management. The second was that this way of tackling (or not tackling) the problem gave power to information technology specialists which they often did not merit either because they had no background in social science or social work, or, even if they did, they were only familiar with one or two proprietary brand hardware and/or software systems which formed the client information system. It was important to establish from the very beginning that this was a system which not only *could* be, but *would* be used hands on by managers without resource to intermediaries who spoke impossible languages.

The most useful software with which I was familiar at that time was MPSS (Monitoring Package for Social Systems) which had been written originally by Andy Bilson for the evaluation of the Juvenile Liaison Bureau in Northamptonshire in 1981–4, to my specification. The advantage of this programme was that it consisted of a database wedded to a 'report generator' which could produce an infinite number of frequency and two or three way cross-tabulations. It also had the facility to add new fields and select groups of records. Andy Bilson came out to Perth to make the necessary changes to the programme and it became the basic analytical tool used by the research team.

The sample consisted of *all* child protection cases referred to the Department for Community Services in Western Australia between 1 March and 30 June 1987. The intention was to read all the files, recording events during the succeeding 52 weeks. Initially all appropriate records in the Perth/Fremantle metropolitan area were brought to a central point in the city and the files read by the research team and experienced social work, child protection and research staff from the agency. Each file was read twice by two readers and file readers were rotated twice over the two-day exercise in order to reduce bias. In addition, photocopies were made of all critical documents on file for the qualitative analysis. The completed survey forms and attendant copies of file material were then numbered, read twice again by the research team and then entered on MPSS computer file. This exercise produced 277 cases which were used as the basis for a preliminary report for the Department for Community Services. After the first 70 cases were entered on computer, the distribution of career types stabilized and then remained constant. It was rather like watching a very practical way of demonstrating statistical significance.

After this, visits were made to the non-metropolitan area offices across the state and the exercise was repeated until data from all 20 of the state's area offices were recorded on the survey sheet and entered on computer file. The research team spent a lot of time sifting and sorting through the photocopied text in order to develop an understanding of why particular child protection careers developed in particular ways.

After the analysis, a final report was written for the Standing Committee of Social Welfare Ministers and Administrators entitled *Patterns of Child Protection Intervention and Service Delivery* (Thorpe 1989). An abbreviated and edited version of this was published by the Crime Research Centre, University of Western Australia in 1991 (Thorpe 1991). The original version contained a lot of material which dealt with the differences between states, so that their existing systems could be enhanced by the results of the research in Western Australia. At their April 1989 annual conference, the Standing Committee resolved to adopt the recommendations of the report.

In those original publications (Thorpe 1989, 1991), the research was based on a total sample of 672 cases – that being the number of what were then believed to be single, exclusive cases of child protection referred to the Department during 1 March to 30 June 1987 period. However, a decision was made to re-enter all the cases using the survey forms and the photocopied file text material after my return to Lancaster to resume my normal academic duties. The main reasons for this were that in the course of the research project I wished to change some of the Fields and Field Values specified on the survey form (see the appendix) and because the Department for Community Services had successfully written a new computer programme, based on MPSS, which was much easier to use in terms of having a relational database and easier Field and Field Value deletion and add-on features (INTERACT). The changes in Fields and Field Values came about as a result of consultations with child protection programme managers and researchers in the eight Australian states which I visited during the writing up of the final report. A second influence came from my colleagues at the University of Lancaster.

After the records were re-entered, the indexing facility of INTERACT was used to reorder the database in alphabetical sequence, an exercise which was not possible on MPSS. This reordering resulted in the identification of a number of cases which had been inadvertently entered twice on the original MPSS database. Several cases showed up simultaneously in two area offices and had been counted twice because there were slight differences in the spelling of names. Since data was often collected separately, no link had been established between them. Other cases were entered twice when they were in fact second episodes in area offices different from those of first episodes. For example a case might have been opened and closed in one area, then several weeks later it might reappear hundreds of miles away and the social workers dealing with the case would not necessarily have been aware of its history. At the time of the research the Department for Community Services did not have a computerized child protection information system, so double counting could not always be avoided. After deleting 17 duplicate entries, the final sample size used for the analysis in this book was 655 individual children referred to the Department for Community Services between 1 March and 30 June 1987.

In September 1990 agreement was reached between a Welsh local authority and the University of Lancaster to conduct a limited study of specific aspects of their child protection operation, specifically the issue of 'parental participation' in child protection services arising out of the 1989 Children's Act. A retrospective 100 per cent sample was used (the first 100 child protection cases referred to that department after 1 January 1990. The methodology deployed was essentially the same as that used in Western Australia with some enhancements, especially in respect of parental participation at each stage of the process. The basic career flow chart was used with little modification in order to ascertain outcomes. Because of difficulties in identifying those 100 cases, the maximum length of time allowed for career development in that study was nine months as opposed to the 12 months of the Western Australian research. The relevant 100 case files were gathered together in one location and read by the University Researcher, Gary Denman and experienced child protection staff from the agency. A survey form based on the flow chart was completed for each file and database reflecting that form created on INTERACT. Data from the survey forms was then entered on computer file. Simultaneously, photocopies of relevant file text were made for the purposes of the detailed qualitative evaluation of issues surrounding parental participation.

Early results

We will now turn to the early results of the Western Australian study and compare it, where appropriate, with the Welsh local authority.

During the analysis phase of the Australian research, I took the opportunity of inviting a number of senior executive members of the Department for Community Services to the office from where the research was being conducted. They were asked to formulate a sequence of questions about the child protection programme. Very generally each executive came up with similar questions

Table 4.1 Allegations in Western Australia

Allegation	Nos	%
Physical abuse	147	22.5
Emotional abuse	14	2
Sexual abuse	143	22
Neglect	309	47
Unclear	42	6.5
Totals	655	100

although not necessarily in the same order. These questions, after some prompting and discussion, could be reduced to the four following questions:

1 What allegations were made?
2 What were the results of the investigations?
3 What were the contexts in which the allegations were made and how did this affect the results of investigations?
4 What happened after investigations?

Seven tables were then produced in an attempt to answer the questions. They will be compared with corresponding six tables from the Welsh Authority.

As shown in Table 4.1, nearly one half (47 per cent) of the allegations in Western Australia were concerned with neglect. Physical and sexual 'abuse' accounted for a further 44 per cent of allegations (approximately 22 per cent each). Very crudely speaking, allegations then were one-half neglect and a quarter each physical and sexual 'abuse' respectively.

In the Welsh local authority, the pattern of allegations shown in Table 4.2 was quite different, even allowing for the difference in classification with Table 4.1. Grave concern (ii) is a Department of Health classification and physical abuse/neglect and sexual abuse/neglect are combined categories which account for 11 (11 per cent) of cases. The biggest difference between Western Australia and Wales lies in the physical abuse and neglect categories.

Table 4.2 Allegations in a Welsh local authority

Allegation	Nos	%
Physical abuse	40	40
Sexual abuse	23	23
Neglect	26	26
Grave concern (ii)	4	4
Physical abuse/neglect	5	5
Sexual abuse/neglect	2	2
Totals	100	100

Table 4.3   Substantiation in Western Australia

Substantiation	Nos	%
Not substantiated	262	40
No investigation possible	41	6
'At risk'	109	16.5
Neglect	91	14
Emotional abuse	10	1.5
Physical abuse	50	8
Sexual abuse	65	10
Unknown	27	4
Totals	655	100

Table 4.3 shows that not substantiated, no investigation possible and unknown account for 50 per cent or one half of all allegations. In effect, in Western Australia, half of the investigations failed to confirm anything of substance. A further 109 (16.5 per cent) of cases were categorized as being 'at risk' and after that, the largest number of substantiated cases were classified as neglect (14 per cent). Sexual abuse and physical abuse were respectively 10 per cent and 8 per cent each. Much of the meaning of the relatively large proportion of 'at risk' and neglect cases will emerge in Chapter 9.

A similarity emerges between Western Australia and the Welsh local authority (Table 4.4) when the proportion of not substantiated cases are looked at. The proportion in the latter case is 56 per cent as compared with 50 per cent in the former. Half the investigations go nowhere. However, the disparity in patterns of substantiated cases is maintained, with a much larger proportion in the Welsh local authority being alleged and then classified as physical abuse – 23 per cent in Wales as opposed to only 8 per cent in Western Australia. Substantiated sexual abuse also retains a similar proportion in both agencies.

Table 4.4   Substantiation in a Welsh local authority

Substantiation	Nos	%
Not substantiated	56	56
'At risk'	7	7
Neglect	2	2
Physical abuse	23	23
Sexual abuse	12	12
Totals	100	100

Table 4.5 Contexts of allegations in Western Australia

Context	Not sub- stantiated	Sub- stantiated/ 'at risk'	Total	%
Custody/access dispute	32	7	39	6
Other family conflict	36	21	57	8.5
Neighbours in conflict	28	4	32	5
Non-conflictual	231	293	524	80
Other	3	0	3	0.5
Totals	330	325	655	100

As Table 4.5 shows, the majority (80 per cent) of allegations in Western Australia were made in non-conflictual contexts, but over a fifth arose in settings where there was a custody/access dispute (as evidenced by the involvement of legal representatives of one or both parents or the Family Court), other conflicts within a family (one person making an allegation about another from the same extended family), or neighbours in conflict with each other. Only seven of the 39 allegations where children were the subject of legal disputes were substantiated, 21 of the 57 allegations were substantiated when family members were in conflict and only four of the 32 allegations were substantiated when they arose within the context of neighbourly rows.

Table 4.6 shows that in the Welsh local authority as in Western Australia, nearly four-fifths (73 per cent) of allegations were made in non-conflictual contexts. Only two out of the eight contexts of custody/access disputes were substantiated, five out of the 15 Family Dispute context cases were substantiated and one out of the three neighbours in conflict contexts for allegations were substantiated. Similarities here lie in the conflictual and non-conflictual proportions, but they are not sustained in respect of families and neighbours in conflict (although in the latter situation there were only three such cases).

Table 4.6 Contexts of allegations in a Welsh local authority

Context	Not sub- stantiated	Sub- stantiated/ 'at risk'	Total	%
Custody/access dispute	6	2	8	8
Other family conflict	5	10	15	15
Neighbours in conflict	2	1	3	3
Non-conflictual	42	31	73	73
Other	1	0	1	1
Totals	56	44	100	100

Table 4.7 Family structure of child protection cases in Western Australia

Family structure	Nos	%
Both biological parents together	193	29.5
Reconstituting families	118	18
Single female parents	276	42.1
Single male parents	45	7
Substitute care	1	0.1
Unknown	22	3.3
Totals	655	100

Nearly one-half (49.1 per cent) of all allegations made in Western Australia were in respect of single parent families (Table 4.7). The overwhelming majority of these were single female parents. Almost one-third of allegations concerned two-parent families (29.5 per cent) and nearly a fifth, reconstituting families (18 per cent).

Table 4.8 Family structure of child protection cases in a Welsh local authority

Family structure	Nos	%
Both biological parents together	26	26
Reconstituting families	22	22
Single female parents	40	40
Single female parents (in extended family)	4	4
Single male parents	4	4
Extended family	1	1
Residential care	1	1
Private foster care	1	1
Unknown	1	1
Totals	100	100

In the Welsh study, a greater range of categories was used than had been the case in Western Australia when attempting to break down caregiver family structures. However, very broadly speaking, a comparison of Tables 4.7 and 4.8 shows that single female parents remain in both cases the largest single category of referred case. Reconstituting families and families with both biological parents together retain roughly similar proportions in both studies while other caregiver categories such as substitute care remain very small.

Table 4.9 Ethnicity of referred cases in Western Australia

Ethnicity	Nos	%
Aboriginal	150	23
Non-Aboriginal	347	53
Unknown	158	24
Totals	655	100

As shown in Table 4.9, non-Aborigines and those of unknown ethnic origin formed more than three-quarters (77 per cent) of child protection referrals in Western Australia. Aborigines constitute approximately 3 per cent of Western Australia's population. In the Welsh local authority, to the knowledge of local social workers, there are no Australian Aborigines, and an attempt was made to measure ethnicity in a very different way – by using a combination of 'first language' and 'religion'. Examination of the files suggested that in 97 per cent of cases it was not possible to know the religious beliefs of clients. Comparison of the two agencies in respect of ethnicity was not really possible, even though an attempt was made to identify those whose first language was Welsh (these are probably the Welsh equivalent of Aboriginal people). In Western Australia the ethnicity category produced what is clearly a remarkable overrepresentation, hence the decision to provide a separate chapter on Aboriginal people in this book (Chapter 9).

Contextual issues

Tables 4.1 through 4.9 provide some important contextual information for those who are statutorily obliged to investigate child 'abuse' and neglect allegations. First, there is no easy way of accounting for the different patterns of allegation especially where, in Australia, half (47 per cent) are allegations of neglect as compared with only 26 per cent in the Welsh local authority. On the question of physical abuse this pattern is reversed and 40 per cent of allegations in Wales concern physical abuse compared with 22.5 per cent in Western Australia. It is difficult to know whey this should be the case. However one explanation may be that standards of child rearing in one community are interpreted differently from those of another. In one area the concern may be that low standards are exhibited in the physical circumstances of a household while in another the focus might be on the means whereby children are controlled.

In both these agencies, roughly half of the investigations drew a complete blank as far as 'abuse' or neglect was concerned. The substantiated neglect and physical abuse categories retained the anomalies of the allegation patterns, while the sexual abuse proportions were similar in both agencies.

Turning to 'contextual' matters, the conflicts surrounding approximately a fifth of allegations with relatively low substantiation rates are a feature of both agencies. The caregiver family structure distribution of child protection cases bears a remarkable similarity in both agencies, with over 40 per cent single female parents referred for investigation. There is little that can be said on the question of ethnicity since there is no Welsh equivalent of Australian Aborigines.

On the whole, it can be said that some of the results are widely divergent in respect of allegations and the consequent substantiation rates, while others show a strong and consistent convergence. They suggest two issues to ponder. The first is that the categorization of allegations may be worth further investigation. The differences could reflect a number of matters of importance particularly as to what different communities regard as important indicators of substandard child rearing practices, whether it is the physical state of a house or a tendency to use corporal punishment to control a child.

The second issue which gives pause for thought is that in both agencies conflict between people who shared legal responsibility for children or came from the same family, or knew each other as neighbours, provided the contexts for approximately a fifth of all allegations. Moreover, investigations do not generally substantiate the allegations. It would suggest that in a significant minority of cases official child protection activity has now become one channel whereby these differences of opinion and concerns about the care of children are dealt with and that within the definitional boundaries of these two agencies, more often than not they are not matters to be considered as far as child protection is concerned. On the question of caregiver family structure single female parents are a substantial focus of child protection investigations in both agencies where there is once more a high degree of consistency in the types of family brought to official attention where the care of children is a matter of concern.

Broad outcome indicators

Finally, in those parts of the developed world where there are relatively easily identifiable disadvantaged ethnic minorities there is a strong suggestion that they may be overrepresented in child protection statistics.

In exploring preliminary background questions to child protection work, it can be seen that the work cannot be divorced from some fundamentally *cultural* and *structural* issues. The cultural considerations about what is important in child rearing may create focus amongst professional workers. As far as those who become responsible for the care of children are concerned, then there is a suggestion that recent changes in respect of family structure and the ways in which families deal with disagreements give rise to uncertainties which surface in the child protection context. In both agencies, half the time and energy devoted to investigating allegations did not result in the identification of 'risk', 'abuse' or neglect. By way of background, there is here the first hint of a suggestion that children in need of official attention may be fewer than is popularly and perhaps even professionally imagined.

Table 4.10 Child protection career types in Western Australia

Career type	Nos	%
Begins care	64	10
Becomes care	40	6
Home-based services	139	21
No further action	82	12.5
Not substantiated	330	50.5
Totals	655	100

Having made a preliminary attempt to answer the questions 'why do children come into the child protection programme?' and 'in what contexts are referrals made?', the next question would be 'what happens to cases after they are referred?'. A rapid and easy way to answer this is to use the career type classification.

Table 4.10 shows the distribution of Child Protection Career Types in Western Australia. Setting aside the not substantiated group, the largest single category of cases was those which received home-based services (21 per cent) while the next largest were the substantiated but no further action cases (12.5 per cent). Only 10 per cent of cases began with an admission to care, while 6 per cent initially received home-based services but entered care later after a crisis – the becomes care cases.

Table 4.11 Child protection career types in a Welsh local authority

Career type	Nos	%
Begins care	7	7
Becomes care	2	2
Home-based services	28	28
No further action	8	8
Not substantiated	55	55
Totals	100	100

As in Western Australia, the largest single group of substantiated cases in the Welsh local authority (Table 4.11) were those which received a variety of home-based services (28 per cent), while the next largest group were the no further action cases (8 per cent). The proportions pursuing different careers are somewhat different between the two agencies although the ranking remains the same. Only 9 per cent of Welsh cases in total were admitted to care compared with 16 per cent in Western Australia – but as will be seen in Chapter 9, the significant ethnic bias of that sample may account for some of these differences.

Discussion of master tables

Thus far, child protection system managers will have obtained a lot of background information by using these tables in order to answer the types of questions posed in interview. We will now turn to a master table in order to bring together some of the key elements emerging from this picture. The master table deals with patterns and the outcomes of interventions in three ways. First, it presents broad patterns of outcomes (career types); second, these are shown in relation to the crude results of investigations; and third, it allows for the further detailed examination of subcareers. Essentially this is a crosstabulation of substantiation with career type. Each one of the interviewed executives in Western Australia got to the master table after producing a maximum of ten other tables.

Information theorists refer to the master table as an association matrix in the sense that it displays associations which ensure further questioning in order to account for the differences which can be discerned by visual inspection. The table excludes those cases which were not substantiated and deals only with those matters where a child protection issue was raised by the investigation. It aims to answer the question 'What did the agency do in response to different types of abuse?'

Table 4.12   Career type and substantiation in Western Australia

Career type	'At risk'	Neglect	Emotional abuse	Physical abuse	Sexual abuse	Total	%
Begins care	21	23	1	8	11	64	20
Becomes care	15	21	2	1	1	40	12
Home-based service	53	25	5	20	36	139	43
No further action	20	22	2	21	17	82	25
Totals	109	91	10	50	65	325	100
%	34	28	3	15	20	100	

As shown in Table 4.12, in Western Australia, the most extensive users of substitute care were neglected and 'at risk' children (76.9 per cent of all children who received a substitute care service). They formed 68.75 per cent of those who began with substitute care after receiving home-based services. This table suggests that substitute care services in this agency focused extensively on children who were not victims of physical or sexual assaults. Other conspicuous groups were the 11 sexually 'abused' children and the eight physically 'abused'

Table 4.13 Career type and substantiation in a Welsh local authority

Career type	'At risk'	Neglect	Physical abuse	Sexual abuse	Total	%
Begins care	0	0	5	1	6	13.5
Becomes care	1	0	1	0	2	5
Home-based service	5	2	12	9	28	63.5
No further action	1	0	5	2	8	18
Totals	7	2	23	12	44	100
%	16	5	52	27	100	

children who entered care immediately or very shortly after allegations were investigated. They were however much less in evidence in the becomes care category, there being only one case each of such assaults.

Over half (52.5 per cent) the becomes care cases were children who had been neglected and 15 of the 40 cases (37.5 per cent) in the becomes care category were judged to be 'at risk' children.

The no further action cases also display interesting patterns. Only 18.3 per cent of 'at risk' cases and 24 per cent of neglect cases were closed after the investigation whereas for physical abuse cases the proportions being closed without any service were much higher (42 per cent). Sexually abused children were only very slightly more likely to not receive service (26 per cent) than were neglected children.

Table 4.13, the master table for the Welsh local authority continues to demonstrate the already identified differences with Western Australia in respect of the relatively large numbers of physical abuse cases. These cases made up five out of the six begins care cases and one of the two becomes care cases (75 per cent of those admitted to care). Physically abused children also were the largest recipients of home-based services, followed by sexually abused children. One could presume here that the caregivers of the Welsh children were excessively violent in comparison with their Western Australian counterparts, or that neglect was not perhaps perceived in the same way in the two agencies.

It is at this point that finer analysis is required of the events represented in the master table. One way to illustrate this is by analysing the computer records and text of begins care/physical abuse cases. First of all, a listing of the harms and injuries sustained by the children in the begins care/physical abuse cells in Tables 4.12 and 4.13 can be obtained by using the Database Enquiry facilities of the INTERACT programme. For the Western Australian sample this produces the Table 4.14 which shows us that five out of the eight physical abuse cases admitted to care in Western Australia shortly after investigation, sustained more than what some would describe as 'minor' injuries. We have here infants with broken bones (three out of these five were under four years of age) and even more importantly, for four of these cases there was no explanation as to how the injuries were caused, or who caused them. The fifth case was injured by excessive

Table 4.14   Begins care/physical abuse cases in Western Australia

Harm/injury	Nos	%
Scalds, burns, fractures	5	62.5
Cuts, bruises, welts, bites	2	25
Unknown harm/injury	1	12.5
Totals	8	100

corporal punishment. Four of these cases were referred by medical professionals. The action causing the unknown harm/injury was listed as 'strangulation'. These are all serious matters. What emerges is a picture of severely injured children without much supporting explanation in the majority of cases.

In the Welsh local authority a very different picture emerges from Table 4.15. Here, the overall majority of cases falling into this category sustained only minor injuries – Cuts, Bruises, Welts or Bites, with only one child having a fracture. Further analysis shows that these cuts and bruises resulted in *all* cases from excessive corporal punishment and, moreover, these were *older* children; only one was an infant. Reading the text of these files reveals a completely different situation from that of comparable case types in Western Australia. For the older children, these injuries arose out of attempts to control what their caregivers perceived as disobedience and when the investigators showed up on the doorstep, in the main the caregivers admitted their actions, yet expressed the view that somehow the child 'deserved' the punishment. Under these circumstances social workers organized voluntary admissions to care. In contrast, the Welsh children in the physical abuse/no further action cell (also five cases) were similarly injured by similar excessive punishments. The differences however lie in the *attitudes* of the caregivers, in so far as the no further action case categories not only admitted their actions but were less inclined to lay blame on the child (Denman and Thorpe, 1993).

Table 4.15   Begins care/physical abuse cases in a Welsh local authority

Harm/injury	Nos	%
Scalds, burns, fractures	1	20
Cuts, bruises, welts, bites	4	80
Totals	5	100

Conclusion

At the end of this chapter on early results, analysis has finally moved from large tables containing lots of cells with large numbers, to very small numbers and text. This is precisely what the monitoring and evaluation instrument was designed to do, to break down information excess into small, comprehensible pieces. The comparisons between Western Australia and the Welsh local authority make much more sense within the context of the details of individual cases – but the evaluator has to know where to start to look for explanations. We have gone here from tables with 325 and 100 cases respectively to the detailed examination of eight and five cases respectively. Critical analysis of this nature becomes possible by means of the career heuristic, the application of the principle of specificity and textual analysis. The Western Australian master table has 20 cells and the next four chapters will consist of a detailed examination of the text hidden in each one of the cells, taking them in 'Career Type' order.

5 Beginning with substitute care

Sixty four children about whom allegations of 'abuse' or neglect were made in Western Australia entered care very shortly after investigations began. These 'begins care' cases were the 'red light' situations which more often than not resulted from an immediate crisis for caregivers. Table 4.12 showed that these 64 cases were distributed as shown in Table 5.1. This chapter will look at these cases in more detail by examining the five separate groups and using text extracted from case files.

Table 5.1   Type of 'abuse' in begins care cases

'Abuse'/neglect	Nos	%
At Risk	21	33
Neglect	23	36
Emotional Abuse	1	1.5
Physical Abuse	8	12.5
Sexual Abuse	11	17
Total	64	100

'At risk'/begins care cases

A third of the begins care cases were judged to be 'at risk', a common enough expression in child protection circles; indeed in this study it represents the largest single grouping of case categories after investigation. It is however important to bear in mind that investigations were unable to establish that children had been neglected, harmed or injured in this category and that there was no evidence of any action or actions which might have caused such harm or injuries. The WELSTAT definition refers to 'reasonable grounds to suggest the possibility of prior or future maltreatment' (WELSTAT 1987a: 9). This definition then continues to speak of 'departmental involvement'. In the absence of specific harms, injuries or actions which cause them, then on what grounds was

Table 5.2   'At risk'/begins care cases – caregiver family structure and ethnicity

Caregiver family structure	Aboriginal	Non-Aboriginal/ not known	Total	%
Both biological parents	1	3	4	19
Single female parent	7	7	14	67
Single male parent	2	1	3	14
Total	10	11	21	100
%	47.5	52.5	100	

intervention justified and why in these cases were these grounds sufficient to warrant removal from home? These matters will be explored, but initially it is worthwhile looking at what further crosstabulation shows.

More than two-thirds of the children 'at risk' came from single female parent families, while almost a half were Aboriginal children. Table 5.2 suggests that these children came overwhelmingly from families which were disadvantaged by both ethnicity and structural factors (single parenthood).

Only two of these children were removed by means of emergency legal powers – Apprehension (the equivalent of an Emergency Protection Order under the 1989 Children's Act in the UK). Care and protection applications followed these apprehensions, but one was withdrawn and the other adjourned. The police were involved with five of these cases, but there were no prosecutions. These 21 children came from 12 separate families. What were the situations of these families and why was care considered to be a necessary service?

Two of these 'at risk' cases involved young men (16 years old) absconding from care. Both were already state wards as a result of offending (Cases 59 and 376). Both boys had limited histories of minor delinquencies, they came from families which had fragmented and none of their parents wished to care for them. A third child was the baby daughter of a young woman who was herself already a care and protection state ward, the circumstances were that

> the mother of the child . . . has very poor mothering skills and tends to lead a transient lifestyle. Due to the problems she was experiencing with her child, [she] approached her aunt to take over the care of the child. Both parties appear very happy with the arrangement.
>
> (Case 612)

Two other youths presented behaviour problems. One was a 15 year old

> who recently returned to [an Aboriginal community] had been petrol sniffing. He dragged a woman into the bushes and had started to beat her, he was stopped by locals – after she had sustained fairly serious injuries. After this he walked away and prowled round the community until he became unconscious.
>
> (Case 353)

This youth was flown to Perth for medical assessment and treatment. A care and protection application was lodged on 'uncontrolled' grounds, but was then withdrawn and the boy was returned to his mother. The other was a 14 year old youth who entered hospital and care because

> the school and hospital were concerned at his conduct. He has been coming to hospital frequently with a variety of minor and even trivial complaints. He has also been missing a lot of school and the teachers find he is very demanding of their time and attention. He is apparently an epileptic, but gets drugs irregularly. He said his mother is often too inebriated to supervise the drugs or look after her children . . . I saw his mother this morning. She was intoxicated (at 11 a.m.) and resentful of the meeting. She said several times that her son was 'sick in the head' and should be put in the 'nut house'.
>
> (Case 354)

The youth was taken to a hostel, where he overdosed and was readmitted to hospital.

The last five 'at risk' children were from a large Aboriginal family and were moved to a hostel after their grandmother decided to cease looking after them. The grandmother reported that they 'were misbehaving and not taking any notice of [her] . . . They are staying out and sleeping at other people's homes . . . We then approached the mother (who is an alcoholic) in trying to find placements' (Cases 352–7). The mother said that 'until such times as she could get a house, she could not care for them . . . [she] then stormed out of the office and said she did not know what to do'. The children were then placed in a hostel.

With only three exceptions, all the remaining 'at risk/begins care' cases were ones where single female parents, with severe difficulties of their own, required help in caring for their children. Cases 336 and 337, a 13 year old boy and his 15 year old sister, were placed temporarily in foster care while their mother was serving a prison sentence. Their father had disappeared some time before.

Cases 205 and 206 were admitted to care when their mother entered a psychiatric hospital. Their mother said 'she is not capable of looking after them and was willing to stay away as long as it was necessary. Her reasons for her depression was that "things just get on top of me and then I find it hard to cope"'.

One isolated single parent mother was looking for respite care for her child: '[The mother] has decided she can no longer care for [the child] who is intellectually handicapped, despite a great deal of counselling [from a psychologist] . . . Looking for long term care but also respite over weekend' (Case 8).

An aboriginal woman 'phoned requesting a 6 week placement for the child . . . [she is] . . . currently living in very crowded conditions – relatives drink and she fears for the safety of the baby' (Case 9).

Isolated single male parents were also in similar situations to their female counterparts

[The child] is at risk mainly due to his father's social isolation; emotional and psychological state; inappropriate parenting skills and the acknowledgement of this. [His] requests for 'help' need to be accepted as serious, although they may be an indirect plea for 'help' himself.

(Case 314)

Another small child was admitted to emergency foster care because his mother was 'underweight, tired and nervous . . . [she] is at the end of her tether. She is feeling guilty about asking someone else to help, she has no immediate family to turn to' (Case 394).

Two exceptions to the sad catalogue of poverty and isolation were cases where children were suspected of being actual or potential victims of sexual assaults. One of these was a 10 year old girl from an affluent family who ran away from home and made allegations about her father to the police and child welfare workers. It took almost three months to bring the case to the Children's Court where a care and protection application was made. Her family opposed the application and the hearing lasted for three days during which time the girl was extensively cross-examined. The court adjourned the case *sine die* and the girl returned home voluntarily (Case 204). The second case concerned a child who was one of a family of three in which the father had sexually assaulted his other children and several others outside the family. He was convicted of these assaults, but the particular 'at risk' child in the begins care group had not been a victim. However because of the acute stresses on the mother and other children during the pre-trial phase of the father's prosecution, she was temporarily fostered with a family friend (Case 606).

In all these cases we find crises, but of three different varieties. In the first group there are older children without caregivers, some already in care, who are 'at risk' either because they are absconding or out of control. Risk is evident here – but these are not risks directly caused by deliberate caregiver intentions or activities. In the second group (the majority of cases in this category) we find single parents who are homeless, addicted to alcohol, stressed and generally unsupported. In part many of their problems are *structural* rather than self-inflicted. The social workers in their accounts have little time in which to make help available and, rather less obviously in their accounts, do not always find these caregivers amenable to negotiation. This will be worth considering again, when we examine 'at risk' children who do not receive substitute care services. In categorizing them as being 'at risk' the question can legitimately be asked 'Who or what has created the risk?' or 'Who is responsible for this catalogue of misery and unhappiness?' The category as defined by WELSTAT, using the term 'maltreatment' seems to be as pointed as 'abuse'. It is only in the last two cases out of 21 that we can see obvious actual or potential child victims of deliberately harmful adult caregiver actions. Seven of these 'at risk' children came to the attention of medical personnel, three for examination, four as in-patients for ailments not related to their reasons for being in care and one because of health problems caused by petrol sniffing.

Table 5.3   Neglect/begins care cases – caregiver family structure and ethnicity

Caregiver family structure	Aboriginal	Non-Aboriginal/ not known	Total	%
Both biological parents	7	2	9	39
Single female parent	9	5	14	61
Total	16	7	23	100
%	70	30	100	

Neglect/begins care cases

The Table 4.12 shows that 23 children were admitted to care because they were neglected. These children came from 12 families and two of these families account for nine of the 23 (one family had five children, one had four children, one had three and two had two children each respectively).

Table 5.3 crosstabulates caregiver family structure with ethnicity. Nearly three-quarters (70 per cent) of these cases were of Aboriginal Ethnic origin while nearly two-thirds came from families where the caregiver was a single female parent.

Table 5.4   Neglect/begins care cases – neglect type and medical services

Neglect type	Medical examinations	Inpatient treatment	No medical involvement	Total	%
Supervision	1	0	4	5	22
Medical care	1	2	0	3	13
Food	1	2	0	3	13
Abandoned/deserted	0	2	5	7	30
Failure to thrive	0	2	0	2	9
Not identified	0	0	1	1	4
Other	0	0	2	2	9
Total	3	8	12	23	100
%	13	35	52	100	

Table 5.4 shows the type of neglect found by investigators, crosstabulated against the type of medical intervention (if any) which was required at the time. Seven (30 per cent) of these neglected children were abandoned/deserted. Only two of these children however actually required medical treatment as in-patients. Five children (22 per cent) had not been adequately supervised by caregiver(s), one of whom was medically examined but did not require treatment. Of the three children whose medical care was neglected, one was examined while two were treated as in-patients. A similar situation pertained with the three children who

were judged to have inadequate or wrong diets. Two children were diagnosed as failing to thrive because of neglect. They both required in-patient treatment.

The most interesting feature of Table 5.4 when considered in comparison with the 'at risk/begins care' cases is the much higher levels of medical examinations and treatment, much as one might expect since neglect on this scale necessitated rapid admission to hospital or care. Approximately half the children were involved with medical services and two-thirds of these (eight cases) or a third of *all* the children in this category were hospitalized for treatment and observation.

Table 5.5 Neglect/begins care cases – care and protection applications and apprehensions

Care and protection	Apprehended	Not apprehended	Total	%
None	3	8	11	48
Adjourned	0	2	2	9
Withdrawn	4	0	4	17
Granted	5	1	6	26
Total	12	11	23	100
%	52	48	100	

Table 5.5 looks at the types of legal intervention made by the Department of Community Services for these 23 children. Just over one half (52 per cent) were compulsory admissions to substitute care by means of the department's emergency legal powers – apprehension. In three of these cases there was no follow up care and protection application in the Children's Court. The department withdrew the application for wardship in four cases (all from one family) and were granted wardship in five (all from one family). A further three children were brought before the Children's Court and an application for wardships via care and protection proceedings was made. In two of these cases the Court adjourned the case and in one case wardship was granted.

It can be seen that neglect/begins care cases are subject to relatively high levels of legal intervention, although two large families account for most of it. Furthermore, of the 23 neglect/begins care cases only six children were made state wards, and five of these came from one family.

Case file analysis (Cases 396–400) shows that this particular family were living in a vastly overcrowded household with relatives in a remote Aboriginal community in the northwest of the state. The father was working some distance away, and when visiting home (once a month) he . . . 'spends a lot of time in and out of prison, on mostly drunk charges'.

The file records the condition of some of the children (aged between two and 13 years old): 'L [an older girl] had sores all over her body and C [a younger boy] also had infected ears and sore eyes. The children had all been to the Regional

Hospital for a medical check-up after we apprehended them'. A few weeks later the youngest, a two year old girl, also became an in-patient when she failed to respond to out-patient treatment for 'sores all over her head'. The community medical services (there were no social services available locally) had summoned the child protection worker who was based 50 kilometres away. He did not know the family other than by indirect contact with the health services and the apprehension took place with little opposition. A few weeks later at the Children's Court, the magistrate ordered that the three older children remain in a hostel while their health recovered, and that the two youngest children should be returned to their mother immediately, even though they had all been made state wards.

The second family (four children aged between five and 12 years) were white, living with a single parent mother in a town in the southwest. The oldest, a 12 year old girl ran away because her mother asked her to stay home from school to look after the younger children while she went to darts every Tuesday. She was asked to do housework and clean up while the mother was 'at work from 5.00 a.m. fruit picking. Home 5.30 p.m.'. The girl had run away before and records describe her as 'extremely distressed, psychologically disturbed' (Cases 462–5). This girl was apprehended and taken to a foster home while the three younger children were apprehended and went to a local children's home for a few days. Within a week, the care and protection application was lodged with the Children's Court, but with a request for an adjournment because,

following a discussion with social workers:

1 There have been changes that have been made by [the mother] regarding the supervision of the children.
2 All children are currently residing with their mother – at their request.
3 The family have agreed to departmental involvement in an attempt to resolve conflicts and outstanding issues.

The focus of the work developed around the conflicts between the 12 year old daughter and her mother. The care and protection applications were eventually withdrawn – they had clearly been used originally as a coercive measure as well as a safety fallback device in case the mother failed to cooperate with the counselling she was offered.

Three children from another family who were apprehended because they were abandoned/deserted lived with their single female Aboriginal parent in Perth. A six year old girl was found walking along a road, late in the evening, carrying her baby brother. The police went to the house and 'had located a very young baby alone in the house and asleep on the bed' (Cases 1–3). The police took the children to a local hospital 'as the 2 year old child was soiled and dirty and distressed'. The Crisis Care workers then went to the hospital where

the three children had been bathed and their clothes changed. Nursing staff said that the children appeared very well cared for and were only superficially dirty. There was some concern about N carrying the 2 year old child as N has [a potentially disabling condition].

The children were then taken to a local post-natal hospital from where the children were collected the next day by their mother. The mother had been to the police station 'where they pointed out at length the errors of her ways last night. She had no previous record there, and no charges were laid. Police felt further lecturing unnecessary'. The medical staff at the hospital considered the children well looked after and the police had no records of the mother. The department closed the case, and there were no care and protection applications.

Two children, originally not apprehended, were subject to care and protection applications which were adjourned. They were a four year old girl and her baby brother of a few months who were abandoned/deserted, being cared for by a single female Aboriginal parent. This woman had been sharing the care of the children with a number of people in a remote community, but she moved unpredictably taking the children into her own care and then equally unpredictably handing them back. This had happened three times in the preceding months. The members of the community reported the fourth incident to the local department for community services. The children were admitted to a local group home. The file names at least three local women as being involved in the care of the children and gives constant reference to the mother's 'drunkard state'. Care and protection applications were lodged with the Children's Court but adjourned because one of the women (a relative) was looking at the possibility of guardianship. A later file note comments

> Talked with [the mother] re her plans for the children. [She] looked tired – sober – and possibly run down. We discussed the good things [she] has been doing lately re visiting the kids, being reliable etc. [She] maintains she has been 'off grog' for a good three weeks. I asked her if someone was helping her and she said she was doing it alone.
>
> (Cases 363 and 364)

The care and protection applications were again adjourned and the guardianship idea dropped. The adjournments continued (at three monthly intervals) for the next year with the children moving from the group home, to their mother's care, to the care of various relatives.

The two failure to thrive children lived under completely different circumstances whereby caregivers were unable or unwilling to fulfil expectations of them. These children were both babies of only a few months old. One was already a care and protection state ward, living in a foster home who had been born prematurely suffering from 'foetal alcohol syndrome'. She was readmitted to hospital three times and did not grow for over four months. The foster mother, after a warning, did not adhere to the requirements of a contract. The child was readmitted to hospital, after she was found to be 700 grams below discharge weight. The contract also stated that the house be cleaned daily but the records indicate the home 'is always filthy' (Case 372). Furthermore the doctor expressed the opinion that the child would die from neglect if she was returned to the foster home. She was then discharged to another foster home.

The other failure to thrive case also involved an uncooperative mother

> From what was observed and discussed today, it is apparent that [the child] is not being cared for at optimum level and that [his mother's] ability to provide a clean home was not evident today. [Her] attitude was one of passive defiance, she answered our questions in monosyllables, was evasive, avoided eye contact.

The baby was admitted to a local post-natal hospital then to a foster home where '[the mother] appeared upset at the prospect of leaving [the baby]' (Case 53). She was still in the foster home a year later.

Two children were admitted to foster care from a police station 'after school – dirty, neglected, scabies'. Their mother was in a psychiatric hospital at the time. The child protection worker took the view that the adults in the house could not 'look after themselves, let alone the children'. The children remained in care until their mother was discharged from hospital and had stabilized on medication.

Another child, who was already a state ward but had been returned home was readmitted to care because the worker

> could see no immediate change in [the father's] lifestyle. [The mother] was too distressed to consider her lifestyle, stating that she just wanted to look after her own baby, and walking out half-way through the conference.
>
> (Case 610)

The parents were described as having 'alcohol and violence' problems which were unresolved. The child went back to foster care and wardship was extended by the Children's Court. The child had returned to foster care after he 'required hospitalization for pneumonia, chest infection, eye infection and malnourishment'. The parents had failed to keep marital counselling appointments. They did however resume care of the child a few weeks later because his mother 'regularly brings [him] into the office to show him off. He is progressing well and community health report that there have been no problems'.

The remaining children in the neglect/begins care category were all Aboriginal children who had been placed by the *biological* parent or parents with relatives, who then approached the department for financial assistance to support the informal placements. In all cases the payments were made by approving the relatives in the kinship network as foster parents. They all lived in remote Aboriginal communities on state income support.

In very many respects it can be seen that the neglect/begins care cases were similar to the 'at risk'/begins care cases. Witness the same levels of poverty, isolation and alcohol misuse – the overrepresentation of deprived sectors of the population. The crises however tended to be of a different order in the sense that the hazards faced by children cared for under these circumstances were of a much more immediately life-threatening nature. Witness here the scale of legal intervention and medical examinations and in-patient hospital treatment. However, in a different sense the decision-making processes show here a sort of 'tariff' in respect of legal intervention. For the truculent and undeserving there are apprehensions which go all the way to wardship in the Children's Courts. Less interventionist are apprehensions followed by care and protection applications which are adjourned or withdrawn and then there are the apprehensions which are not followed up by court proceedings but simply allowed to lapse. A number of factors are present in the situated moral reasoning here, especially the capacity of caregivers to cooperate with child protection workers. A set of interlinked considerations are also brought to bear in judging the moral character of caregivers – the existence or otherwise of a police criminal record and the diagnostic categories of medical professionals who extend 'scientific' judgements to include culpability and value judgements about standards of child rearing. These matters are thrown into much sharper relief by the neglect/begins care cases than those cases with 'at risk'/begins care.

Emotional abuse/begins care cases

In the emotional abuse/begins care cell in Table 4.12, there is only one case. This involved a 14 year old girl who had run away from home. She was found, by her parents, in her boyfriend's house. Her reasons for leaving were recorded as, 'Mum and Dad yelling and picking on her calling her names etc.' (Case 6). She refused to return home as she feared her mother would hit her for running away. Records indicate she was moved, at her request, to her stepsister's home. This case appears to be one of conflict between a 14 year old girl and her parents, but no information exists as to what their views were and why they 'picked' on her, or what happened after the department facilitated the child's move to her stepsister's home.

Physical abuse/begins care cases

There were eight physical abuse/begins care cases in the sample, considerably fewer than those 'at risk' or neglected. Only two of these cases involved Aboriginal children and only one came from a single female parent family. Four came from reconstituting families where one of the parents was not a biological parent of the child concerned. Although the number of children involved in 'red light' physical abuse cases were very small, the caregiver family structure and ethnicity make-up of these cases was quite different from other begins care cases. Four of these children were removed from their caregivers by means of emergency legal powers (apprehension). They all then proceeded to the Children's Court with care and protection applications, as did a fifth case which was not originally apprehended.

Four of these five applications for wardship were granted by the court, the fifth was dismissed. Here we see very high levels of legal intervention and activity by child protection workers. Further examination of the harms and injuries received by these children gives some indication of the seriousness of the circumstances:

Case 593   Fractured collar bone, arm and leg, extensive bruising
Case 434   Fractured leg, burns to the face
Case 180   Healing bruises and sores, cigarette burns
Case 181   Healing bruises and sores, cigarette burns
Case 538   Burns to the face, scalds on chest and shoulder
Case 640   Bruising to the head, healing scars
Case 564   Minor bruises on the body
Case 645   A cut on the neck.

Case 593 concerned a 16 month old child. The doctor's opinion was that the injuries could not have been caused accidentally and he informed the Department for Community Services. The child protection worker interviewed the mother and her cohabitee: 'Both explained that the bruising . . . had resulted from [the child] falling from their bed whilst [the mother's cohabitee] was caring for her and [the mother] was at work' (Case 593). The account of the worker continues: 'I believe that the explanation for the injuries was not consistent with the type or variety of injuries'. The child was apprehended. Her mother went with her to a hospital in Perth. Six weeks later, the magistrate dismissed the care and protection application which had been 'vigorously' opposed by the mother and father separately (they had been separated for some time). In making this decision the magistrate took note of one doctor's description of the mother as 'an excellent mother'. He said he was satisfied with the evidence of the injuries that this constituted legal grounds for the apprehension but that the statutes governing wardships were concerned 'with the acts and/or omissions of near relatives, those having custody and/or guardianship' and in this case there was no evidence that any of those who had care of the child had caused the injuries. The child (who had already been living with the mother and grandparents in Perth since being discharged from hospital) remained with her family.

Case 434 was described to me by a child protection worker as a 'horrible case' which indeed it was. This was a four year old girl, one of five children under the age of six years in a migrant family where the mother couldn't speak English. The child was referred by the family doctor because of developmental delays and was admitted voluntarily to a residential nursery. The father had

stated how difficult it was for both he and his wife to teach [the child] eating skills and habits, as well as toilet training which he claimed [she] was resisting. [The father] demonstrated the methods by which [the child] was restrained in her bed by the use of material straps.

(Case 434)

The father refused the offer of a cot and refused to allow his wife to be interviewed (she sat in another room). A number of other services were provided, a Home Support Teacher to teach the mother English, pre-school services for the other children as well as a female social worker who could look at the reported feeding and toileting problems. The department even arranged 'for [some alterations to the house] to assist with the drying of nappies during the winter months'. These practical measures were used as the basis of work as well as the respite care which had already been used and permits the begins care classification. A further hospital admission however confirmed a fractured femur, 'burns to the chin and lower lip extending to the inside of her mouth, and bruises to elbow and recent fractured thumbs and another fracture higher up the broken leg'. The police interviewed the parents before the care and protection application was made. Wardship was granted and the child placed in a residential nursery after discharge from hospital. Since the parents did not oppose the application, their cooperation was used to work out a phased rehabilitation plan using a parent training centre. Nine months later the family moved to another state and the child was returned to their care; she travelled with them. The wardship was transferred from Western Australia.

Cases 180 and 181 were children aged four and two years who had just arrived in Western Australia from another state where the child welfare agency had become very concerned about them. On the day information was received from that state, the family was traced to a caravan and child protection workers turned up with the police. After a series of hostile and antagonistic exchanges in which the workers were refused access to the children, they were apprehended and taken to hospital for examinations which revealed bruises, sores and scarring patterns consistent with cigarette burns. They were placed in foster care, care and protection applications made and wardship granted. An intensive programme of counselling was created for the parents – the mother wanted the children back and the father, while initially hostile, gradually engaged in the programme. Ten months later the children were successfully returned to their care.

Case 538 was a nine year old boy, referred by his school, who said his stepmother had thrown hot water on him. The stepmother 'feeling pressured' said she 'exploded', and the father agreed he took 'no active role in parenting'. The worker in her report decided against legal action because:

1 Parents readily accepted responsibility for the injury.
2 Parents were willing to enter treatment and address issues leading to the injury.
3 Both children interacted in a positive manner and showed no fear of either parent.

The boy was admitted voluntarily to care with his grandparents who then sought guardianship. A final comment by the worker was that:

It is evident that the blended family had not welded and there are in effect, two families living under one roof. [The child] is definitely an outsider in this household and does not receive the same loving treatment that [his stepbrother] does.

Case 640 was an eight year old Aboriginal girl whose mother, whilst drunk, woke the child and banged her face on the bedroom floor. The child explained how further healed and healing scars 'had been inflicted recently by her mother'. Comments noted by the child protection worker came from interviews with the father:

> [The father] made allegations that [the mother] is an alcoholic and that she is very violent when intoxicated. [The father] also stated that [the mother] on previous occasions inflicted knife wounds on [the child] as well as other physical assaults.
>
> (Case 640)

A care and protection application resulted in wardship and the child was placed in foster care in another Aboriginal community. Supervised access with her mother was organized.

The other Aboriginal case in the physical abuse/begins care category was that of a 14 year old girl in conflict with her parents. The girl had failed to return home on time, and was found by her father, 'visiting a chalet where 2 or 3 young men lived'. She became 'very abusive towards her parents . . . Mum became angry and grabbed her by the throat'. The girl threatened to leave home and the father 'told her to go ahead and leave' (Case 564). As neither the parents, nor the girl, wished for her return, she went to stay with her cousin. After a short, voluntary stay in a local residential unit, she returned to stay with the cousin when the family moved away. On the child protection information system, the action causing the minor bruising is recorded as attempted strangulation.

The last physical abuse/begins care case concerned a 13 year old girl also in conflict with her parents. She claimed she had been 'flogged' by her mother and stepfather. The child complained at length about her stepfather's drunken violence: 'she gets bashed approximately every two weeks' and 'normally he hits with a flat hand' (Case 645). On the file it describes how

> during the time of the [investigatory] visit [the stepfather] on a few occasions tried to get into the [child protection worker's] car and thumped the car while emphasising a point to [the child]. After five more minutes of this [a child protection worker] decided we weren't getting anywhere and it was becoming dangerous so we left.

Late that night the police were called to the house where they found the mother 'badly beaten'. The mother and children were admitted to the Women's Refuge. A few days later the natural father of the child drove up from Perth and took her and her sister with him. The case was closed.

In this group of cases we find the most seriously injured children in the sample: two infants each with broken bones and scars with no explanation as to how they occurred, two children taken at night from a caravan with a police escort, one child with scalding and another whose mother had pushed her face to the floor.

Decision-making by workers here reflects the level of interaction with caregivers, a mixture of questions around cooperation and in these cases, whether there was an explanation and/or admission. The boy who was punished by the stepmother pouring hot water over him was not subject to legal intervention. In one way or another we see varying types of what is loosely called 'domestic violence', but despite this, workers still take account of the *character* of parents and aspects of surrounding circumstances. The last case is a true child protection drama, rescue from a drunken and violent stepfather, when the workers themselves were physically exposed to potential danger. It was the only one in the sample of 655 cases.

Sexual abuse/begins care cases

Table 5.6   Sexual abuse/begins care cases – caregiver family structure and persons believed responsible

Person believed responsible	Both biological parents	Single female parent	Single male parent	Total	%
Parent	4	1	0	5	45.5
Sibling	0	0	1	1	9
Friend/neighbour	1	1	0	2	18
Not known	0	1	2	3	27.5
Total	5	3	3	11	100
%	45.5	27.25	27.25	100	

Eleven children were admitted to care shortly after investigation began as a result of sexual abuse allegations. Six of these came from three families (of two children each), the remaining five children came from one family each. Table 5.6 crosstabulates caregiver family structure against person believed responsible for the assaults. For five of the eleven children in this category, the person believed responsible for the sexual assaults was a parent. Four came from families where both biological parents were together and one from a single female parent family. A sibling accounted for assaults on one child in a single male parent family, while a friend/neighbour accounted for assaults on two children, one in a single female parent family and one in a family where both biological parents were together.

Table 5.7 examines the nature of the harms and injuries sustained by these child victims along with the actions were believed to have caused them. Six of the children in this category were victims of acts of indecency which involved physical touching, all of which resulted in identifiable emotional trauma. Five sustained sexual assaults which involved penetration. In three cases this had physical consequences.

Table 5.7   Sexual abuse/begins care cases – harms/injuries and actions which caused them

Actions causing	Emotional trauma	Anal/vaginal disease/ trauma	No identifiable injury	Total	%
Indecent dealings/molestation	6	0	0	6	55
Penetration	0	3	2	5	45
Total	6	3	2	11	100
%	55	27	18	100	

Table 5.8   Sexual abuse/begins care cases – legal intervention and police prosecutions

Care and protection application	Apprehended		Not apprehended		Total	%
	Pros.	No pros.	Pros.	No pros.		
None	0	0	2	0	2	18.2
Adjourned	1	0	0	0	1	9
Withdrawn	2	0	0	0	2	18.2
Granted	1	4	1	0	6	54.6
Total	4	4	3	0	11	100
%	36.4	36.4	27.2	0	100	

Table 5.8 shows the scale of legal intervention including police prosecutions. It is a three way table. Legal interventions of one kind or another occurred in all 11 cases. Eight of the 11 were apprehended and all apprehensions were followed by care and protection applications. In one other case a child became subject to a care and protection application without first having been apprehended.

In total prosecutions were made as a result of assaults on seven children. Six males were prosecuted, of these, two were the fathers of two children each and one was a friend/neighbour. In one case, two adolescent boys were prosecuted for offences against one child and the boyfriend of an adolescent girl was prosecuted – not for a sexual assault but for 'carnal knowledge' (sexual intercourse with someone less than 16 years of age).

Let us look first of all at those cases where legal activity was at its highest with apprehensions, care and protection applications and prosecutions. Cases 237 and 238 began with a classic story – that of a 14 year old girl running away from home to a relative's house and then refusing to go back. The department had been involved with the child for some time and regarded it as a parent/child conflict.

[A social worker] has been involved with family for some time and [the child's] relationship with mother dreadful. [The child] ran away last night and is with her sister . . . [her mother] doesn't want DCS involvement and also doesn't want [the child] to stay with her sister. . . Advised [the social worker] to tell [the child's mother] to collect her daughter and take her home'.

(Case 237)

Ironically there was a hint of an allegation about this sister's cohabitee, who 'a few years ago tried to get into bed with another sister while she was staying there'. For this reason, the area office manager directed that a 'sexual abuse investigation' should take place. What emerged was a different story. The child reported that over a period of several years her father had asked her to sleep in his bed where he had fondled her breasts and pubic area. On one occasion, digital penetration took place. In fact *all* his daughters had been assaulted:

> There was one more time in Year X. There wasn't much hot water so Dad said. So he ran a bath and got in then we all had to get in with him. D went in first, and she was getting out and I was getting in. Dad washed me and he washed me everywhere. . . Mum knew that Dad was bathing us but she didn't care, she just sat in the loungeroom.

The two girls remaining in the house at the time of the disclosure were apprehended, placed with older sisters and the father prosecuted.

Cases 607 and 608 were somewhat different. The mother reported that her four year old daughter told her that 'Daddy, in the bath, had asked the child to rub his penis'. The husband admitted this, and was 'remorseful, crying, saying it was an isolated occurrence which happened when [the mother] was in hospital'. The mother was concerned that her husband should not be jailed. Both parents were 'willing to talk'. The father said he wished to remain with his family, so the children were apprehended and placed with grandparents. Interviewers said that the mother 'has limited insight into the situation and could not be relied upon to protect the children if on her own'. She was confused, desperate to retain her husband and worried about what might happen to him; she 'initially made statements to the effect that [her husband] was not responsible for his actions'. The child protection workers, following the textbooks

> confronted this issue with [the mother] many times during the interviews giving clear messages that [her husband] was responsible, that he was to blame for the current crisis, that she needed to protect the children, not [her husband].

The father was convicted and placed on probation several weeks later. No conditions were attached to the probation order, but accommodation was found for him and the children returned from grandparents to their mother's care.

The third case of sexual assault involving a father was that of Case 255. Here there was no prosecution, although the child was apprehended and wardship granted by the Children's Court after a care and protection application. The allegations came from a schoolteacher, and concerned a 15 year old girl. An office interview disclosed that

> [The child was] very withdrawn and reluctant to open up. Stated that she was scared of her father – in fact everyone was scared of her father. Sexual abuse has been occurring since [she] was 10/11. Father would complain in front of mother that [the child] did not care about him and did not show him enough attention. Mother would tell [the child] to sleep in their bed with her father. . . Father has threatened [the child] with 'I will deny allegations' and 'If you tell, the family will break up'. [The child] feels both mother and sister won't believe her.

The father did indeed deny the allegations and the child, who was not supported by her mother and sister, refused to talk to the police. She was apprehended and placed initially with friends. Subsequently she went through five more placements in a matter of weeks – an emergency foster home, a psychiatric ward, another foster home, a residential home and then another foster home. During this time one of her male teachers had a brief sexual relationship with her, but no record exists on the file about any action taken in response to this.

Cases 116 and 117 concerned sisters aged six and three years old, living with their father who had separated from his wife. The mother received an allegation from the older child about her father during an access visit. It was found that 'both children [had] genital and anal injuries and scarring' and the older child gave a very clear account of persistent penetrative sexual assaults on her and her sister by her father. A decision was made to apprehend and a care and protection application was lodged because:

– [The Father] looking at all other explanations as to who might have abused the children including [a friend] or [his wife] putting the children up to it.
– Concerns for [the mother's] *present* ability to adequately cope with and protect the children.
– Concerns about [the mother] being successful in a Family Court action for custody given that [the father] is denying he sexually abused the children and no criminal charges being in place.

The mother opposed the care and protection applications, but the father didn't. The children were placed in a foster home for six months after which they were returned to their mother's care.

Case 61 would be described in the literature as a matter of 'sibling abuse', and arose when an older daughter, who had left home, alleged sexual abuse by her father a few years ago. Concern was expressed for her younger sister, who was living in the father's care. The sister, who was seven years old, disclosed during interview that her 19 year old brother had touched her on four occasions in the vaginal/pubic area and her chest. The girl was apprehended and placed in a foster home. A care and protection application was lodged but adjourned. The conditions of the adjournment were:

2 Undertaking by [the father] to attend counselling with a family therapist. . .
3 That [the child] attend the family therapist.

4 Therapist to provide bimonthly reports as to the progress of the counselling to the Department for Community Services, [the father's] legal adviser and [the child's] legal adviser.
5 Undertaking by DCS in the event of a recommendation by the family therapist that [the child] should return home the application could be withdrawn.
6 Supervised access outside departmental premises once a week.

At the core of the decision to apprehend lay the father's failure to tackle his older son. But there were other considerations too:

> There is considerable evidence of frequent physical violence within the family. This primarily has been of [the father] assaulting his ex-wife and [oldest daughter] . . . emotional abuse within the family is demonstrated by [the father's] use of threats to control family members . . . moral risk is present in that [the father] allegedly sexually assaulted [the two oldest girls] over a period of some years.

The girl wished to return to her father's care, but the child protection worker commented that 'I feel she is too young to make an informed decision in this regard'. The father agreed in the Children's Court to seeing the family therapist. A final note clearly demonstrates the theoretical orientation of the worker here:

> Although the Department's statutory role is with [the child] it's clear that she cannot be viewed in isolation from the rest of the family even though they have left the family home. An integrated programme of support should be available to all members of the family in an attempt to reintegrate the family as far as possible.

> (Case 61)

No prosecution of the brother took place and the file offers no clue as to whether or not the police were informed.
Case 224 was a 15 year old girl who disclosed to the police that both her father and a 70 year old family friend had separately been sexually assaulting her over a number of years. The father was arrested, prosecuted and placed on probation with conditions that he 'remain away from the matrimonial home until authorised', 'that he attend for counselling and treatment as directed in writing', 'that he refrain from contacting in any way the child . . . other than as authorised in writing', 'that he attend marriage counselling as directed in writing', 'that at a time and place to be notified in writing . . . he make a complete apology to the child and make known to the child that he accepts full responsibility for what took place'. The reasons for the apprehension and care and protection application in this case was expressed as being

> Because of [the child's] lack of confidence in her mother, due to the latter's ambivalent attitude toward the father's offences against his child, and thus [the child's] doubt about her mother's protectiveness, [the child] spent about 4 months in . . . a foster home.

After that time, the girl returned home but left after a fight occurred between her and her mother 'over [the child's] boyfriend and her having friends in the house'. The background to this was the child's complaints about her mother 'spending so much time with [the father]'. The girl was readmitted to foster care.

Cases 411 and 346 were the only two Aboriginal children in the sexual abuse/begins care category. They were both located in remote Aboriginal communities in the northwest of the state. Case 411 concerned a four year old girl who became a state ward 'after evidence of abuse came to notice'. This evidence was described as 'an initial sexual abuse encounter' when the child's mother 'was unable to provide the necessary degree of protection'. The incident took place at a drinking party. 'The mother was present at the party and admits to consuming a large volume of VO Port . . . in consequence her recollections are hazy and it is clear she suffered alcoholic amnesia'. The child was initially placed in another community then returned to her mother's care.

Case 346 was a 14 year old girl living with an uncle and aunt. She had a boyfriend who worked away from the community but returned at weekends. Departmental officers received confirmation that her boyfriend was sleeping with her and then immediately visited the community. The girl disappeared and her relatives admitted that they permitted the boyfriend to sleep with her, implying that they had little control over her. A few days later the boyfriend appeared – a 16 year old youth. He readily admitted that he had a sexual relationship with the girl and refused to guarantee that it would cease; he also said that the girl 'chased' him round the community every time he appeared (there was a lot of supporting evidence for this from the community). The youth was arrested, prosecuted and fined $25 for having sexual intercourse with someone under the age of 16 years. As soon as the girl reappeared she was apprehended, taken to a placement some distance away and became a state ward. She refused to discuss any of these matters in interviews with child protection workers.

The sexual abuse/begins care cases exhibit virtually all of the issues referred to in the literature. *All* of these children were females and all of the persons believed responsible were males. We see here the problem of child witnesses and denying adults, mothers (and fathers) failing to demonstrate that they could protect their children, as well as adolescent victims traumatized by their experiences and behaving in self-destructive ways. The moral calculation in these cases again is based not so much on what actually happened to children as much as whether or not mothers (and a father) accepted that assaults had taken place and were prepared to take action. We also see here very markedly high levels of legal intervention, cases involving apprehensions, care and protection applications *and* prosecution on a scale which does not exist in other case types.

Conclusion

It is worthwhile at the end of this chapter to reflect on what emerges from these 64 'red light' cases. With the 'at risk' cases, we see high levels of social and personal disorder, structural disadvantage and alcohol-related problems. We also see out-of-control adolescents in this group. 'Neglect' cases demonstrate the same features (less the adolescents), but in these cases children suffered physically, there was more legal intervention and very high levels of medical intervention and hospitalization. In both these groups Aboriginal people and single female parents dominate the social context. While decision-making is reflected in part by considerations of the moral character of caregivers, there is also a complex set of contextual issues – the absence of local support networks, the willingness of caregivers to cooperate and accept the agency's version of situations as well as the actual harm suffered by children. Legal interventions here appear to operate on a 'tariff' which takes account of all these factors, but especially the character of caregivers. The degrees of threat posed to children by caregiver incapacities or the actual levels of harm suffered by children were *not* directly related to levels and degrees of legal interventions.

Physical abuse cases are quite different. There are a very small number of seriously and deliberately injured children, but no prosecutions – and no explanations either. Where explanations existed, the adults more readily admitted to losing control of themselves. Structural disadvantage scarcely features here. What counts is *explanation* in determining the nature of legal intervention. Moral character is rather less of an issue.

With sexual abuse we see a lot of legal intervention and in a significant proportion of these cases, police prosecutions of adult males for criminal offences. The extent of prosecutions though is somewhat independent of civil proceedings, (apprehension and care and protection applications) which again do not necessarily depend on the severity of the sexual assaults described, but on the preparedness of a caregiver (mothers with only one exception) to protect their daughters.

Fortunately, the cases in the begins care category are relatively small in proportion to other cases – 20 per cent of substantiated and 'at risk' cases and 10 per cent of all allegations. Ten per cent however was one in ten of all allegations made during the sample time period and they required very rapid action – placements to be found, legal documents to be prepared, medical examinations and medical treatment to be organized and plans formulated for the future of children under conditions of crisis and uncertainty. This was especially true of the 'at risk' and 'neglect' cases in terms of volume. In terms however of public exposure, of press presence in Children's Courts and potential criticisms from other agencies, this was mostly true of the physical abuse and sexual abuse cases.

6 Home-based services

One hundred and thirty-nine children received home-based services because neglect or 'abuse' was substantiated or they were considered to be 'at risk'. This chapter will analyse these cases in detail.

'At risk'/home-based services

Of these children, the largest single proportion (38 per cent, or 53 cases), were not harmed or injured but judged 'at risk', as shown in Table 6.1. Fifty-one per cent of these children came from single female parent families and only 17 per cent from Aboriginal families – which were however almost entirely single female parent families. Nearly a quarter (23 per cent) came from reconstituting families.

Table 6.1 'At risk'/home-based services cases – caregiver family structure and ethnicity

Caregiver family structure	Aboriginal	Non-Aboriginal/ not known	Total	%
Both biological parents	1	8	9	17
Reconstituting family	0	12	12	23
Single female parent	7	20	27	51
Single male parent	1	4	5	9
Total	9	44	53	100
%	17	83	100	

As shown in Table 6.2, nearly one-fifth of these cases (18.9 per cent) were not given help, but made subject to monitoring and surveillance. The largest single service on offer was that of advice and guidance which was given to twenty six cases, while four cases received services described as 'treatment'.

Table 6.2   'At risk'/home-based services – service types

Service type	Nos	%
Monitoring and surveillance only	10	18.9
Advice and guidance only	26	49.0
Material and practical assistance only	2	3.8
Advice, guidance and financial assistance	2	3.8
Advice, guidance, material and practical assistance	6	11.3
Advice, guidance, material, practical and financial assistance	3	5.6
Treatment	4	7.6
Total	53	100

Monitoring and surveillance

The ten children subject to monitoring and surveillance came from five families (A, B, C, D and E). Families A, B and C had two children each; Family D had three children, and Family E had one child.

It appears that children considered to be 'at risk' and for whom only monitoring and surveillance occurred were either allegedly victims or potential victims of sexual assaults, or whose families/parents were identified as 'problematic' by the authorities. Another pattern emerging is the families' or parents' response to welfare intervention, which played a role in decision-making about the cases.

Family A had two sons, one of whom was referred by the school for 'daily soiling and suspected sexual abuse'. Family D had three daughters (Cases 502, 503, 504) and there was concern about their contact with a man who was being charged for a sexual offence against another child. In both these cases, investigation through interviews and a medical examination of Family A's son failed to confirm a sexual assault. The worker in Family D described the interviews as 'fruitless'. In both cases, the workers continued to suspect sexual assaults because of contextual factors. For example, in Family A's case the father's 'past records of indecent dealings and intercourse' was seen to be relevant and in Family D, the girls were thought to be 'not telling anybody' about suspected sexual assaults.

With regard to the other five children (three families), the reasons for referral can be described by textual material as follows: In Family B (two children), the state housing agency was concerned about the father's 'interactions with his kids'.

Family C consisted of two small girls (Cases 227 and 228) living with their mother, father and grandmother. The reason for referral was unclear because it was not stated on the file. Reference was made on a file note six weeks later to the mother's 'extreme fear' that the department would take her child from her, implying that concerns were expressed about her care of the children.

Family E was a two parent family with a two month old baby (Case 307) referred by a child health nurse concerned about 'lack of bonding' and 'mother's vagueness about the child's needs'.

Workers seemed to use a number of contextual factors to make decisions about ongoing involvement in these cases. This included the families' responses to intervention. In the cases of Family A and Family D, where sexual assaults were suspected, the main contextual factors for wanting to keep the cases open were the adults' past sexual offence records. In addition, in Family A, the worker was concerned that the father 'could give excessive punishments to his children' and there were 'relationship problems . . . between the parents'. The worker was unable to keep Family D's case open because they moved from the neighbourhood. With regard to the other three families, it is unclear for two of them why the cases were kept open. In Family B's case there were no obvious symptoms of 'abuse' or 'neglect', and a note about reasons for continuing case management in a 'hands off' manner. Family C's case record only described the mother's 'extreme fear' of the department, and 'feeling hassled', but did not indicate the reasons for departmental involvement with the family. Finally, Family E received several visits over an eight month period in which the mother expressed her resentment at 'wishing she hadn't opened her big mouth to the Child Health Nurse', so she wouldn't have had to put up with the visits from the child protection worker. Case closure indicated 'offers of help rejected'.

Advice and guidance

Twenty six children from 15 families received advice and guidance (Families F to T). Families F and G each had four children. Families H and I had three children, Family J had two children. The remaining families (K to T) had one child each. Seven children in this group were Aboriginal.

Children considered to be 'at risk' for whom advice and guidance services were given were so defined due to 'home conditions', adequacy of parental care and supervision, the use of alcohol by parents and significant others, and alleged or actual sexual assaults on the children. Decisions to continue case intervention hinged on parental cooperation, the availability of other personal and practical supports and vouching for parents by significant persons. In one case, Family F, the 'conditions of . . . home' were felt to be 'totally unsuitable for the adequate and healthy care of . . . children'.

In five cases, concerns about the adequacy of parental care and supervision of children reflected judgements about parental behaviour and the physical environment, particularly with regard to the special needs of some of the children. Four of the cases (351, 354, 392 and 395) concerned children with disabilities such as intellectual disability or cerebral palsy or epilepsy, or where the babies were newborn. All four children were living in environments where alcohol was recorded as a concern, for example, an 'inebriated' mother who could not supervise the child's medication, parents having a 'history of alcohol abuse', a mother reportedly 'spending more time in town, heavily drinking', 'drunks enter the community'. In addition all these children were of Aboriginal descent and were living in remote communities, far from health and welfare services. In the fifth instance, (Family H) another Aboriginal family in a remote community, the mother left her three children (Cases 348–50) in the care of their grandfather, went into town and 'got on the alcohol again'.

Two other families, (I and N) were referred for alleged 'inadequate supervision' of the children, but the events leading to this judgement seemed to be constructed as 'inadequate control of children's behaviour'. Family I, with three children (Cases 505–7) was referred by the police as the seven year old son had 'stolen from a shop' and the parents 'didn't appear to be concerned'. '[This family had] been the subject of a number of complaints from police alleging that the parents are inadequately supervising the children, neighbours are being bothered by petty stealing'.

Family N, a 16 year old girl (Case 386) was living with her father (the parents were separated). Her mother telephoned from another state expressing concern about her daughter's behaviour, 'reported as having been drinking and going to pubs'. These concerns may reflect judgements about 'suitable behaviour' for teenage girls.

Families K, Q, R and S could be grouped as experiencing 'relationship difficulties' in which the children became the subject of the referrals, defined as 'child protection'.

Families K and Q (each with one girl, Cases 264 and 423 respectively) were self referred. In Case 264 the eight year old girl was the subject of the mother's referral. The mother, a young single parent, was 'experiencing behavioural difficulties with her daughter'. This was described as returning home from school at 6.45 p.m., and being 'disobedient and aggressive'. The mother who had been 'under the welfare' herself, had sought help as she did not want to hit the daughter 'too much'.

In Case 423, a 14 year old girl in a reconstituting family referred herself because of conflict in the household 'worker believed sexual abuse had taken place but it couldn't be proved'. In this case, it appears that the worker is applying a particular theory connecting family conflict with sexual assault. The grounds for the judgement were not specified in the case notes.

Families R and S again concerned contexts of alleged or actual sexual assaults on two girls. In family R, the 15 year old girl (Case 454) had been sexually assaulted by her stepfather who had been imprisoned. The agency's involvement with the child occurred when she was living with her natural father, and appeared to be a follow up 'to clarify the areas of assistance that . . . might be provided'.

Family S concerned a three year old girl (Case 491) in which it appears that the mother had 'suspicions' of sexual assault on the child by her father during an access visit. Questioning of the child by the mother and interviews by the worker using anatomically correct dolls showed that the allegations could not be substantiated. Despite this, concern for the child led to an application to the Family Court by the mother, assisted by the worker, to suspend access.

Finally, referrals about children in families G, J and T reflected generalized concerns about the care of children by single female parents. The case notes imply that the focus was on the competence of the mothers in all cases. Family G had four children under the age of six years (Cases 427–30) living with their mother in a country town. The referral, made by a visitor to the house, alleged that the children were 'neglected', which resulted in a visit by the department the next day. Family J was an Aboriginal mother with two children (Cases 360–1): 'People [were] concerned about the mother's treatment towards the children. [She] takes fits and gets very depressed . . . then starts hitting the kids'. Case 270 referred to a baby who was referred by a hospital because of 'no bonding to the child, no parenting skills'. In all three of these families, an external authority, whether agency or person outside the family, has defined in generalized terms the perceived inadequacies of the mothers of the children.

Despite the variations in the reasons for referral of the children, defined as 'at risk', the patterns of intervention and decision-making that did emerge were not connected to the allegations of harm to the children. They seemed to reflect a combination of 'parental cooperation', arrangements for alternative forms of care and support for children and vouching for parents by persons in authority.

In the vast majority of these 'at risk' cases, the workers either reduced the intensity of intervention or closed cases where the family accepted advice, made changes, or agreed to alternative support and care arrangements.

Family F, for example, whose home conditions were judged to be 'unsuitable' for 'adequate and healthy care of . . . children', initially received a strongly worded letter stating these concerns as potential 'strong evidence . . . that the children may be considered to be in need of care and protection'. The relevant section of the legislation was quoted in the letter as a basis for action if 'an immediate improvement . . . [did not] occur within a reasonable time'. The family's compliance with the advice given in the letter resulted in a commendation 'on the dramatic change in [home] conditions' and the continuation of regular surveillance.

In the cases where children in remote areas had disabilities or were vulnerable for other reasons, such as being newborn or having parents in poor health or disabilities such as 'fits' or 'depression', arrangements were made for the community 'to care for or supervise the care the children received'. These cases then were 'followed up' or 'monitored' at regular intervals, such as 'fortnightly' (Case 395), or 'every 6–8 weeks' (Cases 360–1). In the case of older children, such as the teenage girls in Cases 386 and 454, the cases were closed as soon as suitable care arrangements were finalized, either with the natural fathers or other relatives.

Parents who were vouched for by authority figures also had their cases closed or only 'informally' monitored. For example in Cases 427–30 the mother's competence was approved by a doctor whose examination revealed that one child was a 'healthy and well cared for baby'. Another example was an official at a remote Aboriginal community who said that the 'children are very healthy . . . [the mother always] says . . . I didn't touch my kids, I didn't hit them'.

Action through the Family Court to give some protection to a three year old from alleged sexual assault through supervised access was another arrangement which apparently satisfied the worker (Case 491). Other families, namely I (Cases 505–7) and T (Case 270) were not so cooperative. In both cases the families moved to other towns after 'readily agreeing' to intervention.

Practical and material only

Only two cases received practical and material help with no advice and guidance. Both these children (a four year old girl and a year old boy) lived with their parents in a Perth suburb. Physical assault allegations were made by their grandmother in the context of a couple who kept separating and then reuniting. The child protection worker wrote of his visit that

> [The father] came to the door and looked suspicious but generally welcoming. He was willing to discuss finance and general management, but cautious about discussing his relationship with his wife . . . [The mother] was initially angry and unwilling to enter into any discussion . . . She gave a half hearted agreement to my suggestion for [the little girl] to attend care five days each week . . . The house was filthy and cluttered with all manner of odds and ends, and looked as if it hadn't been cleaned for weeks.
>
> (Cases 188 and 189)

No advice was given by the worker here, merely the offer of help which was somewhat grudgingly and reluctantly accepted by an angry and resentful mother.

Advice, guidance and financial assistance

Two cases received both advice and guidance and financial assistance. Case 82 (a ten year old boy) was referred because his 'alcoholic' parents were on the verge of separating. By the time the child protection worker visited, they had parted and the mother was worried about her husband applying for custody. The mother was supported through the crisis and the parents referred on to marriage guidance counsellor. The mother was given $260 over a period of 13 weeks to help her to meet household expenses.

Case 614 was a 15 year old girl in conflict with her stepfather. The girl was helped to move out of the caravan home by the child protection worker into independent accommodation. While the department refused to subsidise her board and lodging, they gave her two financial assistance vouchers worth $50 and $30 respectively.

Advice, guidance, material and practical assistance

Six children lived in five families which were 'at risk' and received advice and guidance as well as material and practical assistance. All these children were infants, three were babies less than a year old, one was a one year old, one a two year old and one a three year old.

The caregivers in four out of these five families were all young and isolated mothers who were experiencing difficulties with very small children. There were two very reluctant women in this group and one who cooperated to a very high degree. Had her reaction to the presence of child protection workers been different, she might well have had her child compulsorily removed.

The reasons for referral of these families seemed to cover allegations of perceived 'deficiencies' in parenting, or more precisely, mothering. In all cases, the sources of referral were 'external' to the family.

Case 126 concerned a nine and a half month old baby boy, whose brother (Case 125) 'was referred because of a physical assault by the mother'. Case 422, a three month old baby, 'was alleged to have been neglected'. The language implies that a third party had made the allegations about the care of the children. Case 48 could not have been self-referred, because of the mother's 'defensive[ness] about her children, and [angry reaction] at any suggestions that they are not normal'. The worker said that little could be offered to the family 'until they are willing participants'.

The nature of the allegations suggest that the mothers were regarded as not caring for their young children 'adequately' as defined by the referral sources. For example, the mother of a one year old baby (Case 22) who was referred by the police, had spent the evening in a pub and then went home, leaving her baby outside the pub in its pram. The file notes that '[mother] very distressed – says she is an alcoholic and needs help. Quite distraught with her action in forgetting [the baby]'.

Cases 232 and 233 were a baby girl and her three year old brother. An anonymous caller alleged that 'there was no food in the house' and implied that the mother used drugs: '[needle marks] on the mother's arms'. The mother's lack of 'confidence' and 'competence' in feeding the child also were 'revealed' during the investigation.

In another case (48), the child in question had not been harmed in any way, but the characteristics of the child combined with the mother's circumstances seem to have led to a view that the children were 'at risk'. Thus Case 48 concerned a two year old intellectually disabled child, whose 'constant screaming exhausted his mother'. The potential risk to the child resulting from the mother's stress levels seem to have prompted intervention.

As was mentioned earlier, the decisions about the form of intervention offered and case closure seemed primarily to reflect mothers' levels of 'cooperativeness' with workers, their acknowledgement of needing help, and the vouching for them by recognized authorities.

Cases 22 and 422 exemplified these 'cooperating' mothers who accepted the services offered. In Case 22, the mother

> has been genuinely very shaken up by this experience and now openly acknowledges that she needs help and not just with her drinking problem ... her general attitude towards and handling of [the baby] seemed very good and clearly there is a close relationship.

In addition to the mother's acknowledgement of her need for help, her doctor said that she was 'not mentally ill, but is like many young women these days leading a disordered lifestyle and being subject to depression'. The doctor's comments seem to 'normalize' rather than 'pathologize' the mother's behaviour and lifestyle. The mother's cooperativeness and the doctor's vouching for her seemed to influence the worker's views by creating a focus on her needs rather than her shortcomings. The worker noted 'whether with day care ... and counselling [the mother] will have more of the needs met', instead of listing her inadequacies as a parent.

In two instances (Cases 232, 233 and 48) mothers did not want intervention or help and 'reluctantly' allowed the worker into the house (48) or 'adamantly opposed' help offered (232, 233). The former case was closed because the families were not 'willing participants'; the latter stayed open longer than intended because of a conflict between the mother and her family in which protection issues became the focus.

Advice, guidance, material, practical and financial assistance

Only two families involving three children received advice and guidance, financial assistance and practical and material help. Case 291 was a ten year old girl cared for by a single female mother. In interview, '[the mother's] speech was slurred and fragmented. Conversation centred round her deprived background – an orphan, a prostitute, a stripper "pussy cat on parade". It appeared [she] was under the influence of a drug'. The concerns were that she had placed too much responsibility on her daughter who 'had saved her mother's life twice when she overdosed'. Regular visits were made to the home and on one occasion 'three bags of groceries' were given by Christian Aid as well as a limited amount of money. However, eventually the mother voluntarily entered a drug rehabilitation clinic and the child went to live with her father. A letter to the father spelt out the terms and conditions of this arrangement

> stating that she was not to be returned to her mother's care until she [the mother] has demonstrated over a long period of time that she can live free of drug dependency ... should [the child] return to her mother's care prematurely then the Department may lodge an application with the Children's Court for [her] to be placed under the care of the Department.

The letter ended by giving the telephone number of the emergency child welfare service.

Cases 310 and 311 were boys aged four and two living with both parents, following an unsubstantiated allegation of a physical assault on one of the boys. Weekly visits were instigated because of concerns about the

> backgrounds of both parents ... their poor models of parenting style [which] have not equipped them with an adequate base in child management skills. They both display an overall concern for their children, are anxious the children not be removed from their care, and place the children as a high priority in their lives. They have a poor understanding of children's abilities, norms of behaviour and a general lack of tolerance and adaptive ability.

The four year old was enrolled in day care and weekly visits were organized 'to assist with child management skills'. Financial assistance was given on three occasions after the father left the home and there was no income for the family.

Treatment services

In four cases, 'treatment' was organized for 'at risk' situations. This involved a child and caregiver together in one case, and a caregiver of three children in a second family.

Case 82 (referred to earlier in the advice, guidance and financial assistance section) had a nine year old brother (Case 83). A psychologist saw both parents and the child. No information was contained in the case record about what this work consisted of. It might have been a lengthy programme or simply a one-off contact.

The mother of three girls aged 13, two and one (Cases 542, 549 and 560) 'was admitted to [a psychiatric hospital] by DCS Social Worker diagnosed as having a schizophrenic psychosis, partly brought about by excessive marijuana usage. The children were temporarily placed with family members'. The file note on the crisis leading to admission reveals that

> [the mother] answered the door in her underwear then asked me to wait while she dressed . . . [after being invited in] while dressed [the mother] seemed to be having problems with her skirt so she impatiently took off her jumper and skirt again and sat in her underwear.

After hospital treatment she rapidly stabilized and the children were returned to her care.

'At risk'/home-based services were the single largest group of service users in the study. While it is clear that there were genuine concerns for children living in poverty, with isolated single parents, we can also see that some families received intensive service while others merely received warnings. Many parents accepted help reluctantly, others had significant difficulties of their own connected with drugs and alcohol. In many cases, child protection workers facilitated the voluntary placement of children with relatives while the most severely incapacitated parents received other forms of help. The moral reasoning of workers took account of all these factors, but the basic concern wasn't simply with the hazards faced by children with parents who were incapacitated by substance misuse or mental illness; they also took note of matters such as 'parenting skills' and the willingness of parents to cooperate. In addition, most of the allegations were made by sources external to the family, such as police, hospitals or nurses. The opinions of these sources about the lifestyles or characters of the mothers/parents tended to influence the workers' conclusions about the risks faced by the children.

Neglect/home-based services

The neglect/home-based services cell in Table 4.12 shows that 25 of the 139 cases which received home-based services were substantiated as neglect. They

Table 6.3 Neglect/home-based services cases – caregiver family structure and ethnicity

Caregiver family structure	Aboriginal	Non-Aboriginal/ not known	Total	%
Reconstituting family	1	0	1	4
Single female parent	8	12	20	80
Single male parent	0	3	3	12
Not known	1	0	1	4
Total	10	15	25	100
%	40	60	100	

constituted 27 per cent of all neglect cases and 18 per cent of all cases which received services at home.

Table 6.3 crosstabulates caregiver family structure with ethnicity. Twenty (80 per cent) of the 25 neglected children who received home-based services were looked after by single female parents and a further three (12 per cent) were looked after by single male parents. Only two of the 25 cases did not come from single parent households. Aboriginals accounted for ten children in this group (40 per cent).

Table 6.4 Neglect/home-based services cases – neglect type and medical services

Neglect type	In-patient	No medical service	Total	%
Supervision	0	15	15	60
Food	4	1	5	20
Environment	0	1	1	4
Not known	0	4	4	16
Total	4	21	25	100
%	16	84	100	

Table 6.4 looks at the major type of neglect experienced by these children and the medical services they received. Nearly two-thirds of these children received services because of neglect of supervision (15 cases). Of the five children (20 per cent) who had their feeding neglected, four of these received in-patient treatment in hospital. The nature of neglect could not be deduced from the files in four cases.

Table 6.5   Neglect/home-based services cases – service types

Service type	Nos	%
Monitoring and surveillance only	5	20
Advice and guidance only	6	24
Material and pracical assistance only	2	8
Advice, guidance, material and practical assistance	4	16
Advice, guidance, material, practical and financial assistance	8	32
Total	25	100

Table 6.5 shows that nearly a third of these children (eight of the 25) received intensive services from the Department for Community Services. No caregivers in this group received 'treatment' for drug or alcohol problems or psychiatric conditions.

Monitoring and surveillance

Five children from two families were subject to monitoring and surveillance without receiving any help. The first family (Cases 97 and 98) consisted of a nine month old girl and four year old boy living with their mother. The file note reads

> [Mother and father] had separated. [Father] who then resided at [address] was caring for [the boy] and [the mother] retained [the girl] as she was breast-fed. On this occasion [the mother] visited and absconded with [the boy] leaving [the girl] with [the father].

An ongoing custody dispute developed over the children: 'The Department became involved through several accusations of alleged physical abuse/neglect mainly by [the father] who wished [the mother] to be declared an unfit mother'. The neglectful act had occurred when the mother visited her husband who at that stage had the children in his care. He was drunk and asleep. This permitted the case to be classed as neglect. The custody/access dispute was resolved within weeks when the mother was awarded custody of both children. A series of home visits continued when that order was varied and the mother and father continued separately to refer their ex-partner, alleging neglect.

Cases 631–3 were children aged ten, nine and seven living with their father. The allegations came from the police that the children were 'seen out on street unsupervised at 10.30 p.m.'. The father was a shift worker who had not made arrangements for the care of his children when he was not at home. The file reports that

> [the father's] first reaction was anxiety over who made the complaint and why no one else was complained about . . . he appreciated our positions but he was going to ignore it . . . he admitted he was having trouble coping but

felt things were going OK. I pointed out that it was not satisfactory for a 10 year old to look after a 9 and 7 year old at any time especially during the night . . . I suggested to [the father] that he employ a housekeeper or baby-sitter and clean the house and look after the kids . . . He felt children should learn responsibility at a young age . . . I offered to apply for financial assistance for him for help with employing a housekeeper but he declined and said he could afford it. Discussion ensued with the conclusion that [the father] was to employ some help. We would come back in 2–3 weeks and if the situation had not improved, DCS would have to apprehend the children.

Information was sought from the Health Department who replied that the house was no 'untidier than any other single parent's home in [the town]. The view was that this was a malicious complaint about a single father doing his best'. School attendance by the children was good. The investigator noticed that 'There were a few beer cans around the back but nothing else of any concern'. Three weeks later, the child protection worker visited the town again. The school commented that the 'children were arriving at school cleaner, tidier and with lunches'. He called at the house, got the father out of bed and

He said he has got some help to clean the house and to look after the children . . . I wasn't invited in but the house looked very tidy from where I stood. The floor was clear, the table set and the dishes were washed. I congratulated [the father] and told him I was pleased because the children were obviously happy living with him and I wanted it to stay that way.

Practical and material assistance only

There were two cases in the neglect/home-based services category which received material/practical assistance. Both were Aboriginal children, but at almost opposite ends of the state. Case 265 was a six year old boy visiting relatives in Perth. He and his mother were staying with a family described earlier (Cases 1–3, p. 70). For Cases 1–3 this was a second episode, but the mother of the child in question (Case 265) had moved to see other relatives in Perth, leaving her six year old boy with the mother of Cases 1–3. The referral form reads

Last Friday, children wandered down to pre-primary, had been playing with friends and found no one at home when they returned. [The Community Health worker] met [the mother] at home, [the mother] arguing that kids had 'wandered off' and whacked them. [The Community Health worker] blasted [the mother], arranged to visit weekly to monitor and will advise DCS if further concerns arise.

Three days later the Community Health worker, telephoned the department:

visited [the mother] this a.m. found her drunk, not coping. [She] said 'tell [the social worker] to take the children away'. [The Community Health worker] feels [the mother] doesn't really mean this and will visit again this p.m. to see if [she] has sobered.

A Family Resource Worker was allocated to the case and the children found a place in a playgroup. The final note on the file reads that

> [The mother's] lapse from her usually good standards of child care resulted from an acute period of low spirits [due to a multitude of factors] in which she began drinking heavily. Now that she is back on a (reasonably) even keel there is no need for further DCS involvement – especially since Community Health maintains regular contact with her.

Case 393 was a 17 month old Aboriginal child living in a remote northwest community. He was referred by the Community Health agency because of failure to thrive. His care was assumed by his maternal grandmother. Photocopies of the case file in this instance do not include the documents which described the nature of the material/practical assistance given to the child, but basic continuing overseeing of the child remained with community health. Minutes of an interdisciplinary child protection case conference merely state ' Health workers have been involved with the family and some progress made. [The mother] has put in for a transfer to [a local town]'.

Advice and guidance

Six children from four families in the neglect/home-based service category received advice and guidance services. Cases 19 and 20 were nine and 11 year old boys who appeared to be beyond the control of their single female parent.

> [A neighbour] contacted the Unit stating that [the boys] were with her next-door neighbour. She was aware that they had not been staying at their own home for some days, staying with her neighbour on some occasions, and sleeping in the park on others . . . on interviewing the boys . . . [one child] advised me that he and [his brother] had run away from home because they were belted with a leather strap for little if any reason and that his mother had told him that she did not want him in the house any longer. The overwhelming impression I gained from [the child] was that he was worldly beyond his years . . . whilst it was clear that there were some problems with [the mother's] handling of the boys I was not entirely convinced of [the child's] version of events.

In fact the neighbour who made the referral also said that she suspected the boys had been smoking marijuana and that when she went to speak to the mother, she was 'out with her boyfriend'. The mother was interviewed separately and

> it was clear that the efforts to manage and control the boys' behaviour had been unsuccessful. It also appeared that whilst she was concerned that the boys were safe she had no concern or inclination to attempt to take control of the situation this evening. It was her view that any attempt to return the boys to the house would simply result in them running away again. She perceives herself as totally powerless to prevent this.

A few days later, the reason for referral was listed as being 'hyperactive and difficult to control, violence towards family members and fights with peers, verbally abusive, vandalism, marijuana user and suspected of "popping pills", school truancy and mother requests support'. The plan, developed with the mother,

> involves moving into [her boyfriend's] house in [a suburb] which in effect gives her the support she says she needs and provides a male figure in the boys' lives. Mother sees that this will provide a family environment for the boys and a structure that has been lacking.

The child protection worker then added 'Because of the substantial change in plans and because [the mother] has requested the right to continue without our support, we would see it as advantageous for her to follow through her plans'.

Cases 332 and 333 were in an Aboriginal family referred by the police who

> contacted the office requesting our intervention as the above children had been breaking and entering, stealing and shop-lifting. He [the police officer] was also concerned about the lack of supervision in the home and minimal concern from the mother about the seriousness of her children's behaviour.

A number of services were discussed with the mother 'who claimed [the oldest boy] was the main problem' (see Case 331, p. 99). The worker commented that 'The maternal grandmother . . . had offered more stability for the children as she is more at home than [the mother]. She took [the oldest child] away with her for the holidays which was a good strategy'. On checking with the schools, it was established that the oldest boy 'attends (the school) fairly regularly . . . I contacted these schools on [date] – no problems'. The file summary said

> [The mother] appears to be an urban Aboriginal mother with minimum parenting skills. She doesn't appear to have the ability to change and is extremely difficult to contact, leaving the supervision of her children to her mother and sister. Several attempts to engage [the mother] to accept support has failed.
>
> Historically DCS intervention with Aboriginal families like this one has not achieved much and in some cases there have been undesirable consequences for children. As there have been no further complaints and the children are attending school, there doesn't appear to be any urgency to keep this case open.

Case 540 was a 15 year old boy, whom the police apprehended using their powers of emergency removal. The police said that 'Evidence from neighbours suggested that [his mother] frequently stayed over night at her boyfriend's flat . . . and left [the boy] to fend for himself'. The youth had 'been charged with various offences relating to a stolen bicycle and further charges may follow. The police also believe that he has been smoking marijuana'. Interview with the mother confirmed

> that she leaves [the boy] unsupervised for long periods. This is partly due to the nature of her job where she is required to work late several nights a week. She was in the habit of calling in to see her boyfriend on the way home and so

would often not get back until late in the evening. She said there were only occasional nights when she did not return home.

The child protection worker

agreed with the police that we would work with the family on a voluntary basis and in return they would drop the care and protection. [The boy] was fined for the offences . . . Since the court hearing [the boy] has moved to stay with his mother and her boyfriend. He has enrolled with [a new] high school but he has presented problems there.

After checking out the mother's relationship with her boyfriend, establishing that they planned to marry and that they wanted the boy to remain with them, the case was closed.

Case 605 was a six year old girl who was one of a family of six children, all under the age of ten years (see Cases 573–7, p. 136). This girl was one of the children who was not removed from home although a care and protection application was lodged and then withdrawn on all the children. The family had a long history of contact with the department, largely because the oldest child had become a persistent juvenile offender who became a state ward after a prosecution. The father was unemployed and the parents lived in great disorder. The file indicates that after a few weeks (when the care and protection applications were withdrawn)

The family is looking better every week, Mum and Dad don't drink near as much as they did and they appear to have their household under control. They no longer allow people to visit and stay overnight. They only drink two days each fortnight which is usually pension day. The house looked reasonably clean on my recent visits and I have not seen [the father] or [the mother] drunk yet. We also have not received any reports from the police regarding disturbances etc. . . . [The parents] believe they have things at home very much under control and no longer have big drinking sessions or overnight binges. [The mother] helps [the oldest child] with his homework on occasions but not all the time. They make sure their fridge is full of food to last them through before they buy alcohol.

Advice, guidance, material and practical assistance

There were four cases in the neglect/home-based services category which received both advice/guidance and material/practical assistance. These children came from one family and they were all less than four years old (including two-year old twins). The referral came from a doctor who said of the mother, 'Her husband has left her and gone to live with his father . . . there have been medical signs for some time regarding lack of adequate diet and clothing'. The doctor had spoken to the mother about his concerns, but he had been informed that day by a neighbour '[who didn't know where to go about it] . . . that [the mother] went out yesterday evening and didn't return until 10.00 a.m. today'. Someone had been in the house 'because there was water running all over the place and found a lady friend [of the mother] on a bed, but incapable (drink or drugs?) of caring for children' (Cases 102–5). The mother was interviewed

at 8.30 a.m. . . . dressed in night attire. . . .she denied the allegation that the baby-sitter was incapable on the night in question. She also denied there was any neglect of the children by way of diet and/or clothing. Further discussion revealed the following. 1) [Case 102] has an abscess under her arm as a result of an infected cut, 2) the twins have very little hair, and [the mother] claims this is a result of a disorder of the scalp. She states she has an appointment tomorrow at [a hospital] re this . . . The house was in a somewhat dishevelled state at the time of my call and it was clear that [the mother] had no routine for her children. They had no dressing gowns, and [the mother] made no attempt to put warmer clothing on them. [The mother] stated that the baby was due to attend the health clinic yesterday, but she had forgotten. The children appeared to be at no immediate risk, but obviously their health is of concern. [The mother] is in need of considerable support and liaison with medical personnel is essential. [She] will require assistance with day care, Family Resource Workers and possibly [a psychologist].

It transpired that the children's dietary deficiencies were 'somewhat disguised by the fact that [the mother] gives the children lots of milk, hence they appear well fed, but lacking in essential vitamins and iron'. Also, the mother 'was recently involved in a motor vehicle accident, and charged with drunk driving – [she] was vague as to who was caring for the children at this time'. The mother was not keeping medical appointments, but was 'currently "shopping around" medical personnel when she is confronted with the fact that the children's medical problems are diet related'. The twins were admitted to hospital for tests and then treatment by means of dietary supplementation. The practical assistance consisted of the provision of day care places for all the children and the case was closed after medical monitoring and continuing visits to ensure that the day care places were used.

Advice, guidance, material, practical and financial assistance

Eight children, from three families received the most intensive home-based services (advice and guidance, material, practical and financial assistance). Case 331 was the brother of children referred to earlier – Cases 332 and 333 (p. 97), the urban Aboriginal family about which the child protection worker expressed scepticism about the effectiveness of intervention. This particular child was 'given a football and fees paid for his enrolment in a local junior football team. [The worker] attempted to engage [the mother] in a community sewing group but rarely found her at home'.

Cases 535, 544 and 545 were three children aged from three to six years of age. The allegation was that '[The mother] drinks excessively. Supervision of children is inadequate, children seen playing outside without clothes on in the early hours of the morning'. A visit to the home revealed that 'the lounge room was sparsely furnished, untidy and dirty, clothes were strewn over the lounge settee. Papers, toys, shoes and pot plants were lying on the floor. Children had drawn on the walls'. The mother denied that she allowed the children to play outside unclothed, and

> when asked about her drinking habits [she] confirmed that she did drink moselle, in the afternoons or evening but only one or two glasses. She denied that she had a drinking problem. When asked if she had been drinking this day she replied that she had 2 glasses of moselle after lunch before she put the children to sleep. It was evident that [she] had been drinking.

The mother said that she saw nothing of her ex-husband (who had access rights) and her family lived in the eastern states. The worker's plan pointed to financial difficulties, isolation and lack of confidence. She was given money to help with bills (a washing machine repair, mortgage arrears, an electricity bill). She was taken to a playgroup with the children – which she didn't like because it wasn't for 'people like her e.g. single parent – pensioner'. After one visit the worker left the house and noted

> when we left to go to the park and as [the mother] stepped into the car there was a distinct smell of alcohol on her breath. She and [the baby] enjoyed the time in the park. When I left, I made an appointment to see [the mother] the following week however, she phoned the office and cancelled.

A later case summary noted that

> The assessment of [a psychiatric clinic] was that [her] depression was a reactive one to life events and did not represent underlying psychiatric disorder. This diagnosis has been borne out by subsequent events. [The mother] has considerably improved her child care to the extent that there is no longer a concern about neglect of the children. Her financial position has been stabilized and she has made several productive social contacts which notably reduced her social isolation. [Her] alcohol consumption remains a concern. She firmly denies that she has any problem in this regard but observations would suggest she is alcohol-dependent. This is not presently interfering with her child care to any substantial degree but could pose a problem if the dependence increases.

The case was closed three months later, one child was attending a crèche and the mother was going to a voluntary group for single parents as well as enrolling for an assertiveness training course.

Cases 685–8 were four Aboriginal children, again in a single female parent family, referred by Community Health because care for the children had

> deteriorated. The children are unsupervised and have a general air of neglect. They are all below the third percentile in weight. [The youngest child] was admitted to [a hospital] . . . with vomiting and severe weight loss, he was in an appalling condition.

The mother was said to be 'frequently intoxicated'. After a visit by child protection workers a contract was drawn up in which the mother agreed to

> the following conditions and to accept the following support in order to retain [her] children in [her] custody and control: 1) Accept intervention, support and advice from the family support worker 2) . . . ensure that [her house is] kept in a reasonable standard of cleanliness and that there is sufficient food in the home for [the] children 3) . . . accept budgeting advice (withdrawal of only half of her benefits) 4) ensure [the two oldest children] attend school every day 5) . . . take all the children to the . . . [health centre] for a check-up once a fortnight . . . each month they will see the Child Health Sister . . . attend all appointments with the visiting paediatrician 6) . . . make an effort to curb drinking of alcohol . . . and . . . accept counselling from the Alcohol and Drug authority.

The mother was loaned $250 for a washing machine, given vouchers for food, clothing, beds and blankets. One note on the file says

> [date] shows that of 190 hours work [a family resource worker] 115 hours, or approximately 60%, has been spent with [the mother of these children] or working with her specific problems as they relate to her children i.e. alcoholism and home hygiene, or directly with the four children.

On another note, improvements in respect of 'dramatically reduced alcohol intake,' school attendance and children gaining weight were noted as well as improved standards of 'house care and maintenance'.

Emotional abuse/home-based services

Table 4.12 shows us that five children fell into the category of emotional abuse/home-based services. All these children came from five separate families, they all received advice and guidance supplemented in two cases by treatment for two of the children. They were all, with one exception (a seven year old), adolescents.

Case 174 was an 11 year old boy who was left in the care of his grandmother six years previously by his mother. Grandmother's home was 'condemned as unfit' by the local authority, so a voluntary arrangement was made for him to stay with friends. After a few weeks the condemnation order was ended and the boy returned to live with his grandmother. While he was staying away allegations were made about his behaviour; he was described as being

> fairly overweight for his age – literally wolfing through 8 rounds of pressed meat sandwiches . . . it was explained [to him] that we were not taking him away but making a private arrangement [with his neighbour] whilst the house was condemned . . . [the grandmother] was under major pressure from the authorities and DCS did not wish to be offside but seen as supportive and would maintain our support.

Initially the grandmother 'said she'd expected the Welfare to swoop on [the child] and take him away. I said we'd only do that if there was no other option and we did not want a hostile lad on our hands'. The boy saw a clinical psychologist who described him as

> a highly manipulative boy, accustomed to getting his own way. He readily admitted to being 'spoilt' and to deliberately using sulking and tantrums as a means of doing as he pleases and getting what he wants. [He] is actually proud of his manipulative abilities.

The report concluded that

> In many ways he presents merely as a classic example of a child raised by an indulgent grandmother figure . . . emotional damage is more likely to occur as a result of removing him from [his grandmother's] care . . . I would like to see [him] encouraged to attend some social or sports activities with peers in his leisure time and to attend some camping activities during school holidays. [He] does not currently require any psychological inputs.

The case was closed after the boy returned to his grandmother. It was categorized as emotional abuse because he was 'spoilt'.

Case 304 was a 17 year old girl described as 'very unhappy at home or school. Frightened of alcoholic father, disliked bossy, status-conscious mother, scared of older brother'. She was admitted to a psychiatric clinic where she remained 'in shelter' for eight weeks. Child protection workers helped organize the admission, but by the time the girl was due for discharge, they decided to cease their involvement. Her brother was described in the file as 'a very high achiever . . . very powerful, very manipulative'. The family refused to cooperate with both the department and the psychiatric clinic.

Case 373 was a 13 year old girl who was

> kicked out of home by stepmother . . . on Friday they had gone to the [local youth centre] disco. The person giving the girl a lift was running late. When [she] got home at 12.30 a.m. all doors and windows were locked. [She] slept the night at a friend's place. Came home at 9.00 a.m. to find [her] clothing and other bits and pieces on the verandah.

Visits were made to the girl's home where her father and stepmother described the girl as 'the problem'. They said she lied about her whereabouts, didn't help in the home and 'plays upon stepmother [who] does not speak or understand English'. Arrangements were made for the girl to go and live with her mother and a few days later she departed and the case was closed.

Case 409 was a seven year old boy who was left with his brother 'with caravan park caretaker . . . while [the mother] and *de facto* went away – either Bush or to Adelaide'. Child protection workers visited. It transpired during enquiries that the older child was not even registered at a school let alone attending one. None of the allegations of neglect were substantiated but the mother was seen to be

> obviously rather possessive of her son. She says that she has given him lessons herself. She is presently trying to teach him about Aboriginal

dreamtime ... The above may be part of the reason why they have neglected to enrol [him] in a school.

Arrangements were made for the education department to write a formal letter about schooling and to enrol the child. The case was classified as emotional abuse because of the failure by the parents to make educational provision. The plan on the file ends by saying

> Because the allegations were denied and the explanations the couple gave to the allegations appear adequate, I am satisfied that we do not need to go and visit the family again. However if we do receive a further complaint I would not ignore it. The family are aware that if we do receive further complaints we will return to see them.

They had been warned. The worker closed the case with a note on her concerns about the 'somewhat transient' nature of the family, adding that she would ring the headteacher of the school later that week 'and enquire if [the child] has been enrolled'. The letter from the Education Department said

> It has been brought to my attention that you have a school aged child who is not at school. Since this is illegal and subject to a considerable fine I would suggest that you enrol [him] as soon as possible at [a primary school, telephone number supplied].

This was the only Aboriginal child in this group of cases.

Case 417 was a 13 year old girl referred from school because she was about to be suspended for aggressive behaviour (she swore at a teacher). It was established during the investigations that the father 'had a serious alcohol problem and that [the child] was treated very negatively by him'. The mother decided to visit Perth with her daughter and take her to a psychiatric clinic. 'It appears that [the mother] is truly concerned for her daughter and is prepared to do something about the problem'. The girl was eventually expelled from school; she spent a month in a psychiatric clinic from where she was 'expelled' (discharged). Contact with the girl and her family continued for some time with a lot of appointments with a clinical psychologist. A year later the department closed the case because 'the home situation has improved markedly as has [the child's] behaviour. [The father] has reduced his consumption of alcohol due to regular visits and both parents have participated in counselling sessions to some degree'.

Physical abuse/home-based services

Twenty cases appear in the physical abuse/home-based services cell in Table 4.12. Tables 6.6, 6.7 and 6.8 deal with caregiver family structure, ethnicity, harms/injuries, actions causing them and medical services for those cases.

Table 6.6 shows that in this category, Aboriginal people and single female parents are *under*represented in comparison with 'at risk' and neglect cases which had similar service careers (see Tables 6.1 to 6.5). Only four of the 20 children

Table 6.6 Physical abuse/home-based services cases – family structure and ethnicity

Family structure	Aboriginal	Non-Aboriginal	Total	%
Both biological parents	0	4	4	20
Reconstituting family	0	8	8	40
Single female parent	4	4	8	40
Total	4	16	20	100
%	20	80	100	

were Aboriginal and only eight in total were cared for by single female parents. Eight children (40 per cent of this group) came from reconstituting families.

The injuries and the causes of them are shown in Table 6.7. Eighteen (90 per cent) of these children were injured by means of excessive corporal punishment and in 15 (80 per cent) of these cases, children sustained injuries in the nature of cuts, bruises and welts (there were no bites). Two children were thrown.

Table 6.7 Physical abuse/home-based services cases – harms/injuries and actions which caused them

Harm/injury	Excessive corporal punishment	Throwing	Total	%
Cuts, bruises, welts, bites	15	1	16	80
No identifiable injury	0	1	1	5
Not known	3	0	3	15
Total	18	2	20	100
%	90	10	100	

As shown in Table 6.8, none of these 20 children required medical treatment of any kind as a result of their injuries, but seven were medically examined.

Table 6.9 shows that three-quarters of these cases received advice and guidance only, while three cases received financial assistance and one case material and practical assistance in addition. Only one case was subject to monitoring and surveillance.

Table 6.8 Physical abuse/home-based services cases – harm/injury and medical services

Harm/injury	Medical examination	No medical service	Total	%
Cuts, bruises, welts, bites	6	10	16	80
No identifiable injury	0	1	1	5
Not known	1	2	3	15
Total	7	13	20	100
%	35	65	100	

Table 6.9 Physical abuse/home-based services cases – service types

Service type	Nos	%
Monitoring and surveillance only	1	5
Advice and guidance only	15	75
Advice, guidance and financial assistance	3	15
Advice, guidance, material and practical assistance	1	5
Total	20	100

Monitoring and surveillance

This latter case (Case 303) was a 16 year old girl living with her single female parent, who referred herself because her mother

> drinks publicly and privately . . . [and she] was forced [by her mother] to get out of her bed and do the dishes at 3.00 a.m. Her mother also hit [the child] about the head. On this occasion her brother . . . 16 years, who lives down the road with the father . . . happened to be staying the night, intervened to prevent any further physical harm to [the child]. Apparently on [a recent date], the mother tried to drown [the child] in the bath. These physical attacks appear to be prompted by heavy drinking. [The child] says that everything else – food, care is satisfactory in the home.

The child had a 'very slight swelling to the left cheek bone'. The mother was interviewed, she

> acknowledged that she drinks but not to excess. She states that the two incidents of 'physical' attacks on [the child] were related to [the child's] involvement with her father. [The mother] does not like [the child] going to the father's flat.

The conclusion was that 'there is little doubt, that [the mother] does care for her children and tries to protect them. However, the elder children are caught in the adult conflicts'. The case was kept open by telephone contact with the school. There was a visit a month later as a result of concern at the school about the mother's boyfriend who had moved into the house and who was said to 'drink heavily'. The worker

> suggested to [the mother] that it would be in the interests of herself and the children if a social worker visited her once a week to monitor the situation. In this way, accusations re poor care could be dismissed as not true. Such action would protect the family and curb some of the extreme activities i.e. drinking, verbal abuse in the home.

A few days later during a visit to the school, a teacher described the mother as 'a lovely person when she is not drinking'. Weekly visits were agreed. The file notes later that mother was 'reluctant to accept my presence, but agreed to visits for approximately one month'.

Advice and guidance

Fifteen children – three from one family, the rest from 12 separate families – received advice and guidance only after physical abuse was substantiated. Case 12, an eight year old boy, was referred by his school where he had attended 'with cut on head and bruise under right eye. Says his mother threw a can at him and kicked his head when he was in trouble about homework yesterday'. The boy was interviewed at school:

> He was frightened about our intended visit to his home. [He] said that [his stepmother] had told him not to tell anybody or she would belt him again. He said that his father was in bed when he left for school this morning and had not seen any of the injuries.

After discussing the situation with the boy's father and a very hostile and aggressive stepmother it was decided that the boy should go to live with his aunt. The worker

> then rang [the aunt] who readily accepted care of [the boy] and said that she wasn't surprised at the situation as she had heard rumours of his poor treatment by [stepmother]. I then rang [stepmother] back and told her I would be collecting [the boy] within thirty minutes to take him to his aunt's.
> On my arrival [she] had all [the boy's] gear packed in garbage bags but had neglected to tell [him] what was happening to him. He dutifully picked up the bags as she snarled at him to get out and don't come back. I briefly asked her for an explanation for his bruises and she snapped back 'I lost my temper' and added 'But I didn't kick him in the face'. With that happy and jovial place left behind I conveyed [the boy] to his aunt's place ... The [aunt] made us both very welcome and assured me [the child] would be fine with her. She went on to say that she had been concerned [for him] for some time but family politics had not allowed her to be more vocal.

Cases 32–4 were an Aboriginal family of three children all under four years of age. They were referred by a doctor who was concerned about the mother's 'current stress level'. He said that she had 'got to the stage of trying to keep the children contained by hitting them'. The mother was interviewed, she was

> very tired almost to the point of lifelessness. Children with their grand-mother. Aunty there visiting, says she's prepared to have the children, also . . . [the mother] admitted to losing her 'cool' with the children and sometimes hitting them too hard . . . advised DCS would not tolerate abuse of children . . . recommended strongly that she find alternative care for children before hitting [them], by phoning [her family] DCS [Emergency Duty] or a [family centre]. She is going to the [family centre] this afternoon re playgroup etc. at [another location].

The mother moved to live with the grandmother and child protection workers organized a lengthy correspondence with the doctor and housing agency to try and get the family relocated nearer the grandmother. However, the housing transfer was held up for some months because of rent arrears. Notes on the file about finding the $180 to pay off the arrears did not result in any help forthcoming with regard to rehousing.

Case 38 was an eight year old girl referred by her school which reported 'bruises seen on [her] buttocks by [the referrer] and principal Mistress'. She said that she had been hit with a stick by her mother's *de facto*. The child was interviewed at school, but refused to get into the child protection worker's car. She was walked towards the house by one worker, the second followed in a car.

> As [the child] left the school grounds she met with [the mother] and [*de facto*] who had been driving around looking for [her]. (I was later told by [the *de facto*] that [she] was often late home from school, sometimes stopping to play on the way). Because [the mother] refused to return to her home for an interview, saying that [her partner] was about to leave on a journey, [the worker] had to speak with her in [the street] outside the school grounds. This lasted for approximately 25 minutes and was not conducive to forming a satisfactory working relationship.

Eventually, 'an agreement was reached for the mother to meet with myself to examine ways of intervening. [Her partner] will not be able to be involved as he will be away for one month'. Five months later the closing note on file read 'The situation at home is good and has been so since my early involvement, (once the family accepted the fact that changes needed to be made . . . (the school) will maintain a "watching" brief . . . and will contact (me) if the need arises'.

Case 125 was a four year old boy whose mother had 'hit him on to floor, damaged teeth and swollen lip took him to GP and dentist. Says it has only happened once before – previous week. Lady very frightened of what she has done'.

At interview, the mother said 'that her anger was not caused because of the child's behaviour but because of feelings which she was unable to control within herself'. The mother began to attend a psychiatric clinic 'she has been very keen to listen to and act on suggestions . . . she has now adopted a different daily routine and hence starts the day off by feeling relaxed and comfortable with her husband and children instead of feeling stressed . . . A very satisfactory outcome due to [the mother's] desire to alter the situation and her preparedness to take full advantage of any opportunity offered'.

Case 292 was a 12 year old boy referred by a counselling service which had been seeing his mother: 'Abuse occurs after [the *de facto*'s] drinking bouts and takes the form of pushing, twisting of ears, stripping of clothing etc.'. The family was interviewed and the mother said she would attend for counselling.

> Since [the mother's] attendance at [the centre] her insight and awareness have increased greatly. Departmental officers have been attempting to further support her in making some protective decisions regarding [the child]. However [the mother] now appears to be changing her behaviour to cope with the home situation thus leaving [the child] in a position that remains abusive. [A psychiatric] assessment has been requested to clarify the current effects of abuse on [the child] and also to provide greater understanding as to the impact of statutorily removing [the child] from his present family situation. This is an option which may need to be considered in the future, should [the mother's] position remain unchanged.

A few days later the boy expressed a wish to return to the care of his natural father in another state. He was interviewed again and

> remained adamant about returning to his father . . . Initially [the mother] was opposed to [his] request though now appreciates that [his interstate move] appears to be inevitable. [The mother] will probably allow [the child] to move at the end of the year though she does not view this move as a positive one.

The boy left to live with his father four months later, and his mother was helped to 'let go' by means of a grief counselling course.

Case 385 was a 15 year old Aboriginal girl referred from a hospital

> on [date] night [the child] had been over [at] her auntie's place until quite late. When she returned home, her mother was very upset with her. She began hitting [the child], [she] ran to get away, hit a chair and consequently started to bleed. She was sent into [a hospital] to be checked.

The girl was pregnant, and she stayed in the town at a relative's house instead of going back to her community. A few days later the mother was seen. She agreed to girl's version of events and said

> There is a problem revolving around [the child's] boyfriend . . . There are tribal problems surrounding their relationship . . . It appears [the child] does not understand the problems that could arise if she continues seeing [him]. [She] has been staying with her Auntie in [a town] for the past week. She knows very little about her father's side of the family. This has given her the opportunity to meet some of her relatives.

The child protection worker then noted 'During visits [to the community] visit the family just to monitor the situation, make sure [the child] is okay. She may need to discuss any problems she is having'.

Case 405 was an eight year old boy referred by his school: 'Apparently last Friday [the boy] had been hit with the tubing from a vacuum cleaner and has bruises on his thighs, hip and around his temple . . . [his teacher] . . . confirmed that there was extensive bruising'. The boy's mother, a recent migrant to Australia from another part of Asia, 'presented as a very tired, emotional woman. Being [from another Asian country] she kept apologising for the state of the house (which was clean and tidy) and her appearance (which was okay).' The mother

> became very upset and started crying . . . she appears to be on the verge of a breakdown – [she] talked about the fact that she is pregnant again and doesn't want to be, the baby's cough and not sleeping at night, the bookwork for their business which is behind, and about how angry and frustrated she gets when [the boy] disobeys her.

The mother was offered, but refused 'a couple of days' rest in hospital'. The worker

> spent a long time discussing alternatives to disciplining [the boy and] that the school was concerned and would be keeping an eye on [him] . . . [the mother] was not at all defensive and readily admitted that she often felt like killing [the boy] . . . [she] cried the whole time.

The investigation concluded that the mother 'is going to need support but that she will not take it for fear of being seen as not coping. She is aware that people will be keeping an eye on [the boy] so I feel that beating will not occur again'.

A week later the father was contacted by telephone, he

> was very understanding but said his wife had a very hot temper . . . He is aware that [his wife] needs assistance and support with the children – especially [the boy] and said he tried to spend time with them after work and weekends so [she] could have a rest . . . He was adamant that the beating was a one-off incident and said that he had got angry at [her] and told her the punishment had been excessive.

A few days later after checking with the child health services that all was well, the file noted that the mother had gone to hospital for a 'couple of days' rest . . . she appeared quite happy and relaxed when I visited. [The boy] appears well and [she] said her husband had been spending more time with the children and had taken over disciplining [the boy]'.

Case 416 was a three year old boy with a stressed mother, referred by a neighbour who reported that at a darts match the night before

> [The child] had been pestering his mother for something and in a fit of temper, [the mother] had picked him up and thrown him heavily onto a table. [The boy] had sustained a cut cheek from the incident when his face hit some chairs nearby.

The injury was confirmed by the pre-school centre and the boy was interviewed there where he confirmed the story and the mother attended at the office the next day for an interview.

> She was very distressed and admitted that she was under a great deal of stress. She has made previous contact with [the Emergency Duty Team] recently when she felt she could no longer cope. She had also sought the help of [a community health nurse] who she said was giving her 'counselling'.

Three factors were listed as 'influencing her inability to cope'. First there were gynaecological problems (she was due shortly to have a hysterectomy), second 'she sees [the child] as hyperactive and says he has been diagnosed as such' and third, there were 'personal conflicts with other people' in a self-help single parents group to which she had been referred. The file comments '[she] sees her relationship with both her children as positive . . . she feels [the child] as continually testing her and this wears her down'. The child protection worker established that the children were to stay with their father during the school holiday and after that her mother would be coming to stay during and after the operation 'so it looks as though [the mother's] attention will be diverted for at least a few weeks'. She was given a form which was designed with the worker to look at her interaction with the child. A follow-up appointment was made to look at the daily schedule of interactions between the mother and children.

Case 424 was a 15 year old youth who came into a departmental office on the advice of his doctor who had examined him after he complained about being hit around the head and abdomen with fists by his mother's *de facto* partner. There was one bruise on his scalp behind an ear. The youth said that there had been arguments with this man about clothes and shoes, one of these arguments resulted in the fight. The mother was telephoned, she came to the office and confirmed the youth's story – adding that a few days earlier he had shouted obscenities at this man who was

> surprised, deeply offended and hurt by [the youth's] verbal abuse. She explained that tension had been building since [the youth] had been picked up by the police after stealing money from the video shop . . . I explained [to her] that the department took such an assault [on the youth] by his stepfather very seriously. She assured me and [the youth] that she could ensure [his] safety and would inform [her partner] that I wished to see him about the matter. I asked [the youth] to return to the office on [date].

The youth returned two days later 'and told me that things were much better at home. He appeared less tense and unhappy'. The mother's partner was seen later, he described

> his disappointment and hurt and anger at [the youth's] involvement in stealing and swearing at [him] . . . he justified his attack on [the youth] and said he could not guarantee that he would not do so again, if under provocation.

The worker explained the department's role and responsibilities and the man considered he wanted the same protection as the youth was 'younger, taller and possibly stronger than he is'. A week later there was a joint meeting of the whole family in which everyone expressed the view that 'there had been better communication between family members'.

Case 489 was a 14 year old youth who was referred by a school nurse because he 'received a belting from his stepfather and things haven't been very good at home'. The mother was interviewed; she described a very tense and difficult relationship between stepfather and her son: 'She said the air is electric the whole time between them and is very unpleasant'. Apparently the stepfather gave him 'quite a hiding for no apparent reason other than being initiated by the noise of the children having fun'. There was no record of any interview with the stepfather on file, but the youth was seen on eight occasions by a student social worker 'to build [his] self-esteem and to provide him with insight into his behaviour, and to look at the way [he] interacts with others around him'.

Case 531 was a 16 year old girl who came to a departmental office saying that

> her home situation was extremely stressful, the main factors being her step-father's alcoholism and his conflict with her mother. (She) also disclosed some incidents of physical abuse by her step-father which occurred in the past.

The stepfather 'had hit her once across the face with an open hand. This was for truanting'. The mother was interviewed at the office and after much discussion it was decided that the child should go to her grandmother's home while the mother could get counselling from another agency.

> In discussion [the mother] fully accepted her responsibility to protect her children, both in the short and long term . . . during the interview [she] cried a number of times, especially at having to choose between her child and her husband . . . [In conclusion] although low on personal resources at present, [the mother] is aware of her responsibilities for her children, and wants a better life for herself. I believe that, given time, she will be able to reach a decision in regard to her marriage.

The mother then took her daughter to the grandmother's home and the case was closed six weeks later after checking that the girl had settled with her.

Case 563 was a three year old girl referred by her mother's solicitor after she came back from a weekend access visit with her father, with a bruise (confirmed by medical examination). Apparently the father had hit her 'with a strap for wetting her pants'. In interview, the child confirmed this along with a medical certificate. The mother said that her estranged husband's 'upbringing had been that a strap was appropriate punishment. Discipline was usually a source of conflict between [husband and wife] and resulted in being the main reason why [she] left him'. The mother had immediately set in motion steps to end the access arrangements; the file note reads '[The mother] would like us to investigate basically to provide support for her court applications'. She was told by the child protection worker 'that we would consider the children as being at risk if [her husband] had further unsupervised contact'. The case was closed ten weeks later after the mother confirmed that since receiving a solicitor's letter she had had no further contact with her husband.

Advice, guidance and financial assistance

Three children from two families were in the physical abuse/home-based services category, who received financial assistance as well as advice and guidance. Case 279 was a three year old boy. The file notes that

> [The mother] and [child] presented at office for financial assistance [first time] . . . [she] was very distressed – alternating between weeping and laughing hysterically. [The child] presented with a bruise under left eye. [The mother's] explanation for the bruise was that she had been angry with [him] and threw him onto his bed where there was a bucket under the cover and [he] had hit his eye on the edge of the bucket. [The mother] has had lots of stress to cope with. [The child's] father . . . is a heroin addict in [eastern state] . . . Her family is not particularly supportive . . . I suggested part-time day care might give her a break which she agreed was a good idea. [The mother] needs support in arranging this and in plugging her into other community resources to give her personal support. She may want to return to work – she is a professional [person]. She said she felt relieved at end of interview. I gave her a $60 FAV.

The file summary said

> [The mother] does not receive much support from her family . . . despite the pressures of recent years, and the lack of support. [She] impressed me as a competent and independent person. Her rapport with [the child] was obvious.

The case was closed two weeks later.

Cases 382 and 383 were 12 and nine year old girls referred by the school health nurse. These children were assaulted 'for no reason at all' by their mother's *de facto* partner. One child

> said they were both sitting on a pool table when [he] asked them to go outside. He was shouting and swearing at them and then hit both of them with the palms of his hands over their ear drums. [The child] said that she could not hear for a while after this.

Hospital examinations of both girls confirmed minor bruising behind the ear of one child and on the arm and chest of the other child 'due to falling over and injuring herself after being hit'. The mother and children were interviewed at their home, the referrer had mentioned that the mother 'was very drunk' the night before. During the interview her *de facto* partner arrived: 'he was drunk, he did not see me in the room and started abusing [the mother] and yelling at the children. He then saw me and fell onto the bed'. The man then 'aggressively' made a series of loud complaints about his partner accusing her of sleeping with [another man] etc., condemning her for not washing his shirts . . . I told him I was not there to listen to his domestic arguments. I was there because of the children . . . He admitted that he had hit them and would do it again if they were naughty. I told him that he was not to hit them, that if he did I would consider taking out a charge against him.

The heated row continued between the partners. '[He] came outside to talk to me on his own. [She] took this chance and walked out with [the children]'. There is no record of the conversation with the *de facto* partner, but a few minutes later the worker

> caught up with the mother outside the police station. She got into the car and we talked about what she was going to do. It appears she has been trying to get him to leave – he won't – she wanted to take out a restraining order against him but wasn't optimistic . . . We talked about the death of her husband for some time – she said she had never been able to talk about it – she blames him for the predicament she's in. She has a lot of anger. We also talked about her life in [an eastern state] and all the things she has left behind. [She] had a good cry and said she would like to talk to someone . . . she got out of the car and I told her I would see her the next day.

The next day the worker called round; he asked the mother to come to his office and fill out some forms. The *de facto* partner wanted to come too, but 'she said no. Whilst [a colleague] talked to [her] I rang round getting info to support her story . . . sent fax to [a supervisor] re fares to [eastern city]. [Teacher] returned [children] to the office'. The worker then booked the family on flights to the eastern city. Ministerial approval was obtained for airline tickets to the eastern city and a repayment request was signed. The file ended with the note 'I will take them to the airport and make sure they get off'.

Advice, guidance, material and practical assistance

Case 130 was a two and a half year old boy whose parents received advice, guidance, material and practical assistance. The child had an intellectual disability and the family had been receiving services from another government agency for some time. One of the workers visiting the family (a twice-weekly routine) watched the father drag the child

> by the arm into a bedroom and threw him on the floor (i.e. carried momentum of dragging). Belted him with thong (not able to see but could hear muffled slaps) . . . came out . . . no red marks observed. [The father] sat him down and gave him an apple. Few minutes later, it was as if nothing had happened . . . [The mother] sat there passively during the incident. She has as little as possible to do with [the child] and asks [the father] to do most things for him . . . [The child] tries to gain attention from [the mother] by pinching or hitting. This has worsened to biting and face slapping.

Apparently the worker had long been aware that the parents had tried to cope with the child's continued screaming ('Parents believe he needs discipline for screaming'), but 'this was the first time [the worker] saw [the father] lose control'. The family were offered and accepted day care as well as a home care worker to help in the house.

In this group of cases two issues stand out from the text – conflicts between step-parents and children in reconstituting households and stressed parents. In the former group of cases, workers resolved problems either by arranging for children to live with other relatives or by working on the communications between adults and children. In the latter group of cases workers intervened to reduce stress levels by means of the provision of day care or counselling. None of these cases stayed open for very long.

Sexual abuse/home-based services

Thirty six cases appear in the sexual abuse/home-based services cell in Table 4.12. Tables 6.10 to 6.15 summarize details such as family structure and ethnicity, age ranges and gender, persons believed responsible for actions which caused harms and injuries, medical services and treatment and service types.

Table 6.10 Sexual abuse/home-based services cases – family structure and ethnicity

Family structure	Aboriginal	Non-Aboriginal	Total	%
Both biological parents	1	11	12	33.3
Reconstituting family	2	10	12	33.3
Single female parent	0	12	12	33.3
Total	3	33	36	99.9
%	8.3	91.7	100	

Table 6.11 Sexual abuse/home-based services cases – age range and gender

Age range	Male	Female	Total	%
1–4 yrs	1	3	4	11
5–10 yrs	9	3	12	33
11–14 yrs	0	15	15	42
15–18 yrs	1	4	5	14
Total	11	25	36	100
%	30.5	69.5	100	

Table 6.10 shows that these children were drawn equally from families where both biological parents were together, families which were reconstituting and single female parent families. Only three of these 36 children were Aboriginal.

Table 6.11 shows that over half of these children (56 per cent) were over 11 years of age, the largest single category were females aged 11 to 14 years, but the genders of these victims of sexual assault was approximately one-third male and two-thirds female.

Table 6.12   Sexual abuse/home-based services cases – persons believed responsible and action causing abuse

PBR	Indecent dealings/ molestation	Penetration	Not known	Total	%
Parent	5	5	0	10	27.7
De facto parent	4	1	0	5	13.8
Sibling	2	0	0	2	5.5
Step-parent	2	2	0	4	11
Other relative	1	4	0	5	14
Friend/neighbour	5	0	1	5	17
Loco parentis	1	0	0	1	3
Not known	1	1	1	3	8
Total	21	13	2	36	100
%	58	36	6	100	

As shown in Table 6.12, just over one quarter (27.7 per cent) of the persons believed responsible (PBR) for these assaults were parents. *De facto* partners of mothers were believed responsible for 13.8 per cent and step-parents for 11 per cent of cases. Siblings and other relatives accounted for nearly a fifth (19.5 per cent) while friends/neighbours, loco parentis and not known (only three cases) accounted for just over a quarter (28 per cent). Over one third (36 per cent) of the assaults involved some form of sexual penetration while assaults involving touching and physical contact constituted over one-half (58 per cent). Non-family members (friends/neighbours, loco parentis) were not involved in penetrative assaults.

Table 6.13 shows that over half of the children in this group (53 per cent) experienced emotional trauma, while a quarter suffered anal/vaginal trauma or disease as a result of penetrative assaults. In a fifth of the cases the harms/injuries were either not known, not identifiable or not recorded.

As shown in Table 6.14, half of these children received no medical service, while the rest (who received out-patient treatment) were medically examined. In 15 of these cases, treatment services were supplied. This involved six individual children, one child and the person believed responsible, and four adults believed

Table 6.13   Sexual abuse/home-based services cases – actions causing harms and injuries

Harm/injury	Indecent dealings/ molestation	Penetration	Not known	Total	%
Emotional trauma	15	4	0	19	53
Anal/vaginal trauma	0	9	0	9	25
Not identifiable	0	0	1	1	3
Unknown	6	0	1	7	19
Total	21	13	2	36	100
%	58	36	6	100	

Table 6.14   Sexual abuse/home-based services cases – medical services and 'treatment' services

'Treatment'	Medical examination	Out-patient	No medical service	Total	%
Child	3	0	4	7	19
Family	1	0	0	1	3
Caregiver	0	0	2	2	5.5
PBR	3	0	2	5	14
Child and PBR	1	0	0	1	3
None	9	1	10	20	55.5
Total	17	1	18	36	100
%	47	3	50	100	

responsible for assaults on five children. This group demonstrates a very high rate of 'treatment' interventions with a high rate of medical examinations but a low rate of medical service.

Additionally, the police were very active in investigation and prosecution activities in twenty eight (77.7 per cent) of cases. Eleven adult males were prosecuted for sexual offences against 17 children – nearly half of this sample, while criminal investigations, but not prosecutions, were undertaken by the police in respect of a further seven adults who were involved with nine children. All the persons believed responsible for assaults were males.

Table 6.15 shows that sexual abuse/home-based services cases received a smaller variety of services. None of the cases in this group were subject to monitoring and surveillance activities; they *all* received some form of continuing and active intervention with high rates of 'treatment'. Compared with other cases in the home-based services career types they received relatively little financial or material and practical assistance. Table 6.10 indicates they were less likely to be

Table 6.15   Sexual abuse/home-based services cases – service types

Service type	Nos	%
Advice and guidance only	21	58
Treatment	14	39
Treatment and financial assistance	1	3
Total	36	100

drawn from Aboriginal and single parent families which normally experience greater social deprivation. There is here the suggestion that these children came from families which were more broadly representative of the state's population.

Advice and guidance

Twenty one children from 19 families received advice and guidance only. Fourteen children from 13 families either received treatment themselves, in combination with family members, or the offenders received treatment.

The overwhelming pattern of these cases is that males were the persons believed responsible for the sexual assaults on young or teenage girls and in four cases on young boys. The majority of the male offenders were parents (fathers) or live-in partners of the mother. Whilst the female victims ranged in age from pre-schoolers (four years old) to late teenage years (16 and 17), the boys were all at lower primary school age (six to seven years old).

Tables 6.12 and 6.13 show that 58 per cent of the sexual assaults were categorized as 'indecent dealings/molestation', and 36 per cent involved 'penetration'. The circumstances and contexts of these sexual assaults on the children were diverse, for example, some assaults were current/immediate, whilst others had occurred some time previously and were only revealed by the children at a later date. Some vignettes taken from the files are reproduced as examples.

Case 41 was a 16 year old girl who referred herself to the department. She

> revealed that she had been sexually assaulted by her stepfather since the age of 14 years, until six months ago when she left home. She said the assaults included full sexual intercourse and had commenced around the time her older sister left home.

Case 443 was a 16 year old girl. She and her sister (see Case 442, p. 120) were referred by their mother who had just discovered that her husband had been sexually assaulting his daughter for a long time. The sexual assault was intercourse and the father was charged with incest.

Case 568 was a 17 year old woman who came to the attention of the department when a young man came to the office saying that his father, who employed the young woman, had 'had intercourse' with her. The young woman, when interviewed, was described on the file as being 'in shock (crying and shaking) and was uncertain whether penetration actually took place'.

Cases 533 and 548 were eight and 12 year old boys whose father had been convicted and imprisoned for sexual assaults on other children. Several months later, his own sons disclosed similar assaults to their mother. The older boy had been penetratively assaulted, but not the younger one.

Cases 647 and 648 were a five year old girl and a seven year old boy in an Aboriginal kinship network. It transpired that sexual assaults by their uncle had been going on for several years, often involving masturbation, anal and oral penetration of the boy. More recently, the five year old girl had also been assaulted.

Case 72 was a 14 year old Aboriginal girl who had abdominal pains and a vaginal discharge. She complained that she had been raped by an uncle.

Case 195 was a nine year old girl referred by her teacher who wished to 'assist in apprehending a door-to-door "Christian" preacher who is at present sexually assaulting one of her nine year old pupils. The mother is not fully aware of what is happening and is refusing to take any action'. This child had been left alone at home at night whilst her mother worked a night shift.

Case 69 was a 15 year old girl who disclosed at school that her 33 year old brother had fondled her breasts and made sexual suggestions.

Cases 67 and 68 were a seven year old boy and his 12 year old sister who disclosed that their father had been sexually assaulting them on weekend access visits. The father had engaged in oral sex with the girl and 'incited the boy to engage in mutual masturbation. [The boy] had observed his father assaulting [his sister] . . . and reported it to [his stepfather] who informed the police'.

Case 402 concerned a four year old girl whose mother came to the department after visiting the police station. The police had charged her 19 year old nephew with a number of offences. The young man had in his possession 'several pairs of women's knickers and pornographic books . . . [the mother] spoke to her daughter aged 4 and a half years [who admitted to her mum that the youth] had been playing with her [vagina]'. An interview with the child, using toys and an anatomically correct doll confirmed that she had been touched on her vagina.

These case examples indicate the range of the sexual assaults on children. The other cases not cited here are of similar diversity, covering complaints of penetration of the children, masturbation of the offenders, fondling ('touching') of the victims, and other behaviours only hinted at, through descriptions of harm or effects on the children. For example, Case 301, a six year old Aboriginal boy who told his parents that his 13 year old male cousin had 'played with his doodle', had also complained about having a sore bottom and sore penis. The parents became suspicious because the cousin was always wanting to shower or sleep with their son.

Case 302 was another six year old boy who wouldn't 'let his mother touch him especially around the bottom'. There was no other statement on the file about the nature of any assault, but reference was made to the child playing with some older boys at a building site where they all took their clothes off.

Another significant issue was the legalistic framework within which the investigations and interventions were carried out, compared with action taken in other forms of 'abuse' to children. The investigations usually involved the police, with prosecutions following in many cases. In the cases of seven children (302, 306, 213, 647, 648, 312 and 251) the police were not involved, and there were no explanations on the files as to why they were not involved. In addition, therapy or 'treatment' services seen to have been provided without any clear pattern emerging as to why seven children were offered treatment and others were not. For example those assaults involving rape or sexual penetration which might have been regarded perhaps as 'more serious' than assaults involving 'fondling' or 'making sexual suggestions' were no more likely to involve 'treatment'.

Case 306 was a 13 year old girl who was 'touched on the breasts and bottom on 4–5 occasions over the last 6 months [by the mother's *de facto* partner] while passing her in the passage way'. Most of the intervention appears to have involved attempts to arrange alternative care with relatives, including the girl's older sister, an uncle and her father and his new wife. None of the relatives was able or willing to have the girl stay with them. Eventually, at the end of several months, the family situation was described as conflictual: '[The child] is often at loggerheads with mother and it seems she has attempted to get rid of them by playing one off against the other'. Again, there is no indication of why the police were not involved, especially as the file reports that the boyfriend refused to leave the house, and the mother was described as 'unprotective' of the child. The mother and the girl did not want any further contact with the department.

It would appear that in Case 213, the police may not have been involved because the assault by the stepfather as disclosed by the 12 year old girl had ended about three to four years previously, when the marriage had ended. The family had been living in another Australian state at that time. Treatment services were offered to this girl who

> seemed very sad and cried at times during [the first] interview . . . she expressed the belief that the abuse was her fault because her dad 'took a liking' to her because she was pretty, she said she loved him and missed him, but he did 'a very naughty thing'.

In Cases 647 and 648, where a five year old girl and seven year old boy had been allegedly assaulted by their 16 year old uncle, the police were not involved. This may be because the file itself did not present any clear evidence for the allegations. However, the families of the children were rehoused, and the 16 year old offender commenced psychological treatment for a four month period. The case was closed when the psychologist considered she had achieved her goals.

Treatment for the child

The family of the 12 year old girl in Case 312 received treatment services more for the parents' alcoholism than for the sexual assault by the mother's boyfriend, who allegedly 'fondled' the daughters' breasts and put 'his hand between their legs'. The boyfriend left the family immediately after the allegation was made, so it may have been one reason for not involving the police. A case conference was held with the family (mother, daughters and estranged husband) and a placement with the paternal grandmother was considered. The child refused to go there, but as she wanted time away from her family, she went on a weekend camp. Other family crises such as car accidents and financial and housing difficulties kept the case open for many months until the family moved from the area, their problems still unresolved.

Finally, in Case 251, the 16 year old male offender who 'touched his seven year old [niece's] private parts and exposed himself to her', was given weekly therapy sessions. The police were not involved in this case either, for unstated reasons.

In some of the cases where treatment was offered, it seemed to have resulted in changes to the family structure while in other cases it seemed to have personal therapeutic goals for the children. Case 441 was a 13 year old girl referred by the police who had just interviewed her mother. The child had alleged that over three years her stepfather had been 'fondling and digitally penetrating her'. The girl was medically examined and temporary alternative accommodation arranged for the family first at a refuge and then with a relative. Despite the mother being described as 'unreservedly' believing her daughter, she was ambivalent about the prosecution of her partner. She reacted '[explosively] by throwing things around the kitchen' when the partner was imprisoned for nine years for the assault. The daughter who had been attending a group for children who had been sexually assaulted eventually decided she no longer wished to live at home. Foster care was arranged for her. She came to the conclusion that she was being 'doubly victimized' first by the assaults and second by being blamed by her mother for the imprisonment of her partner.

Case 442 was a 12 year old girl, the sister of Case 443 described earlier (p. 117). The 12 year old had only been assaulted once by her father who had 'touched her breasts and vagina', unlike her older sister who had been a victim of incest. However, the 12 year old was given treatment services because she 'found it hard to deal with the changes occurring in the family'. The worker considered that the mother was more emotionally distant from this child than from her elder daughter.

In Case 536 a 14 year old girl had been a victim of repeated non-penetrative sexual assaults by her stepfather over several years. The mother used the counselling centre which the stepfather attended about his alcohol problem instead of police involvement, to get the stepfather to leave the house. This was successful. The daughter began attending a victim's support group, and the case was closed soon after that.

Treatment for the PBR

In three cases, the offenders chose treatment services, sometimes as part of the prosecution process.

Case 71 was a 12 year old girl who alleged that her father had 'touched' her breasts and 'requested that she should masturbate him on a number of occasions'. He admitted this and was prepared to apologize to the child for his behaviour. He had already voluntarily contracted into a programme run by a psychiatrist. The final note on the file indicated that 'assessment of [the father's] attitude and ability to change has the highest priority, and the question of when he is to return home is of great concern to the family'.

In Cases 277 and 278, two boys aged six and seven years old (neighbours) were sexually assaulted by another neighbour, a 13 year old boy. The sexual assault was oral penetration of one child and attempted anal penetration of both boys. The police were involved and the boy was prosecuted but the charges were dismissed. However he continued to attend for the psychiatric treatment which he had commenced prior to the court hearing. The cases were closed after this.

Finally, in Case 620, a father touched his three year old daughter on her vagina, following a family row. The father was arrested and charged. As the workers considered that 'the problem is based in the marital relationship and personal dynamics of the couple' they offered family counselling. The father's probation agreement required that he participate in family counselling. After six months, the case was closed with a note that 'Family dynamics functioning at a much improved level . . . No concerns held by [the mother] towards [the father's] relationship with either of the children'. However, a 'watching brief' for three months was considered necessary 'due to the seriousness of the charge of indecent assault'.

Reaction of parent to the abuse

A third and final significant pattern emerging was the number of instances where mothers disliked having to 'choose between' their children [usually daughters] and their male partners. Even believing the child implied some form of disloyalty to the partner. In many cases, the children continued to be exposed to risky situations or they left home.

For example, the 16 year old girl in Case 41 left home due to 'sexual intercourse' with her stepfather. The child's mother 'didn't really want to believe her and stayed with her husband'.

Cases 67 and 68, where a seven year old boy and his 12 year old sister had been assaulted in access visits to their father, did not have to leave home or suffer their mother's disbelief. However, the mother indicated that

> she is having difficulty with her feelings towards the children. She wants to hold and hug them but feels she cannot – presumably due to her own emotions being in turmoil and conflict . . . the children. . . are feeling alone and without . . . love and support'.

In Case 293, the 12 year old girl being interfered with by her mother's boyfriend, was aware that her mother 'would be upset as [the offender] is her boyfriend'. The mother 'was totally distraught at the news and this state of shock continued for a long period'. She said it would be best if her daughter stayed with her father. No charges were brought against the alleged offender and the girl remained in her father's care.

In Case 306 described earlier where the mother's live-in boyfriend was 'touching' the 13 year old girl's breasts and bottom, the mother said 'she realised she had to make a decision between her boyfriend and daughter'. The mother's decision to 'help the boyfriend' resulted in many unsuccessful attempts being made to find alternative accommodation for the girl. The case closed with the child still living with her mother and the alleged offender, in a conflictual situation. Neither mother nor daughter wanted outside help.

Case 441, a 13 year old girl referred by the police because of the stepfather 'fondling and digitally penetrating her', was believed 'unreservedly' by her mother, who was simultaneously

> still keen to maintain her relationship with [the stepfather] and underplayed the serious needs of the situation for [her daughter] . . . [the mother] was afraid of being alone and felt there were many positive things about her relationship with [the stepfather].

The mother's feelings for the stepfather were revealed by her very strong ('explosive') response to his nine year prison sentence. The girl's eventual decision to leave home was partly influenced by her mother blaming her for the stepfather's imprisonment.

The mother of the 14 year old girl (Case 536), a victim of 'repeated non-penetrative sexual assaults by her stepfather' also was reluctant to involve police because she feared the 'possible break-up' of her family'. The file notes that the mother repeatedly excused her husband's behaviour as being due to alcohol. 'She was unwilling to consider her daughter's welfare above that of the family's as she sees it'. The mother's strategy to use the counselling centre attended by the stepfather to get him to leave the home was successful.

Finally, a whole family (Case 313) was described as

> united . . . against [the department] and the different members were at various times quite antagonistic and resistant to counselling. In this case, the father, whilst drunk, had pulled [his daughter's] top over her head . . . while he kissed her on the neck, stomach and breasts.

A condition of bail was that the father was not to return to the family home, which resulted in strong family reaction. As a result the girl 'had internalised her guilt and was accepting all the blame for the family's current predicament'.

As can be seen, although children, particularly girls, had experienced a range of sexual assaults by males, usually their fathers or mother's male partners, the responses in terms of service provision varied, without a clear pattern emerging. Police involvement often leading to prosecution appeared to be mandatory due to the legal framework covering sexual assaults. In a few cases, police were not involved, but the files do not explain why not. The ambivalence of many mothers who were forced to choose between their daughters and partners was a key issue.

Conclusion

Very varied responses to the care of children can be seen in the delivery of home-based services, since the nature of the problems outlined in this chapter were so different. More than half of the cases (56 per cent) were 'at risk' or neglect matters covering out-of-control adolescents, drunk and isolated single parents and generally poorly resourced families. With the adolescents, work focused on bringing them under control, while with the alcohol and drug misusing single parents, the emphasis was on the normalization of child rearing practices. Only five cases in these two categories received 'treatment' services. In many respects the outcomes of interventions in these cases were not satisfactory because of workers' inability to come to grips with drug and alcohol problems, the limited material resources available (to deal with poverty) and their failure either to articulate or in many cases to enforce a minimum standard of child rearing. Workers clearly struggled with many of these cases especially because of the lack of cooperation and resentments expressed by many parents.

The physical abuse cases were much more clear-cut and generally more successful, with relatively brief interventions to deal with conflicts (with step-parents) either by relocating children with other relatives or working on communication problems. As far as very stressed parents were concerned, the services were provided specifically to relieve some of the burdens of child rearing.

Responses to the sexual 'abuse' cases revolved around prosecution, 'treatment' and measures designed to get mothers to 'protect' their children from adult male sex offenders. For many mothers this created problems which were not easily resolved. Fifteen instances of 'treatment' occurred in this group, but it was not clear why this service was offered to some children and not others.

7 Late admission to substitute care

Table 4.12 shows that the smallest group of cases in the career type category were becomes care cases. These were children who began with home-based services after an investigation but subsequently had to be admitted to substitute care.

Becomes care cases constituted only 12 per cent of all those substantiated or classified as 'at risk'. Table 7.1 shows that the overwhelming majority of these cases were in the 'at risk' and neglect categories (90 per cent).

Table 7.1 Becomes care cases

Substantiation	Nos	%
'At risk'	15	37.5
Neglect	21	52.5
Emotional abuse	2	5
Physical abuse	1	2.5
Sexual abuse	1	2.5
Total	40	100

There were 15 cases classified as being 'at risk'. Table 7.2 crosstabulates caregiver family structure against ethnicity. Two thirds of these children (66.67 per cent) came from single parent families and 60 per cent were Aboriginal children.

Ten of these children were boys and five were girls. Only two children out of the 15 were apprehended and they were also subject to successful care and protection applications. The 15 children came from 12 families.

Case 49 was a 12 year old Aboriginal girl, originally referred along with her siblings when they were all admitted to hospital because they 'had apparently eaten some mince the previous night – then became violently ill . . . [the parents] have apparently left all children to fend for themselves [for the night] . . . they had told youngsters they would be returning [the next day]'. It is not clear from the file

Table 7.2 'At risk'/becomes care cases – caregiver family structure and ethnicity

Family structure	Aboriginal	Non-Aboriginal	Total	%
Both biological parents	2	2	4	26.67
Reconstituting family	1	0	1	6.66
Single female parent	3	4	7	46.67
Single male parent	3	0	3	20
Total	9	6	15	100
%	60	40	100	

what services were received by the family, but three months later the eldest child (the girl in question) had again been left by her mother with the younger children. She said she wanted to leave home and go to a hostel in Perth or live with a relative in a country town. The file notes that

All of us on reflection feel that there is nothing to be gained by making [the child] a ward. [She] is seeking an alcohol-free and quiet environment and we can assist her in that regard without having to use the legal process. Of great concern is the fact that [the child] is old beyond her years. In the two months that she was missing it is rumoured that she was in a sexual relationship with one of the local boys. Her mother did nothing to locate her. [The child] is also the youngest of an older gang who spent their time drinking and indulging heavily in the hormonally stimulating 'Rites of Spring'! If [the child] was in Perth there is no doubt she would gravitate back to [a suburb]. On the positive side [she] is a delightful child with a pleasant and kind nature. She is attractive and is very conscious of her personal hygiene. [She] seeks structure and despite truanting from the local primary school, [she] attended [a local culture centre for Aboriginal people]. If her aunt is well enough and prepared to take [her] we would pay her fare and support private foster rates. [The child] would be given our undertaking that if she went to her aunt and subsequently wished to return home that we would again pay her fare. The proviso would be that [the child] at least try to see it out until the end of the school year.

Cases 186 and 187 were a three year old girl and a one year old boy originally referred because of their mother's drug and alcohol problems. The department maintained a watch over the situation. Nine months later a refuge rang 'wanting assistance with [the mother]. They were concerned that [she] had (1) been drinking, (2) been taking Serepax [a type of tranquillizer], (3) had not been adequately caring for her children'. Child protection workers agreed she could continue to keep the children 'on the condition that she did not drink or take tablets further. If she attempted to do same, it was explained that we would apprehend children'. She was told that there would be follow-up visits. Three days later the mother had a fit on a railway station as a consequence of drug withdrawal. She was taken immediately to hospital 'given a bed but was informed that her children could not stay with her'. The children were voluntarily placed with foster parents since a long stay in hospital followed by a residential rehabilitation programme was planned. The file comments 'NB the current arrangement is private and mutually agreed, as I am trying to avoid further statutory involvement'. Three weeks later the children briefly entered hospital because of '[the boy] gastro problems – [the girl] – bad cough'. The hospital reported that

> [the mother] was there wanting to take the children home. At this time [she] appeared to be very much under the influence of drugs/and or alcohol. [She] has just separated from [the father] and has her possessions [with her]. All Refuges are full so – if she did take the children she would have no accommodation. The children have been placed under Apprehension and an Order to Hold given to the hospital.

The children were returned to foster parents and the family situation reassessed a few weeks later when the mother was 'drug free'. That assessment noted that

> It has become clear to me that [the mother's] periods of crisis coincide with domestic upheavals with [her partner]. It appears [his] concern for [her] addiction manifests in his adopting a policing and monitoring role. This is a significant stress factor in itself for [her]. If, as in the past, [he] suspects [she] is again using Serepax/alcohol he erupts in outbursts of anger, and sometimes violence due to feelings of frustration and powerlessness. This ultimately results in [her] entering a very public, self-destructive binge behaviour.

Workers took account also of

> current parental relationship, appears to be positive and improving . . . I also note [his] positive relationship with the children [who] as time passes are becoming distressed and unhappy about not being with their parents . . . the current arrangements whilst stable and satisfactory . . . have the potential to become emotionally damaging.

The conclusion was that the children should 'return home to their parents as soon as appropriate and feasible'.

Cases 218 and 219 were a one year old girl and a seven month old boy referred by their GP because they 'looked' neglected. The mother was interviewed with the grandmother present. A family resource worker was offered as help, but refused by the mother. The situation was monitored, but a few months later the one year old girl was admitted to hospital with alcohol poisoning. The mother said that wine had been put in her bottle by a friend who had disappeared to a city in an eastern state. After a further health crisis caused by alcohol misuse, the mother was hospitalized. The social worker then conducted a series of complex negotiations with extended family in order to provide care for the children. The following file note indicates the complex nature of the considerations involved:

[the mother] had to go into hospital for alcohol poisoning [following a party over the weekend]. He [the grandfather] wondered if [the oldest child] shouldn't be with him permanently – told him that had to be a family consensus decision with [the mother] and him, being the person whose opinions carried the most weight – [she], because she is the mother – him, because he is the one who can have both children. Asked him if the placement of the children would cause complications of an unwelcome sort re: his relationship with [his current partner] (erstwhile girlfriend of his who is mother of his son – aged 1). No. [Partner] does not want to live with him – therefore there is no danger of his son and grandchildren being in the same house and becoming confused in identities and claims of affection etc. [His partner] is too preoccupied with her hassles with the teenage children from a previous marriage.

The children were then transferred by the department to their grandfather's care and the department subsidized the placements.

Cases 220 and 225 were 12 and ten year old Aboriginal boys living with their widower father. Case 220 was already a juvenile justice state ward placed at home and waiting for a residential placement (which he did not want). A report from the emergency duty team describes the nature of their frequent contact with this child

[He] makes a regular habit of coming into the city, and late at night demanding transport home. Since the last visit in September which amounted to a worker from the Unit transporting [him] and his brothers home to an empty house we have had more than one call making this demand. The staff at [a youth centre] have been providing 'support' to [him] and usually referring the matter to us for action. Last night I was called by the worker who informed me that the [youth centre] was again requesting assistance to transport [the child] home. After discussion I supported the worker's suggestion that we should refuse to assist by providing transport. It was not appropriate to send the boy home in a taxi given that on every occasion when we have returned the boy home in a taxi no one has been there.

(Case 220)

Great efforts were made to find a suitable placement for the boy, and the placement had to be provided with a full-time aide to assist him because

[the child] does not appear to fit into any existing education facility or programme. Most principals that have tried to accommodate him in the past refuse to have him back . . . [this is] a multi-problem family with extensive [department] involvement over many years. There has been a history of marital discord, violence, alcohol abuse, financial problems and inappropriate child care.

It was decided to apprehend the boy and his brother. The boy had run away when the worker arrived.

As we arrived [the father] was in the front yard speaking to two police officers in a van. [The father] had rung the police as [the child] had absconded after [the father] attempted to take him to school. [The child] jumped over the fence and took off.

The boy was eventually found and placed briefly in care, but was brought before the court for stealing. The Court Report said

> [The child] is the fourth of seven children of an extremely deprived single parent family. He is the only child left in his father's care. Although the home environment is a welfare concern and unacceptable [the child] refuses to live anywhere else. Efforts by DCS to alter this situation have failed due to [the child] and his father's non cooperation. Although [the father] wants [the child] in his care he is unable to provide consistent or adequate supervision and [the child] is often left on his own to fend for himself. This is reflected in [his] school record where he barely attended in 1987 and in his criminal record of at least 34 court appearances totalling over 144 charges.
>
> (Case 220)

This boy's younger brother (Case 225) was apprehended on the day the child protection workers visited the home. The father resisted this.

> He initially stated that he would not allow it to happen and then stated he would find a lawyer and oppose the application . . . [He] eventually stated he could agree with our reasons for removing [the older child] but could not see any reason for removing [the younger child] as he was not petrol sniffing or offending. [The father] stated that if we removed [the child] he would kill himself. He then asked us if we would do that to [the child] (inferring that his death would be our responsibility because we removed [the child]). We again outlined our concerns and that we had apprehended [the child] and we attempted to give him the summons. [The father] initially refused to take them but did later in the interview. We agreed to allow [the child] to stay with him until the Siting tomorrow and arranged for a taxi to pick him and [the child] up to bring them to Court. [The father] assured us that he would attend court tomorrow . . . during the interview [the father] attempted to bargain with us saying he would accept a homemaker and counselling. He became angry and stated that the department had not provided any of these services for him, but later stated that he often sits in the backyard and chooses not to answer the door if he doesn't feel like it.
>
> (Case 225)

Case 334 was a 14 year old girl who had been a state ward.

> [The mother] approached the department for assistance with her relationship with [the child] saying that [the child] no longer wished to live at home. There was ongoing conflict and strife all the time . . . She disliked [the child's] friends and felt she was failing at school . . . she felt [the child] was boy crazy and needed a father figure . . . [the child] wanted to live away from home in a foster placement with horses. She felt the home situation was

intolerable . . . Initially the situation at home improved with [the child] deciding that home wasn't so bad after all. Then another issue emerged [the mother] started going out with [an ex-*de facto*]. [The child] was very angry about this as [he] had previously lived with them several years ago and treated her mother badly. [He] is an alcoholic and on a number of occasions in the past [the child] had to phone the police to protect her mother. [The child] will not forgive [him] for what happened and generally distrusts him. [She] basically delivered an ultimatum to her mother, 'It's either him or me'.

The child protection worker found a place for the child in a children's home and she entered care. The final file comment was '[The child] has been indulged by her mother . . . she has received most of what she has wanted if her mother has been able to afford it, [she] tends to have a poor ability to compromise and sees life in a straight forward, black and white way'.

Case 344 was a 15 year old Aboriginal youth who was already under the control of the state as a result of offending. He had been sentenced by the Children's Court to three months in a maximum security institution and was released and sent home. Very shortly after his return, he committed further offences. The court report said that

[The child's] parents are separated. He sees them occasionally. He reports that his father would like to have him stay with him. Other adults correctly or otherwise, say that father will not receive him. Mother is unable to look after him. [The child] has no pocket money.

He received a community service order sentence and went to live with his grandfather on a station. Four weeks later he was again in trouble with the police for breaking into cars; he was sentenced to two months of maximum security. After the sentence was completed he was placed in his older brother's care, but

[his brother] was only there for two weeks at a time when he would be away at [a mine] for the remaining two weeks in the month. [His brother's] wife was unable to supervise – having her hands full with two babies . . . [the child] has asked to go to [a station] and his family support this placement . . . there is no obvious alternative to the [station] placement while [his brother] is working at the mine.

A child progress review three months later noted that the placement was 'succeeding'. It was subsidized by the department financially, so the child was legally and technically in care. Very shortly afterwards he left the station and travelled to another state. The file notes 'NFA at this stage until he comes back into town'.

Case 362 was another 15 year old Aboriginal youth who was placed on probation by the Children's Court after breaking a shop window and stealing bubble gum. The court report said that '[the child] travels around a lot with his father, going from cattle station to station'. Eight weeks later the child had left his home.

He is living independently of his parents at [an Aboriginal community] while their residence remains [in a town] about 20 kilometres away. [The child] is not being cared for, or fed, by his parents. The boy depends on his application for Special Benefit being successful to ensure that he will have food to eat. While out at [the community], he will be working without wages to help the community in their day tasks. His mother has signed that she will exercise care and control over him during the probation period. But her signature does *not* mean that she is feeding and caring for him. It means that she has accepted the Court's ruling that he be placed at [the community].

Two weeks later the child had influenza and returned to town for hospital treatment. On discharge from hospital he went to stay with his grandfather – the placement was subsidized by the department, so the child formally entered care. Four months later, more trouble with the police led to a three month sentence in maximum security. Following discharge the child was convicted of unlawfully driving a motor vehicle and sentenced to reside at an Aboriginal community in another state for 12 months.

Case 365 was a 13 year old Aboriginal boy referred by the police.

[The child] is 13 years old and was living with [relatives]. He says he has been kicked out by them so has gone to [another relative]. She says she doesn't want him, that she has no control over him and is only feeding him. She also says that she and [the male relative] have had arguments as [male relative] says he wants [the child] to return. However [the child] says that he gets belted up by [his male relative] when he's drunk and thrown out. [The child] doesn't want to be at [the male relative's]. The police phoned today to report the above as they were concerned for [the child]. His last offence was committed at 4.00 a.m. and they consider him to be a neglected child apart from an offender.

The next file note comes up with an interim solution.

Discussed [the child] with [the relatives]. Agreed that [he] lives at [male relative's] camp. If [male relative] is drunk, then he goes over to [female relative] until all is okay – but this does not give him justification to wander around town at all hours of the night nor to avoid going to school.

The child was sent by his grandfather to be with his mother in an adjacent state. Four months later the child was back in Western Australia and refusing to return to his mother's care: 'Saw [the child] and he said he would go anywhere but back to [his mother]'. Eventually the child's mother agreed to accept him back and the placement was subsidized, so he formally entered care. However, that placement broke down and he returned to live with the relative he was with when the case opened.

Case 371 was a 16 year old Aboriginal boy who had been prosecuted for offending and was a state ward. His two most recent sentences had caused him to be sent to remote tribal communities and then a secure institution after which he was returned to the care of his parents. He committed further offences and received a community service order with which he was sent once more to serve in the tribal community ahead of his parents moving with him. Before being joined by his parents he was placed in the care of a relative and the placement subsidized by the department. The file note says that the community was

Strongly supportive of placement as it is good for [the child to be] among his own countrymen and away from temptations of town or lack of control by parents . . . alcohol was a routine problem for his parents. He used to sleep at an aunt's house in town on occasion to avoid his father's anger.

A few months later however after several more court appearances as a result of offending, he was again sent to a maximum security institution.

Case 488 was a two year old boy referred by a health centre because of weight loss. He was admitted to hospital for tests and '[the mother] was worried that she will lose him – reassured on this point . . . [the mother] working nights at [a local factory]. Friends have been caring for [the child]'.

A few days later

[the mother] giving up job at mill. Physically worn out, has lost weight. Concerned about [the child] but too tired to put much effort into it. Has offer of week's holiday with a male friend. Taking [the child] and going. When returns is keen to become involved again with Department. Explained to her that we would be happy to assist in non-threatening way and that the medical checking/weighing would need to be sorted out between herself and medics.

A few months later the child was again losing weight and 'she signed the necessary papers to proceed with Wardship' (a voluntary measure). The reason for this was that the

Office has been instrumental in placing [the child] on several prior occasions. The tenuous nature of previous placements necessitated us making firmer arrangements at the last time of placement. [The mother] was told that if she intended making further requests for placements we would need to consider Wardship as a means of providing some stability for [the child] . . . [The mother] was not prepared for us to offer any further support to keep she [sic] and [the child] together. She suggested we proceed with Wardship and if possible [the child] be placed with foster parents who had cared for him previously.

The child eventually returned to his mother's care but the department remained involved.

Case 638 was a six month old Aboriginal baby boy who was reported by the Health Department as 'progressing poorly at the moment and losing weight . . . concerned that his condition is related to the fact that his mother is a heavy drinker'. Arrangements were made for admission to foster care: 'In the past [the child] has been neglected at times due to his parents drinking . . . This has resulted in a spate of visits to hospital'. The child was fostered into another Aboriginal family.

Case 694 was a newly born Aboriginal baby girl. File notes are very sparse, but indicate again problems of alcohol and child care. The mother received advice but the child was medically examined and kept in hospital where she was apprehended and then placed with foster parents before becoming a state ward. Evidence suggests that the mother was uncooperative since the child protection worker involved referred her to the police because of threatening behaviour.

Neglect/becomes care cases

Twenty one cases appear in Table 4.12 defined as neglect/becomes care. This was the largest number of becomes care cases (52.5 per cent) and nearly a quarter (23 per cent) of all the 91 neglect cases in the sample.

While the numbers of children in this category stand out as having much significance, both within the context of all neglect cases and all becomes care cases, these 21 children came from only eight families. Indeed, four families account for 17 of these children.

Table 7.3   Neglect/becomes care cases – caregiver family structure and ethnicity

Caregiver family structure	Aboriginal	Non-Aboriginal	Total	%
Both biological parents	3	1	4	19
Reconstituting family	5	4	9	42.9
Single female parent	6	0	6	28.6
Single male parent	1	1	2	9.5
Total	15	6	21	100
%	71.4	28.6	100	

Table 7.3 looks at these cases by caregiver family structure and ethnicity. Nearly three-quarters (71 per cent) were Aboriginal children, but only just over two-thirds (38.1 per cent) came from single parent families.

The original neglect types (neglect at referral) are shown in Table 7.4. One-third of the children (33 per cent) were originally referred because their supervision was neglected, while a quarter (24 per cent) were abandoned or deserted.

Table 7.5 shows that legal interventions occurred with three-quarters (76 per cent) of these children. Sixteen of the 21 were removed from home under emergency conditions and they were all then taken before Children's Courts with applications for care and protection. Wardship was granted however in only six cases, while it was adjourned in five cases and withdrawn in five.

Table 7.4 Neglect/becomes care cases – original
neglect types

Neglect type	Nos	%
Supervision	7	33
Medical care	3	14
Abandoned/deserted	5	24
Environment	4	19
Shelter	1	5
Not known	1	5
Total	21	100

Table 7.5 Neglect/becomes care cases – legal interventions

Care and protection application	Apprehended	Not apprehended	Total	%
None	0	5	5	23.8
Adjourned	5	0	5	23.8
Withdrawn	5	0	5	23.8
Granted	6	0	6	28.6
Total	16	5	21	100
%	76.2	23.8	100	

Case studies

Case 71 was a 13 year old girl living with her father. The matter was referred to
the department by an aunt who complained that the girl was being 'neglected (not
fed) and may possibly be at risk of physical/sexual abuse'. A home visit brought
no reply and the girl in question was not attending school. Because of the sexual
abuse allegations the police became involved and confirmed that the father had a
criminal record: 'His offences are alcohol related and include assaults . . . it is
believed that [the father] could be dangerous if drunk and/or upset'. The child
was eventually interviewed at school (12 days after the first referral).

> [The child] did not reveal sexual abuse, but rather expressed concerns that
> her father would make advances to her. [She] was subsequently appre-
> hended, as she also revealed information about her family's lifestyle that
> would indicate that her father is not a suitable caregiver . . . [she] was placed
> on a temporary basis with her stepmother.

A lengthy list of the father's habits was compiled:

> That [he] drinks heavily . . . he is drunk at least every second day, but usually
> every day . . . when his pension money runs out he borrows from friends . . .

there is little food in the house on the few days prior to pension day . . . telephone and electricity accounts were in [the child's name], as [the father] has large debts in his own name.

The remainder of the list dealt with the father's sexual remarks directed at his girlfriend over the telephone, a sexual relationship with a 19 year old woman and the overt sexual behaviour of one of his friends. When the father was interviewed '[the child's] allegations were read to him. He denied them all in a vague sort of manner . . . he stated that he believed that the complaint was a result of vicious lies on the part of [relatives]'. He said he would contest the care and protection application. The application however was successful and the child remained in the care of relatives.

Case 135 was a five year old boy living with his parents and six year old brother, referred by the police.

> Both [parents] are 'mad' and violent, dirty, threatening suicide constantly. Police hear from them regularly, kids come to station after school – dirty, neglected, scabies. Police feel they are not in a very suitable environment – constant domestic warfare. At the moment [the father] is unbalanced himself, is in charge of the children as [the mother] is once more in [a psychiatric hospital].

That day the mother had been admitted back into hospital only hours after being discharged. The hospital told the police 'that she was too difficult to treat'. She was taken to another hospital 'continuing to go berserk, she assaulted a female police officer and kicked [the referring male officer]. The police officers had been called to a bottle shop where [the parents] were fighting'. Three more reasons for referral were given, one of which was 'the inability of the adults to look after themselves, let alone the children'. Checks were made with the boys' school. The headteacher commented that 'both boys seemed pretty typical of kids from that sort of environment'. The older child entered foster care immediately, while the younger child followed a few days later. They were accommodated by a voluntary child welfare agency but returned to their mother's care several weeks later after she had stabilized on medication. By that time the father had left the house.

Case 226 was the youngest child of an the Aboriginal family (see Cases 220 and 225, pp. 127–8). The child in question remained at home in the care of his father after his brothers had been removed. This eight year old boy was referred by a relative with whom he had been staying several months after the crisis occurred which caused his brothers to enter care.

> [He] was found at 1.00 a.m. this morning unconscious under the house (after being missing for some time). He had passed out after sniffing petrol. His aunt reported that [the child] had been sniffing petrol on a daily basis for several months now.

The child was taken to hospital, but the apprehension was delayed because the father could not be found. Eventually he appeared, but by that time a care and protection application was under way and the child was placed with one of his brothers in a children's home.

Cases 366–70 were five children in one single female parent Aboriginal family. Their ages ranged from four to 14 years old, two were girls and three were boys. The family was already well known to the department and on this occasion the 14 year old girl was referred by the school as 'she was suspended from school last week for being disruptive and abusive'. The case remained open, since the older boys were 'in trouble with the police' each time the mother 'went away'. The mother was politically very active in an Aboriginal group concerned with land. She frequently attended meetings and left the children with her sister. She was warned that unless suitable child care arrangements were made the next time she left home for a meeting, then the children would be removed. At a meeting in the community a note was made of the agreement with the mother:

> Placement plan for the children. Informed the mother that if no suitable placement is planned [by her] within one week, DCS will be taking out Care and Protection Orders for control of her children. [The mother] informed us – 1. her children will be taken out of [the local school], 2. [three children] will be going to meetings with her . . . [The mother] was informed that these plans would have to be carried out or she would be facing court.

The file note continued

> The day after we had seen her, we made enquiries and found she had gone to [a meeting a long way away]. I spoke to [the oldest boy] and he explained that the car had broken down and they couldn't take the children to [the other community]. After [the mother] returned to [the town], [a child protection worker] and I went down and saw her and warned her that things had gone too far, and the children were going to be taken and there would be a court case because she hadn't followed through with the plan. We went back to the office and [the mother] came back separately to see my [manager]. She saw the [manager], but refused to talk because there was a policeman in the office. Next day, [a child protection worker] and I went down to see her and informed her that we had come to pick the kids up. She said 'yes' and after we had talked to her and she agreed the children should go to her sister in [another community] went inside to get some clothes and she gave [one child] a bath. Then [another worker] arrived in a police car to apprehend the child. Then [the mother] helped us put the children in the car and [another child] who had to be taken to [that community]. Then we drove into [town], stopped at a shop and bought some food and delivered then to their aunt. We had collected clothes and blankets for them.

In fact only four of the five children were taken that day since one had absented himself from the scene. He was apprehended six days later: 'I visited [the mother's] house to see [the child]. The house appeared dirty with old rags scattered around the yard and front veranda'. The boy was not there, but was found two days later and flown out. All these children were categorized as being abandoned/deserted and care and protection applications were lodged but adjourned. Six months later they were back in their mother's care.

Case 380 was an 11 year old Aboriginal boy referred by the community in which he lived with his mother, 'It is believed this lad is left to fend for himself at times. The mother has spent most of her time in town'. The mother was interviewed. The file comments that

> [The mother] is a type of transient lady who spends more time in town than at [the community] . . . From the information I can gather from [the community] she spends more time in and out of the local lock-up on drink related charges.

The parents were separated and the father described as 'looks very old . . . blinding slowly . . . a recipient of Old Age Pension'. The mother agreed for the child to go to his older sister, but within a short time a relative complained that the mother 'was drinking in the bush' with her children. Child protection officers went to look for her, 'and found her drinking with her mother and a few members of [their community]'. The child was asleep on the ground, covered only by a blanket. The mother was advised to provide cover, but she was 'partly drunk when we called her over'. The child was then apprehended because the mother 'refused to budge'. A successful care and protection application was made and the child placed with a relative in a non-nomadic tribal community.

Cases 573–7 were five Aboriginal children from one large family (see also Case 605, p. 98). The department originally became involved with the family when an older child was in trouble with the police. The family were watched carefully; they often had other people staying with them and held frequent drinking parties. The parents were warned, but apparently to no avail and the children were apprehended, split up and moved to a hostel, a children's home and foster care.

However, within a matter of weeks they were returned home and the care and protection applications withdrawn. The children were apprehended because they were left to wander around the streets late at night when their parents were drunk.

> Reason for lack of parental control relate in the main to excessive alcohol intake. [The mother] has spent past month in prison following assault on hospital staff . . . Concerns were initially that youngest child had extensive bruising to lower back. This however was later confirmed by GP as being genetic marking. [The second oldest child] has developed scabies, otherwise all children physically healthy. Behaviourally the two oldest boys show lack of respect for property and limited self control . . . Members of conference concluded that ideally aim should be return of children to parents, that parents' willingness or ability to change drinking behaviour was marginal, especially as mother clearly indicated to field officer she intended to continue to drink.

Cases 664–6 were three Aboriginal children under the age of four years. They were initially referred by members of their own community.

For the past 6 weeks–2 months people at [the community] have been complaining about [the mother's] care of her three children . . . situation needs to be viewed as serious when community complains about child care . . . according to [a neighbour] when [the mother] is not drinking she provides adequate care for the children . . . As 5-day Easter break commences [in four days] . . . [a neighbour] suggested making arrangements for one suitable caregiver to take responsibility for children when [the mother] is drinking – suggested [another neighbour]. [A worker] will follow up this possibility as temporary measure to ensure children's safety – and allow time to look for suitable longer term placement – if there is evidence to suggest the children need to be removed from [the mother's] care.

The situation temporarily improved. 'Immediately after these arrangements were made, the appearance of both [the mother and the two older children] improved. [The mother] also took the boys to [a health centre] for a medical check'. However, further contact with the community gave rise to concern – and then a visit.

[The estranged father] was caring for the boys while [the mother] was in town. He did not know where the boys were and said he saw them an hour ago. With respect to [the baby] he said he had been looking after her most of the weekend and told [the mother] to take the baby to hospital. In general he was vague and contradictory in what he said. We located the boys on the street about 100 metres from the house and brought them home. [The mother] arrived in a taxi with grocery shopping which included a large quantity of alcohol.

The children were apprehended and the baby flown to hospital; she required intensive care because of dehydration. The children were placed in foster care and care and protection applications lodged. File notes state that

The parents of the children regularly drink alcohol to excess. Their relationship is stormy and includes physical violence. During drinking sessions the children were neglected. Both parents have chosen to avoid DCS staff, though they have both been invited to discuss future issues . . . DCS support has frequently been offered in an effort to assist [the mother] to demonstrate that she could offer the children an improved standard of care. It appears however, that [the mother] could only be motivated in this area if the children were physically returned to her, which is an unsatisfactory situation.

Cases 695–8 were four children aged from two to six years. The family had been living in isolation in a remote country area. They moved into a town but

they quickly developed poor household management and have moved around quite a lot, staying with other families. [The father] has been unemployed and drinking has been a prominent feature of his behaviour. When drinking he tends to drag [the mother] (who in turn drags the children) to various places for drinking and cards. The children seem to be receiving less than minimal care. The problems are:

1 Lack of basic nurturing – the children's needs are not considered in any way.
2 Cleanliness. In general, family's lifestyle is deplorable. Basic cleaning of the house rarely occurs. Faeces lying around the place, clothing not washed, personal hygiene not attended to.

A homemaker was introduced and she

spent a lot of effort with the family including helping them in a very practical way in the physical cleaning of the house and cleaning of the children. Her efforts to raise [the mother's] self-esteem and the raising of the quality of care of the house and children has been unsuccessful despite the efforts. It is important to separate what are real welfare issues i.e. the care of the children as against the more general lifestyle issues. Undoubtedly the family has a lifestyle that doesn't easily fit in with the rest of the community, but it is important to identify the exact points which concern the children's well-being. That is, we must specify what are the minimal physical conditions that we require. The nurturing and quality of emotional care is much harder to pin-point. We need to give the family a very firm message about what we regard as minimal care. That is, at least they should be living in their home, and at least the children should be attended to in terms of clothing, basic food, medical attention as necessary, and not being dragged around all over the place.

A pattern of respite care was successfully negotiated with the parents while further attempts were made to help the parents provide the minimum standards of care.

Emotional abuse/becomes care cases

Two children appear in Table 4.12 as having been 'emotionally abused' while initially receiving home-based services and then being admitted to care. These cases are the only two in the emotional abuse/becomes care category.

Case 444 was a six year old girl who was adopted at the age of five months. The child was not a native Australian, but was brought by the adoptive parents from another Asian country. Shortly after the adoption, the adoptive parent's marriage ended and the child remained with her adoptive mother. However, her early life was not easy. Many problems between her and her adoptive mother were reported and various respite placements were organized over the years. The file notes at the point of referral say

[The child] was initially referred following a request by her mother, for a foster placement because of allegedly disturbed behaviour within the context of the family. Previous Departmental records indicated several previous respite care placements and there was concern that the nature and frequency of requests for placement and the continuing patterns of disturbed behaviour reflected a disturbed and possibly rejecting relationship between [the mother] and her adopted daughter.

A psychological assessment was made over the following weeks and the psychologist took the view that further respite placement merely reinforced the status quo – that the family should choose 'to consider long term placement or change family functioning. These options need to be clearly stated to the family, and their attitude regarding these options should be clarified'. A few months later they had not made their minds up although foster care was organized:

A suitable foster home was found for [the child] and arrangements were made for [the mother] to meet the foster parents. She then informed me that a foster home was no longer required for the following reasons: it was too close to the new school term, it would have been okay for the holidays, her husband refused to allow [the child] to be fostered.

A few weeks later a placement was organized but the child returned to the adoptive mother's care. The case was closed because '[the mother] was invited to attend a Case Conference, however, elected not to attend . . . the Field officer's attempts to arrange appointments were resisted and despite several months of efforts, the situation had not improved'.

Case 609 was a four year old boy referred by a clinical psychologist 'suggesting that [the child] was the subject of possible emotional abuse and that he was significantly developmentally delayed'. The mother regularly received out-patient treatment for 'residual schizophrenia'. The child was enrolled in a day-care programme which included speech therapy. During the investigation it was noted that

[the mother] presented as tired, yawned frequently, spoke very slowly – very vague, sometimes incoherent. She could not recall certain details about recent things, she appeared not to have heard the telephone that had been ringing for at least one minute. She gave conflicting stories – e.g. not on medication, then, I took some tablets. [The mother] had not cooperated with DCS attempts to assess his developmental levels, attend speech therapy and day care. She was also believed to be psychiatrically disturbed and was not agreeing to undertake an assessment of her condition. It was believed that the child's delays were the product of his environment. Attempts to modify the environmental factors had failed, therefore placement in foster care was required. The possibility of continued placement with [his mother] had been canvassed, with [the child] still being made a ward, however, [the mother] did not keep to the arrangements made.

The child was apprehended and care and protection application resulted in wardship. Shortly after that the mother was compulsorily admitted to a psychiatric hospital.

Physical abuse/becomes care cases

Only one child was categorized as a physical abuse/becomes care case (Case 258). This was an eight year old boy who was in fact already a state child protection ward and who had been in care but was returned home. The case was reopened when a neighbour

> rang because she was concerned about [the child]. Yesterday he was in the street playing when mother called him in but he refused to go in . . . he was still outside (four hours later) but then threw stones down pathway towards door. Dad came out and chased him and then took him inside slapping him on the way. [The mother] was heard yelling to stop it and [the child] was screaming. There was a lot of thumping around.

Child protection workers called to see the family and saw bruises on the boy's neck which were not caused by his father, but by his mother who said 'that she had gone and hit [him] and marked his neck because she had been uptight about his running off earlier and then throwing rocks'. The boy gave a similar account. The file continues:

> There appeared to be minor problems in the family . . . when [the child] was stealing and generally being difficult with the parents being unable to cope and in open conflict over management of [the child]. [He] was very unhappy, wanted to leave home and stated he was frightened of his father. He was placed in temporary foster care [for two weeks]. Upon his return home [the family] had ongoing therapy on a fortnightly basis and [the child] appeared to be accepting his parent's limits . . . The situation once again deteriorated when the school contacted the Department with concerns. He had become very non-compliant and disruptive at school and has tried to strangle himself by tying his wind-cheater around his neck and a railing . . . Various strategic interventions have been attempted, however [the child] appears to be able, due to the power he holds on the family and school situations, to sabotage these interventions.

The boy was then admitted to a residential setting where an intensive programme of family therapy and behaviour modification was set up with the boy going home at weekends. By the time the case had been open for 52 weeks, there were signs of improvement with the parents 'working better as a team in supporting each other'.

Sexual abuse/becomes care cases

As with physical abuse, there was only one child classified in the sexual abuse category as a becomes care case. This was a ten year old girl (Case 28) whose parents suffered from multiple sensory disabilities. The girl had been sexually assaulted by her stepmother's father (stepgrandfather). The details of the assault were not recorded on file, but there was a successful police prosecution in this case. The girl became the subject of a long and drawn out custodial battle between her natural parents. She was voluntarily admitted to care at the father's request because of the tensions created by the prosecution and the custody conflict. After a few weeks she left care to live with the mother's family although she did have access visits from her father. The case was closed; 'Given that there will need to be a legal resolution, it appears inappropriate for the Department to reintervene'. The stepgrandfather was by then living in the country; he had no contact with the child. The major focus of the parents' interaction was a renewed maintenance battle in which lawyers were involved.

Conclusion

The 40 cases which fall into the becomes care category are important primarily because they indicate the general area of child protection where services designed to protect children palpably failed in one way or another. That does not necessarily mean to say that, given the resources at their disposal and the general training orientation of the child protection programme in the agency, that workers are necessarily to blame. It may be useful to ask, in what situations did interventions fail and why?

The answer is clear and obvious. Only two out of the 40 cases (5 per cent) concerned physical or sexual assaults and the primary focus of both child protection training and the literature is confined largely to this type of case. Indeed, identifiable harms and injuries occurred for only nine of these 40 children. The conspicuous feature of these cases is that of problems relating to drug and alcohol misuse, a matter which is mentioned in 31 (77.5 per cent) out of the 40 cases. In these 31 cases, there were only four children who were further harmed or injured. Alcohol and drug misuse are good predictors for children appearing in child protection statistics. They are *not* however good predictors for further harm or injury to children.

The irony is that while alcohol and drug misuse are easily identifiable as problems, they become reasons for bringing children into care rather than the reasons for remedial actions. In many of these cases the background–dependent assumption is caregivers who drink and take drugs harm children in some way – yet this assumption is rarely connected in case records with direct, observable effects on children. In that sense the records here give accounts about the moral character and disabilities of adults rather than their obvious effects on children.

There is however an interesting exception to this. One of the main benefits of file studies is that good practices are revealed by workers which can never be found in 'painting by numbers' practice guides or in 'scientific' studies. In this instance, it is worth returning briefly to Cases 695–8 (pp. 137–8).

The situated moral reasoning of the child protection worker indicates an early attempt to separate out the character of adults from the condition of children.

Undoubtedly the family has a lifestyle that doesn't fit in with the rest of the community, but it is important to identify the *exact points* (emphasis added) which concern the children's well-being. That is, we must specify what are the minimal physical conditions that we require. The nurturing and quality of emotional care is much harder to pin-point.

(Cases 695–8)

Here we have the beginnings of a potentially important development in child protection which clearly incorporates the principal of specificity. The worker in this case can see three interconnected areas, those of caregiver lifestyle, minimal physical conditions and emotional care. She recognizes that this is a starting point for assessment.

8 No further action

As shown in Table 4.12, a quarter of all those cases 'at risk' or substantiated as neglected or 'abused' were closed without service. The agency took no action whatsoever beyond the investigation, after which formal closure procedures were instituted. By any standards this is an important finding of the research, particularly in view of the legal responsibilities of child welfare agencies and the mass of child protection literature devoted to models of 'protective' service. There is an unwritten assumption in this literature that the identification of 'risk' or neglect or the substantiation of 'abuse' automatically triggers intervention. In a quarter of cases in this study, it did not.

Table 8.1 'At risk' or substantiated no further action cases – caregiver family structure and ethnicity

Family structure	Ethnicity		Total	%
	Aboriginal	Non-Aboriginal		
Both biological parents	9	27	36	44
Reconstituting family	1	5	6	7.3
Single female parent	11	18	29	35.4
Single male parent	0	5	5	6
Unknown	1	5	6	7.3
Total	22	60	82	100
%	27	73	100	

Table 8.1 shows that approximately half the children in this category came from single parent families, half of whom were Aboriginal.

While Table 8.2 shows that with the exception of emotional abuse, these cases were drawn more or less equally from the different categories of 'abuse' types, it must be remembered that of all cases originally classified into 'abuse' types, they

Table 8.2 'At risk' or substantiated no further action cases – 'abuse' type

Substantiation	Nos	%
'At risk'	20	24.3
Neglect	22	26.8
Emotional abuse	2	2.4
Physical abuse	21	25.5
Sexual abuse	17	21
Total	82	100

demonstrate marked differences. The 20 'at risk' cases are only 18.3 per cent of the total of 109 cases placed in that category, the 22 neglect cases are 24 per cent of all the 91 cases originally so classified and in marked contrast, the physical abuse/no further action cases are 42 per cent of the 50 cases originally substantiated as physical abuse. With regard to sexual abuse, no further action decisions were made in 26 per cent of cases. What stands out here is that the category of physical abuse has a no further action closure rate approximately twice as high as that of other categories.

'At risk'/no further action cases

Twenty children were judged to be 'at risk' by child protection investigators. The nature of the risks varied, but they were all associated with the difficulties faced by adult caregivers since none of these children were harmed or injured. Cases 30 and 31 were small children living in a family where the mother was under considerable stress due to a failing marriage. 'A complaint was lodged by [the sister-in-law] on the severe methods of child disciplining. Apparently she would scream at the children and hit them badly'. Interviews with the father, school and family doctor failed to identify 'any evidence of abuse' and 'litigation is pending regarding a likely separation'. The mother was interviewed:

> she admitted hitting the children but not severely and this is considered to be culturally acceptable. She is extremely isolated and a possible custody battle is pending . . . Investigation has highlighted a mixed race marriage (mother Asian and father Australian) which is failing . . . [the mother] has been made aware of the implications of this sort of discipline and is agreeable to utilising time out methods and removal of privileges etc.

Three elements here combine to stop intervention, they are the perception of a less culpable mother who is Asian, isolated and cooperative, a father who is seen to be 'protective' because of the custody application, and children without injuries. It is worth noting that the referral originated from a sister-in-law who was clearly taking sides in a marital dispute.

Case 115 began with a complaint about a single female parent's 'care of [her son]'. It transpired that an older child of hers had been knocked down and killed by a drunk driver the previous year. The child protection worker reported that '[the mother] presented as a very depressed lady with both a grim financial need, and requiring someone to help her talk through her grief'. He concluded that

> I believe, from the hour or so I spent with her, that [the mother] is a caring mother unable as yet to come to terms with her own grief. She is aware of her son's physical and emotional needs and caters as best she can with both . . . It would be, in the most polite terms I can think of, a *bloody travesty* if we were brought in on an investigation at this stage.

Here we find a worker really struggling to keep faith with child protection, the context of the investigation in his view was so obviously one where help was required that he was led to question the morality of classifying the case as child protection in the first instance. The child was seen to be 'at risk' because of the emotional and financial effects of bereavement on his mother.

Cases 340 and 391 were mentally handicapped children living in remote communities. In both instances problems were perceived in respect of caregiver's abilities to look after children without the types of educational and medical support available in urban areas. Case 391 was a nine year old girl living on a caravan site with

> [both parents], their 6 daughters, 3 sons, 2 daughters-in-law, son-in-law, 2 *de facto* husbands and their daughters, the grandmother, 16 grandchildren and 2–4 casual visitors from time to time; making a total of 33–37 persons in all . . . The family exists primarily on welfare payments – the son-in-law taking casual employment when available . . . Accommodation consists of: one 12 foot caravan, 3 large tents and several lean-to shelters.

The only identifiable risk to the child lay in the fact that

> [the child] has had a fit and fallen into the river on several occasions – to be rescued by her father. Moreover, although the risk from crocodiles in this area is low, it cannot be discounted entirely and thus, also remains a concern for her parents.

Here we see a lifestyle well at odds with the conventional view of how Australians should live, and despite the child's learning difficulties, lots of people around to give supervision. However, because of her disability, the child could not appreciate the dangers of the river and crocodiles.

One large family (Cases 597–602) accounts for six of the 20 'at risk' cases. This family also lived in a remote area and the children were 'not attending school at all'. The social worker from the school gave the following information:

> [She] first went to their home on [date] and although the front door was open, no one would answer. She noticed that the house was in an appalling state, filthy and chaotic. In her terms, she did not want to go in unless [sic] she came out with things crawling on her. On [date] she returned and once again no one would answer although the cars were there, door was open and

the TV was on. [The school social workers] said that the home was still in exactly the same condition as she had seen it 5 months earlier ... [she] believes the children are emotionally abused and suspects physical abuse although there is no evidence to substantiate this. Also suspected is undernourishment.

A visit by a child protection worker revealed that the mother was

quite happy for [the children] to attend school but that they did not wish to go to school because they were 'hassled' by the other students ... regarding the concerns of neglect, although the garden and little I saw of the house were filthy, and the girls and [the mother] were dirty, I found no real grounds on which to make an issue. The girls were adequately clothed and looked to be well fed so I decided not to pursue it at this stage ... the problem is an educational one rather than a welfare matter at this time and so have informed [the school social worker] of this.

Notwithstanding the concerns voiced by the school social worker, the child protection worker did not consider intervention was necessary. She agreed with the mother that the 'problem' lay in the school setting rather than at home, but because of the truancy matter (which was held to be the school's responsibility) and the contextual environmental conditions, the children were judged to be 'at risk' rather than 'not substantiated'. It is these contextual factors which appear to make the difference.

Neglect/no further action cases

There were 22 children who were classified as neglected but the cases were closed with no further action. Half of these children came from two large families. These neglected children fell into four broad categories: first, children whose supervision was temporarily neglected and where the investigators viewed these as 'isolated incidents' in which parents admitted and regretted their brief and temporary absences; second, cases where such absences were cyclical and periodic but contextual factors never suggested intervention; third, cases where children were left temporarily with resentful relatives and fourth, children whose parents did not comply with the detailed requirements of medical care.

Cases 35–7 were children in the first category.

Both [women] arrived from [another state] ... leaving their husbands to start a new life. [One mother] has changed her mind and has planned to return to her husband ... The complaint was that there were 5 children living in the caravan, this turned out to be 3. The children have been left at times in the caravan by themselves, but both mothers suggested that the next door neighbour was looking or keeping an eye on them. I explained the risk involved ... they acknowledged this. All children presented clean and appeared well cared for ... I suggest that the issues and the concerns were not major problems with these families, just adjustment issues.

Within the context of clean, well looked-after children the brief neglect of supervision is seen as a matter of 'adjustment' given the circumstances of the families.

Cases 321 and 322 were children in a family where brief neglect occurred periodically within the context of having to be cared for by a resentful 16 year old sister who was '13 weeks pregnant and did not want to take on a caring role for her siblings'. On this occasion the mother 'has been spending days at a time away from her children. She is in the company of her male friend'. Mitigating factors here were the ages of the children (15 years and 13 years). The children knew where mother was, apparently one of them (the 15 year old) had been to ask mother to come home. She refused 'and [the referring maternal aunt] says mother usually cares and has great concern for the children'. The 16 year old sister was described as 'an extremely immature, irresponsible and demanding young woman'. The final summary noted that

> The pattern of this family is that they have 2 or 3 incidents a year where they need crisis intervention, therefore this case should be closed with no further action. If a crisis occurs in future, it should be dealt with on that basis and not reopened as a preventive case unless there are serious concerns about [the 16 year old daughter's child's] safety.

It is interesting to note here that the worker makes a distinction between family conflicts involving adolescents as a 'preventive' matter and the as yet unborn child of the 16 year old which is viewed potentially as a child protection matter.

Cases 624–8 were five Aboriginal children referred by relatives because the aunt 'is concerned that [the parents] often come into [town] for weekends and leave the kids with [her or another relative] at [a community], while they go on a drinking binge'. The Aboriginal child protection worker noted that

> I spoke with [the parents] and gave them a lecture on leaving their kids with relatives. All the kids are back at [their own community] now. I spoke to the school headmaster and advised him of the situation. I spoke to the [community] Chairman and advised him of the situation. [He] will raise this matter with the family also.

There is no suggestion on the file that the children were actually neglected. The inference is that had the parents left their children with relatives to undertake activities other than drinking, then the case might not have been classified as neglect. Once more, it is the moral character of the parents rather than harm or threat to children which determines the classification. The outcome – a decision to close the case with no further action is a consequence of ensuring that the school and community leaders were agreeable to maintaining a watching brief.

Cases 656–61 were six children aged between 11 and four years. They were referred by a community health nurse.

> Her basic complaint was that she was sick and tired of continually sending head lice eradication material – and instructions – home and the material either not being used or not being used correctly. She stated that the matter

was one of basic hygiene and could be remedied by two weeks of regular washing with soap and water and the correct treatment for lice which included washing clothing, bed linen, towels etc. Allied with this was a recommendation that the children have their hair cut shorter to make it easier to keep clean and prevent reinfection.

The file was concluded as follows:

1 The children are not in immediate danger;
2 The problem is basically health and hygiene and not therefore the province of this department.
3 Because of [the mother's] uncooperative attitude and anti-authoritarian stance there would be little if any cooperation with any support offered by this department.

Besides this does not come under the duties of [the child protection laws]. The issue has therefore been referred back to Community Health.

This summary was written after the mother had been interviewed. The worker could perceive a formal classification of neglect, but he interpreted this as a medical problem. Significantly the uncooperative mother is seen as a reason for non-intervention in the sense that her 'attitude' suggests that intervention would in this instance achieve nothing.

Emotional abuse/no further action cases

Two children were categorized as being victims of 'emotional abuse' when cases were closed with no further action. Case 157 was a 14 year old girl whose stepmother was described as 'shouting, screaming, overly punishing, lack of affection'. The child protection worker interviewed the child at school; she 'begged [the worker] not to talk to either her father or stepmother as she was frightened of the consequences'. The child's older sister (who had left home after receiving similar treatment) was contacted. She in turn talked to the stepmother who appeared to develop a more positive relationship with the child – she 'bought presents for [the child and] was showing [her] some affection'. The case was closed when the school social worker agreed to 'monitor the situation'.

The second case, number 46, was a younger sibling of Case 47, a child categorized as 'physical abuse, no further action', and described on p. 150.

Physical abuse/no further action cases

As has been mentioned before, while physical abuse was substantiated in 50 of the 655 child protection referrals, 21 of these (42 per cent) were closed with no further action. Table 8.3 shows that the action responsible for this was excess corporal punishment in all cases but that minor injuries (cuts, bruises, welts or bites) were identified in only eight cases.

Table 8.3 Physical abuse/no further action cases – actions causing harms and injuries

Harm/injury	Excess corporal punishment	Total	%
Cuts, bruises, welts or bites	8	8	38
No identifiable injury	6	6	29
Other	3	3	14
Unknown	4	4	19
Total	21	21	100

Three types of situation were referred for investigation. The smallest group – two cases – were recent migrant families from non-European backgrounds, living in isolation from their own communities, with large families and none of the child care support normally available from the kinship networks. Case 7 was a nine year old girl who

> appeared in school with bruises on her arms and legs which the child claimed was a result of being beaten by mother with a wooden spoon. On a previous occasion she had arrived in school not having had dinner the previous day nor breakfast. It seems she was not given food due to misbehaviour.

Child protection workers interviewed the mother and reported that

> This is a large family, (non-European) in origin and is made up of a 17 year old daughter who works; two 16 year old partly retarded sons, one of whom is working; an 11 year old daughter and the child in question. The father is a shift worker, sleeping most of the day ... [mother] is responsible for managing a rather large family. She confirmed having hit [the child] for misbehaving. Her husband was unaware of the incident and was surprised ... I expressed concern about the severity of punishment ... They refused an offer of assistance ... The school has agreed to monitor the child's welfare.

In deciding to take no further action, the workers took into account the fact that the father 'agreed to take over part of the family management, which, combined with school monitoring seemed sufficient to deal with the case'.

The second type of situation involved single female parents caring for intellectually handicapped children (three cases). Case 54 was a three and a half year old boy who was seen with bruises at a special school which he said were a result of his mother hitting and kicking him. In interview the mother 'categorically denied the allegations'; in this she was supported by her sister who assisted with the care of the child and said that 'the injury had occurred at school, and was due to a push bike accident'. The worker commented that 'This denial, and its support [by the sister] in my view leaves the situation at stalemate'.

However, the mother

> said she wanted to move out, and that she may return to her *de facto* (leaving the child with his aunt). The school report that [the child] has never been seen to have bruises before this, and his relationship with his Aunt appears to be better than with his mother. I believe risk to [the child] would be much less if his mother moved out.

A final note on the file indicates that the school would 'monitor the situation and report any injuries'.

Case 47 was a 4 year old boy staying in a women's refuge with his mother and younger brother (Case 46). He was referred by a refuge worker after the mother had 'lost her temper with her son – gave him a hit across the face which lifted the little fellow off his feet and flung him across the room'. The refuge was visited and the mother interviewed, she 'presented as a very disturbed person, completely unwilling to communicate or cooperate'. The worker neither examined nor talked to the children who were present during the interview because the worker feared antagonizing the mother. The refuge worker attempted to evict the family because she felt the mother was potentially violent towards refuge staff and residents, but the police refused to assist in the eviction and instead referred her for psychiatric care. The worker recommended no further action after the family had moved to another refuge close to the psychiatric facility.

Ten cases fall into the third type of situation – fathers using physical punishment to discipline children for misbehaviour. Typical of these was Case 341, a 12 year old boy. In this instance, a five year old boy had taken $90 from his home and given it to the 12 year old in question, at school. When the five year old's father discovered what had happened, he telephoned the 12 year old boy's father: 'Over the telephone he heard [the father] yelling at [the boy] and allegedly belting him. That's when he made the report to the police'. A visit to the family confirmed that the boy had been hit across the face once and punched in the stomach. The mother said that she and the father 'found the boy difficult to manage and he is backward with his school work. She could see no cause for real concern as she said [the father] is usually very fair but is the disciplinarian of the family'. A home visit the next day found the parents

> angry at the interference of [the five year old boy's father] but although not delighted with DCS involvement were cooperative. We discussed punishment and discipline and the need for them to be appropriate and realistic. Both said that they had tried all sorts of discipline with [the boy] and that physical punishment was apparently the only one that worked ... [the mother] said they had tried depriving him of television or outings or sending him to his room. None of these were effective.

The father was described as 'a very down-to-earth sort of man'. Counselling by a psychologist was offered but not accepted.

Case 500 was the only one of the 21 cases which fell within the crude catchall category of 'domestic violence'. Once again, a child (a nine year old girl) came to school complaining that 'her father had hit her on the bottom. She was having trouble sitting down'. Two days later it was established that the mother had left the home and taken her daughter and three other children with her to a refuge: 'She said that she will stay there a little while'. She then put out a restraining order on her husband and indicated to the social worker that he had been violent to her and the other children. A telephone message completed the file: '[the mother] says she will contact us if she requires any assistance or there are any problems with [her husband]'.

These cases were closed either because workers judged that within the context of isolation and stress, mothers had lost their tempers or fathers had used corporal punishment in excess and were able to acknowledge that was the case.

Sexual abuse/no further action cases

The 17 sexual abuse/no further action cases involved five types of situation. The first type (nine cases) occurred when children were exposed to non-penetrative single incident sexual assaults by adults. In none of these cases was there any prolonged exposure to systematic sexual exploitation and family members were not involved in the assaults except in one case. Typical of these were Cases 140 and 141, 13 and nine year old girls who were assaulted by the grandfather of a neighbour; 'he exposed himself to one child and showed the other blue movies'. The man was prosecuted and placed on a good behaviour bond for 12 months. The mother of the girls felt the situation was resolved since she had talked to the girls at great length. Child protection workers saw both girls on their own; the file concluded with the interview notes from the older child:

> quite a determined nature. Expressed prior feelings of guilt however like her sister, stated that she had discussed the abuse many times, with many people, and now wanted to forget about it. Determined to have no further contact with perpetrator and recognised that abuse was not her fault. Felt no further contact is necessary with these children. They have looked at the abuse in depth and in terms of their own development.

In the second type of situation, children turned down offers of help after one-off assault incidents. Case 236 was a 16 year old girl who had been assaulted by an uncle three years previously.

> She said she hadn't seen [her uncle] since the incident . . . we discussed support for [her] but she said she was fine and didn't want to talk about it . . . support and counselling has been offered to [her] but it is doubtful whether the offer will be taken up.

The case was closed.

The third case type concerned young women who, like the case described above, disclosed being victims of sexual assaults several years previously (two cases). Case 282 was a 21 year old young woman who had been assaulted five years previously. She was referred on to another agency 'for counselling . . . considering her age'.

Another type of situation (three cases) arose where fathers were believed to be responsible for assaults and the mother succeeded in ejecting them from the home or moved house with the children in order to secure their safety. Cases 484 and 485 concerned 14 and 16 year old sisters who disclosed assaults by their father to teachers. The girls and their father were interviewed by the police (who did not prosecute because the statements did not 'corroborate each other'). The mother, who believed her daughters, quit the house and moved to another town where child protection workers followed up with a home visit. The worker noted that 'I reinforced that what the girls had done was the appropriate course of action – the fact that the police chose not to prosecute was not their fault. Similarly, I assured the girls they were not responsible for what happened'.

The fifth case type involved situations where 'sexual abuse' was substantiated, but it was of a verbal nature. There were two cases in this category. Case 532 was a 14 year old girl who experienced an unwanted sexual approach from her older married male cousin. In interview, the child

> confirmed that [her cousin] has been harassing her over the past twelve months. The harassment has been verbal, [he] asking her to have sex with him and telling her he would teach her about sex. The harassment has been verbal not physical and occurred on about fifteen occasions . . . she learnt to cope with the situation by walking away from [him] when he started talking about sex . . . on [date she] told [her cousin's wife] about [her cousin] – she flew to his defence accusing [the girl] of lying. Discussion with the girl indicates that she handled the situation with maturity; we talked about powerplay, adult responsibility, her guilt feelings etc. Recommendations: No Further Action.

Conclusion

The no further action cases all involved genuine incidents of 'abuse' as defined by the agency, but in all these cases there was evidence of cooperation and/or an awareness of a problem by adult caregivers. Where help was offered, there was a reluctance to accept any further professional involvement and when workers were anxious about this, a reassurance of further monitoring was sought from schools.

The question inevitably arises, how safe were the no further action procedures? In the 52 weeks which succeeded each referral, only six (7.3 per cent) of these 82 cases were referred again after they had been closed. In all six cases, further investigations took place. The outcomes of these six second investigations are shown in Table 8.4.

Only two of the rereferred cases were kept open after second investigations, both received home-based services. Case 466, an eight year old boy (previously excessively punished by his father) was again reported by his school as having

Table 8.4   Outcomes of re-referred NFA cases

Case no.	Substantiation	Career
319	Neglect	No further action
322	Neglect	No further action
458	'At risk'	No further action
466	Physical abuse	Home-based services
532	Not substantiated	Not substantiated
628	Emotional abuse	Home-based services

bruises. It was clear from the child's accounts at interview that his father had not ceased hitting him; 'last night after ten dad noticed that more dog food had been used than normal, he became angry with me (it's my job to feed the dog) and strapped me across the arms a few times as punishment'. These punishments appeared to occur 'about three times a month'. The investigator concluded that 'from the [boy's] remarks and reactions he either believes or wanted me to understand that a certain level of physical violence is normal and generally more amusing than a reason for concern'. Arrangements were made for the boy to go and live with an aunt and uncle. A year later the aunt was requesting help. She wanted the boy to stay with her family 'as she is very aware of her brother's methods of discipline and [the boy] is stating that he will not return to [his mother and father's] care'. At his aunt's house, he had been 'acting out and lying and deliberately causing arguments with her children'. The boy was still receiving help from a psychologist a year later. The other case staying open for services was that of an Aboriginal infant originally the youngest child in a large family where there had been neglect. The child was diagnosed as having a heart defect and in need of an operation which could only be obtained a very long way away from her home. She had the operation and returned home, but when her parents went on a 'drinking spree' she was left with an aunt who contacted the agency. This was classed as 'emotional abuse' and the case kept open for surveillance.

On the whole, no further action appeared to be a safe procedure to follow judging from the 12 month rereferral rates. It also illustrates the extent to which child protection workers, as with many of the monitoring and surveillance cases, made arrangements for continuing oversight even when they were not formally involved. This was very much an indirect policing activity.

9 Aboriginal people and child protection

Introduction

As the child protection file studies in Western Australia expanded beyond the metropolitan areas of Perth and Fremantle, it became necessary for the research team to travel to remote regions of the state to read case files with child protection workers and obtain data for the study. One such trip took the researchers to two of the 20 area offices where 90 per cent of the cases concerned Aboriginal children. During the visit to the first of these offices, discussions were held with social workers during the first two hours of the working day, then the researchers settled down to read files. After about an hour one of the social workers came into the office and said, 'I have a "greenie"'. She was referring to the green form on which details of new child protection referrals were entered.

It is not uncommon in action research which closely involves field workers for researchers to become involved in office conversations about current cases which are not part of the research, but which nevertheless can often provide useful background data. In this instance, the social worker, who was alone in the office, was signalling that a new case posing particular problems had landed on her desk. A few minutes after the first discussion that day the police had telephoned her in her capacity as duty officer, to say that the previous evening they had arrested an Aboriginal woman for non-payment of a small fine of $20. Apparently the woman came from an Aboriginal community some distance away and the original fine – which had not been paid – was for public drunkenness. Because of the non-payment, the police had obtained a warrant for her arrest and duly executed it when she showed up in town. Approximately half an hour after she had been placed in a police cell, someone appeared in the police station with her six month old baby. At the time of the arrest the baby was in the care of various people the woman was associating with; it was not in her physical possession when the apprehension took place. The police took the baby to the hospital for the night and then telephoned the social worker the next morning.

In discussion with the social worker, my advice was that the department should pay the woman's fine – this seemed to be the fastest and cheapest way of avoiding prolonged separation of the child from its mother. The social worker commented, 'We have no departmental provision for doing that'. She then said that they could however spend money on chartering a flight and flying the baby back to its mother's community some 200 kilometres away. Another option was to persuade the hospital to release the baby and persuade the police to allow the woman to keep it in her cell until the necessary number of days had been served in order to deal with the unpaid fine. Two days later when the research team left that office the position had not changed. The police apparently did agree to allow the baby into its mother's care, but the hospital refused to release it because 'infected scabies' had been diagnosed – a common complaint for people living in remote areas without the medical care facilities normally available in most rural areas.

This case joined the child protection statistics for that year and was classified by the worker completing the form as *Medical Neglect*. The definition of this condition according to the Department for Community Services orientation and training guidelines was as follows:

Medical Neglect
The lack of adequate medical or dental treatment for a health problem or conditions, which, if untreated, could become severe enough to constitute a serious or long-term harm to the child. Lack of immunization in some circumstances can be considered as contributing to medical neglect. This definition also includes failure on the part of the caregiver to follow through with prescribed medical treatment.
(Department for Community Services 1987: 16)

Inadequate Supervision
The placing of a child in a situation which is likely to require him/her to make judgements or undertake actions at a level beyond the child's maturity, physical condition or mental ability.
Examples are: Young children being left alone, caregiver present but unable to supervise children because of intoxication etc., children having unsupervised access to electricity, poisons, drugs, matches, traffic and pools.
(Department for Community Services 1987: 26)

On the statistical return, the 'Perpetrator' was described as 'Mother'. In reaching this decision the worker indicated that she took account of several factors. First, at the time of referral the police informed her that the woman had been living with a man who was hospitalized as a result of an assault. The man had to be flown to Perth for medical care. While the woman was not prosecuted, the worker was given the impression that she had been responsible for the assault and injuries and was somehow or other dangerous. Second, at the time of arrest, the woman was outside the local pub with a group of Aboriginal people who were or who had been drinking. Third, the woman had previous convictions for drunkenness. Apparently the police were aware that she had a small baby, but explained that they did not execute the warrant until they were sure that the baby was not with her.

In this first hand account of the process of child protection there are two important issues. The first one concerns the way in which the moral character of the woman was considered to be of equal importance to other factors in the definitional process, while the second relates to the role of the state agencies. These agencies were all doing their statutory duty. The police were acting on a warrant, the Department for Community Services was acting on a child protection referral and the Health Department was giving treatment to a child who was sick. In one way or another, the actions of all these agencies were such as to maintain the separation of the baby from its mother. In so doing, the state was arguably continuing the perpetration of legally sanctioned activities which have a long and significant history in Australia.

Australian Aborigines and white settlers

Much has been written in recent years about the British invasion of Australia since Captain Cook landed in Botany Bay in 1788 and the way in which Aboriginal people have been treated by successive generations of white settlers. It is not the intention in this chapter to replicate that work, but rather to focus on one aspect of that history and explore its implications as they are laid bare within the context of child protection research and relate to the story described at the beginning of this chapter.

For Australian Aborigines the term 'protection' has a very special meaning since it was the term used to define the policies and practices adopted by the Australian state towards Aboriginal people for over half a century. The policies and practices of 'protection' did not end until the eve of the Second World War and the experiences of Aboriginal people placed in reserves, settlements and mission stations is still a living memory for the older generation. The history of white contact with Aborigines is well summarized by Healy *et al.*

> Permanent European settlement from 1788 onwards ushered in a disas-
> trous period for Aboriginal culture and society, with continuing clashes
> between the two cultures. The pre-contact Aboriginal population is thought
> to have numbered over 300,000, but this fell rapidly after European
> settlement, until by 1933 it was about 74,000, one fifth of the original size.
> Aborigines, with their stone and wood weapons, were slaughtered by
> punitive expeditions sent out by settlers. This destruction was hastened
> because the Aboriginal population of the isolated continent had no
> immunity to introduced European diseases, such as smallpox, measles and
> venereal diseases (Lippman 1981).
>
> Public policy towards Aboriginal people has moved through several
> phases over the last two hundred years (Rowley 1972, 1978). Alongside the
> unofficial destruction of Aboriginal people and their culture, the official
> policy was one of protection. For over a century, Aborigines were perceived
> as a dwindling savage race, and the aim was 'to smooth the dying pillow'
> (Elkin, 1978). Some remote people remained relatively untouched, but in

other areas, unrelated groups were herded together on small reserves, often away from their traditional lands, with resulting disruption to familial and cultural ties.

By the 1930s, the policy had shifted to one of assimilation: the aim was to submerge Aborigines into the larger Australian population. It was a dual policy, involving the acculturation of the mixed-race fringe and urban dwellers, and the segregation of traditionally oriented Aborigines. The Aboriginal population were not consulted on their future.

(Healy *et al.* 1985)

British laws were applied to Aboriginal people in Western Australia from 1840 onwards on the recommendation of George Grey who was in correspondence with the colonial office. Rowley comments that

Grey's approach was to discount native custom altogether, which shows how little understood was the tenacity of human groups in adhering to the bases of social relationships ... In the century or so since Grey made his recommendations, much more has been learned of the nature of human societies: of the fallacy of applying unitary standards of civilisation and morality and of the resistances to social and political change when the people concerned have not been harmed and enthralled by encroaching culture

(Rowley 1972: 70)

Rowley's message about 'applying unitary standards of civilisation' apply as much to the standards assumed, but not articulated by child protection laws, policies and practices. In this chapter we will see more of what happens when the impositions about which Rowley warned reap their unintended consequences.

The Aborigines Act of 1905 in Western Australia increased considerably the powers of the Aborigines Protection Board first established in 1886. A Chief Protector was appointed who had protectors in all districts who were also police. The new powers, covering everyone defined as 'Aboriginal', included the granting, withdrawing or renewing of work permits to those who employed Aborigines – in effect legally binding Aboriginal people to one employer. Reserves were established on Crown land – but a restriction on size ensured that they would be confined to the least productive land. A third provision dealt with sexual relationships between white people and Aborigines, effectively making them illegal.

While the intentions of the 1905 Act were technically 'protective', in effect they gave the police exceptionally extensive powers over Aboriginal people. Henceforth the police would be able to move Aboriginal people round at will, from employers to reserves. The equivalent Northern Territory legislation, passed in the South Australian Parliament in 1910, made the Chief Protector

the legal guardian of 'every Aboriginal and half-caste child, notwithstanding that any such child has a parent or other relative living, until such child attains the age of eighteen years ... The implications of this were quite definite, and in due course it became usual for a protector to remove the children with light skins from their mothers.

(Rowley 1972: 231)

This early twentieth-century model of child protection automatically made all children of one particular ethnic origin into state wards. Some might call it 'the King Herod Syndrome'.

Nearly 40 years later these measures were adopted and strengthened in Western Australia by the 1936 Aborigines Amendment Act. Under this legislation all Aboriginal people, now referred to as 'Natives', under 21 years old, were made wards of state. Their legal guardian was the Commissioner of Native Affairs. Ironically this massive increase in powers was a result of the protective and assimilationist views of the Chief Protector. The Report of the Royal Commission whose recommendations were incorporated into the 1936 Act suggested abolition of:

> the native camps which, without exception are a disgrace, and provide settlements where families may be taken, where the grown-up members of those families may be housed according to their needs and be usefully occupied either on the settlements or, at periods, at work on surrounding farms, and where the children may occupy quarters of their own, attend a school of their own, be taught such matters as hygiene and other elementary principles of a civilised life, and where, although not debarred altogether from seeing their parents, they may be gradually weaned from the Aboriginal influence.
>
> (Moseley 1935: 8)

Here we see the plan to separate Aboriginal children from their caregivers, to destabilize and destroy the existing kinship networks and the existing protective and caring mechanisms which were part and parcel of customary cultural practice – all in the name of 'protection'.

Aborigines and western child protection practices

How do contemporary child protection polices and practices based on the relatively recently developed ideologies and definitions of the 1960s and 1970s which originated in North America affect Aboriginal people? The research and some subsequent consultations within Western Australia by the Department for Community Services with Aboriginal people gives an interesting picture.

In Chapter 4, Table 4.9 showed that 23 per cent of all the allegations of neglect or child 'abuse' concerned Aboriginal children. As stated before, Aboriginal people form approximately 3 per cent of the state's population, suggesting that Aboriginal children are overrepresented by a factor of eight.

Table 9.1 looks at the results of investigations and ethnicity. Over two-thirds (68.6 per cent) of the allegations made about Aboriginal children were substantiated or children judged to be 'at risk', compared with under half (44 per

Table 9.1 Ethnicity of referred children and substantiation

Ethnicity	Substantiated/ 'at risk'	Not substan- tiated	Total	%
Aboriginal	103	47	150	23
Non-Aboriginal	156	191	347	53
Unknown	66	92	158	24
Total	325	330	655	100
%	49.6	50.4	100	

cent) of non-Aboriginal or unknown ethnic origin children. Not only are Aboriginal children more likely to be referred for child protection investigation than their white counterparts, but allegations are also more likely to be substantiated. Aboriginal children are 23 per cent of all referrals and 32 per cent of all substantiated or 'at risk' cases.

Table 9.2 Career types and substantiation – Aboriginal cases

Career type	'At risk'	Neglect	Emotional abuse	Physical abuse	Sexual abuse	Total	%
Begins care	10	16	0	2	2	30	29.1
Becomes care	9	15	0	0	0	24	23.3
Home-based services	9	10	1	4	3	27	26.2
No further action	2	14	1	2	3	22	21.4
Total	30	55	2	8	8	103	100
%	29.1	53.4	2	7.75	7.75	100	

Tables 9.2 and 9.3 provide a clearer picture as to the influence of ethnicity on the total child protection picture. They show that Aboriginal children feature predominantly in the 'at risk' and neglect categories where they received substitute care services. Of the total 'at risk' and neglect begins care services (44 children), Aboriginal children account for 26 cases (59 per cent). In the 'at risk' and neglect becomes care cases (36 children) Aboriginal children constitute 24 cases (66 per cent). However, they are relatively underrepresented in home-based services for both these maltreatment classifications – 19 cases only as opposed to 59 for non-Aboriginal or unknown ethnic origin children. These tables suggest that the most likely outcome for Aboriginal children after an investigation has demonstrated the existence of risk, neglect or abuse, is substitute care sooner or later (52.5 per cent). For other children these measures are the least likely (22.5 per cent).

Table 9.3   Career types and substantiation – non-Aboriginal/unknown ethnicity cases

Career type	'At risk'	Neglect	Emotional abuse	Physical abuse	Sexual abuse	Total	%
Begins care	11	7	1	6	9	34	15.3
Becomes care	6	6	2	1	1	16	7.2
Home-based services	44	15	4	16	33	112	50.5
No further action	18	8	1	19	14	60	27
Total	79	36	8	42	57	222	100
%	35.6	16.2	3.6	18.9	25.7	100	

Table 9.4   Apprehension and ethnicity

Ethnicity	Apprehended	Not apprehended	Total	%
Aboriginal	26	124	150	23
Non-Aboriginal	19	328	347	53
Unknown	2	156	158	24
Total	47	608	655	100
%	7	93	100	

Table 9.4 shows that 47 out of the 655 referred children were apprehended, and that of these 47 children, 26 (55.3 per cent) were Aboriginal.

Table 9.5   Care and protection applications and ethnicity

Result of application	Aboriginal	Non-Aboriginal	Total	%
None made	123	483	606	92.5
Adjourned	7	2	9	1.4
Dismissed	0	1	1	0.2
Withdrawn	6	8	14	2.1
Granted	14	11	25	3.8
Total	150	505	655	100
%	23	77	100	

Table 9.5 looks at activity in the Children's Court in respect of care and protection applications and the ensuing decisions as to whether or not wardship was granted for Aboriginal and non-Aboriginal children. Of the 49 children in respect of whom care and protection applications were made, 27 (55 per cent) were Aboriginal and Aboriginal children's cases were much more likely to be adjourned or wardship granted than was the case for children from other ethnic backgrounds.

Tables 9.1 to 9.5 present a very disturbing picture. They suggest that the more coercive and intrusive the child protection operation becomes, so the over-representation of Aboriginal children increases. The sequential picture created is as follows:

- Aboriginal people are 3 per cent of the state's population. Aboriginal children are the subjects of nearly a quarter of all child protection allegations. Over two thirds of these allegations are substantiated or judged to be 'at risk', compared with less than a half of allegations on non-Aboriginal children.
- Four-fifths (82 per cent) of Aboriginal children in the child protection system are either judged to be neglected or 'at risk' as opposed to only a half (52 per cent) of children from other ethnic backgrounds.
- Aboriginal children were 60 per cent of all neglect cases.
- Over half of the cases of Aboriginal children substantiated as neglected, abused or 'at risk' received substitute care services, as compared with less than a quarter of comparable cases involving children of other ethnic origins. Aboriginal children were over half of all children subject to the use of emergency removal measures – apprehension – and they were half of all children who became state wards as a result of care and protection applications in Children's Courts.

How do Aboriginal children come to be so grossly overrepresented in child protection? What are the factors within Aboriginal social life as it interacts with the Eurocentric notion of child protection which bring about this situation? Evidence from the case files suggests two issues, those of poverty and those of the continuing remnant of traditional child rearing practices within contemporary Aboriginal communities.

Poverty in Aborigine families

The 54 children shown as receiving substitute care services in Table 9.2 came from 32 families. Table 9.6 shows the caregiver family structure of these families.

Examination of the files reveals that with one possible exception (Case 49, see p. 124) none of the caregivers of these 54 children – whether they were single parents or two parent families – were in employment of any sort at the time the children were admitted to substitute care. *All* the children came from financially disadvantaged backgrounds and were existing on state benefits of one kind or another. One obvious structural context to the overrepresentation of Aboriginal

Table 9.6 'At risk'/neglect Aboriginal children in
substitute care – caregiver family structure

Family structure	Nos	%
Both biological parents	13	24
Reconstituting family	8	15
Single female parent	27	50
Single male parent	6	11
Total	54	100

children in the substitute care sector of child protection is that of financial disadvantage. These children came from impoverished families.

In her introduction to her study of child poverty amongst Aboriginals, Choo says that

> It is widely acknowledged that on a range of social indicators the Aborigines emerge as the most disadvantaged group in Australia. These indicators include health, housing, education, employment, income and criminal justice. The average life-expectancy at birth is 20 years less than that for other Australians. Infant mortality is nearly three times that of non-Aboriginal children. 32 percent of Aboriginal children aged 0–9, as against 1.6 percent of non-Aboriginal children, have some form of trachoma. Aboriginal unemployment is six times the national average. On average, Aborigines earn half the income of other Australians. Aboriginal imprisonment rates are up to twenty times those of other Australians. A large proportion of Aboriginal families live in substandard housing or temporary shelter.
>
> (Choo 1990: 1)

It is interesting to note here the parallels between overrepresentation in the criminal justice and child protection systems. Both are state-governed activities whose aim is to preserve order of one kind or another. Both appear to select disproportionately disadvantaged groups. This matter will be returned to in the final chapter, since it suggests that whatever the high-flown rhetoric of social policy, once an instrument has been created for the identification and processing of 'deviant' and 'disorderly' individuals – those who for whatever reason do not conform to some unwritten norm – then that system will catch within its net those social groups which do not easily match the ideal citizen, family or child. It is a good example of how child protection cannot claim to be any different from those apparatus of the state which discriminate.

Aboriginal child rearing practices

Not only are the structural circumstances of Aboriginal people very different from their non-Aboriginal Australian counterparts, but their child rearing practices are – to European eyes – utterly bewildering. In traditional Aboriginal society (of which but a remnant remains) responsibility for child care arrangements are completely different from patterns which have long been established in the Western world.

> For the first year of life, Aboriginal babies are seldom apart from their mothers, are breast fed and experience constant social and physical contact with adults and older children. From early on, babies are held and carried in positions that require them to develop early physical strength and co-ordination. Until the child is about eighteen months old, it is discouraged from moving far away from its mother. By 3 years, the child is weaned and is changing from physical and emotional dependence upon the mother, to being drawn into its camp peer group, from which it learns such things as toilet training and language development. Security and love are emphasized throughout childhood, not discipline. Parents do not intervene or correct the children unless they are in some distress and then they usually give them what they want. From age 5–15 years, Aboriginal children have a great deal of freedom and continue to be indulged. At Miligimbu, *yolngu* [Aboriginal] children are often away all day with their peer group swimming or fishing, and can sleep at the camp of other relatives if they wish, sort out their own quarrels, and do not have to return at set times or meal times (Harris 1980: 34–4). Thus independence and freedom are encouraged.
>
> (Healy *et al.* 1985: 310–11)

In his case study of the Maran, a Western Australian desert-dwelling group, Tonkinson comments that

> Children are free to do very much as they like most of the time and are given very few explicit instructions by adults. Elderly people, particularly those who are too old or infirm to participate actively in daily hunting and gathering activities, spend much of their time in the camp as guardians and entertainers of the small children. As tellers of stories and singers of songs, and as 'grandparents', they normally enjoy a relaxed and affectionate relationship with the children. From these elders, children acquire much of the lore of their people; a great deal is also learned from their observations and emulation of peers and older members of the band.
>
> (Tonkinson 1991: 84)

Tonkinson also makes the point that 'parents who allow their small children to cry for long periods risk criticism from others for not looking after them properly'.

It is clear from these accounts that a number of important differences exist in child rearing practices between Aboriginals and non-Aboriginals:

1 Close attention is paid to the *physical* care and supervision of very small children by biological parents.
2 Thereafter, the care of children becomes a communal responsibility within the context of the kin network.

3 Children come and go as they please; this includes spending nights away with other relatives.
4 Much of the supervision and socialization of children is undertaken by grandparents by means of stories and song.
5 Parents who let their children cry and do not attend to them are criticized.

Remnants of this mode of child rearing appear to have survived the holocaust of disease, massacre and 'protection'. Of the 91 neglected children in the sample, 55 (60.4 per cent) were Aboriginal. Even in urban conditions, the 'hands off' mode of socialization occurs, as can be illustrated by Case 49:

> [A relative] informed us that [the child] was located at her mother's house. [Her mother] had gone to Fremantle and [the child] was looking after the younger children. [The child] repeated her wish to [the relative] that she either go to a hostel in Perth or go to her mother's aunt [in another town] . . . of great concern is the fact that [the child] is old beyond her years. In the two months that she was missing it is rumoured that she was in a sexual relationship with one of the local boys. Her mother did nothing to locate her.

Here we see the elements of traditional child rearing practice re-emerging in a different context as seen through Eurocentric 'child protection' eyes. What is in the context of Aboriginal culture *normal* child rearing (leaving children unsupervised, not looking for them, letting them go to relatives) is now neglect supervision. Customary practice becomes pathologized.

The child protection worker noted in Cases 576 and 577 that

> [The child] and [his brother] did not attend school regularly and were often seen roaming the streets at night with no adult supervision. They were taken home by myself and the police on several occasions to find that a drinking party was being held with usually everyone drunk and the children not even being missed by the parents.

The theme of 'roaming the streets' and parents being unaware that this was an issue runs through many of these neglect cases, but it is interesting to note that *small* children are kept close to parents.

Cases 399 and 397 for example were the very small children of a large family. The child protection worker noted that 'the smaller children are always with their mother and just on regular visits the children when called by the parents answer back in a grumpy and aggressive tone'. According to the anthropological information however, just as it is normal for small children to be with their parents, so the adverse tone of the children's response to parental summons may also be normal given the child-rearing practices of traditional Aboriginal groups which by Western standards would appear to be ultra permissive. According to Tonkinson

> Temper tantrums are tolerated with great patience and resignation by adults and less so by older siblings. The offended child is rarely disciplined unless it is jealously threatening violence against a younger sibling or one of the

parents at a time when they feel unwell . . . Screaming, writhing on the ground, hurling whatever it can lay hands on at the offending adult, the child, if able to talk, also lacerates the alleged oppressor with foul language drawn from a supply of obscenities and blasphemy that children master very early in their speaking careers.

(Tonkinson 1991: 83)

This description makes the 'grumpy and aggressive tone' of Cases 397 and 399 look very mild indeed, along with the worker's observation that 'The attitudes towards both parents are very negative at times'. What the worker is doing here amounts to a racist interpretation of children's behaviour.

Aboriginal use of the kinship network

Perhaps one of the most interesting features of the substitute care arrangements organized by the department for Aboriginal children was the extent to which the kinship network was used. Mention has already been made of the way in which some workers placed children with relatives, formally accorded them foster parent status and ensured that financial resources were injected into the network to strengthen it. This appears to be a regular and routine measure which is most certainly an invisible but culturally sensitive form of social work practice.

Table 9.7 Placement patterns of Aboriginal, non-Aboriginal and unknown ethnic origin children in substitute care

Placement	Aboriginal	Non-Aboriginal/ unknown	Total	%
Foster care	13	22	35	33.6
Residential/hostel	22	7	29	27.9
Friends/relatives	15	13	28	26.9
Respite	0	6	6	5.8
Independence	0	1	1	1
Other	3	1	4	3.8
Unknown	1	0	1	1
Total	54	50	104	100
%	52	48	100	

Table 9.7 compares the placement distribution of Aboriginal children in care with that of non-Aboriginal or unknown ethnic origin children. This table shows that over a quarter (28 per cent) of both Aboriginal and non-Aboriginal children were placed with friends or relatives. Proportionately nearly twice as many non-Aboriginal children were placed in foster care, but three times as many Aboriginal children were placed in residential or hostel accommodation.

There are two hidden factors here. First, since the majority of Aboriginal children in the study came from two very remote country areas, they were either placed in residential or hostel settings or they remained in the kinship network. Foster placements did not appear to be available. Second, however, even when they were available, they much more clearly resembled kinship placements.

Cases 638 and 639 for example were classed as being in foster care. The worker noted that

> Recently [the children] shifted from their mother's care to that of [the foster mother]. This was an arrangement conceived by the parents in conjunction with [the foster mother who] is a well respected Aboriginal elder . . . [she] is a member of a large extended family all of whom will assist in the care of [the children]. [The mother] is happy with the placement because [the foster mother] also reared her from when she was a small child. [The foster mother] is very happy with the way [the children] have fitted into the family and she states that he is no trouble.

The worker then made a recommendation that

> [the foster mother's] foster application be accepted and that she be given an *identification number*. It is recommended that [the children] remain in this placement until his parents are able to resume adequate care. A stable placement such as that offered by [the foster mother] will be of great benefit to [the children] and a relief to [the parents] who do not want to be separated from their children.

The worker saw the placement, arranged by the biological parents, as their way of making provision for the care of the children which would not have the effect of creating a separation. This was much more closely in accord with traditional Aboriginal child care practices than a simple statistical analysis suggests.

Case 371, an 'out of control' adolescent Aboriginal youth, was placed in his grandfather's community. The Children's Court order placing him under the control of the department wrote the following condition into the order 'conditionally upon being taken to the bush by tribal elders for bush law, counselling and punishment'. Both his parents had requested this placement; the court report recommended that 'whilst [the child] is out bush arrangements are to be made for [him] to be sent to an out station at the request of both his parents and himself'. The youth's grandfather, it transpired, was the station manager.

Aboriginal alcohol abuse

Most of the difficulties experienced by Aboriginal parents were related in one way or another to chronic or acute alcohol misuse. The agency's attention was often drawn to the problem by members of communities who had clearly attempted to care for children themselves but lacked the resources to control either drinking or provide alternative care.

A typical example of this was Case 380 where the worker reported that he received a phone call from [a woman] of [a remote] community in regards the welfare of the above lad (an eleven year old). It is believed that this lad is left to fend for himself at times. The mother has spent most of her time in town . . . she has been [there] since Christmas. The father also spends a lot of time around the shady trees in [town] also drinking and away from the community.

The worker ascertained that the mother 'spends more time in and out of the local lock-up on drink related charges'. The child was placed with his sister, but subsequently was returned to the care of his own community after her neighbours contacted the agency to report her as drunk and incapable. In this case we see two communities reporting on the care of children and participating in decisions about placement when neither the child's parents nor his sister were able to care for him as a result of alcohol misuse.

Aborigines and 'protection' v. 'welfare'

These ethnically sensitive practices do not appear to conform to the kind of advice offered in the agency's *Guide to Case Practice* (Department for Community Services 1987). Indeed that guide makes no mention of Aboriginal people, a most extraordinary omission considering the nature of child welfare in Western Australia. However, many social workers and managers at all levels within the agency spotted this omission very shortly after the guide was published and a series of consultations were set up with Aboriginal people which reflected the realities of child protection practices with them.

The result of those consultations, published and endorsed by the executive of the department some 20 months later, was entitled *Enhancing Child Welfare in Aboriginal Communities (Child Protection Issues)* (Aziz 1989). Note the change in terminology, the lesser emphasis on the term 'protection' and its replacement by the expression 'welfare'. Some of the material in that report is very revealing; one social worker made the following comment:

Drinking mothers with children are seen generally to be irresponsible but this is further differentiated. The mother who continually drinks and neglects the supervision of her children is the most 'neglectful'. The continual drinker who leaves her children in the care of another is less neglectful.

The binge drinker who will be drunk for 1 or 2 days following pension days, who leaves her children unsupervised during this period, but cares for them for the remainder of the time is again less neglectful, while the mother who is a binge drinker by leaving her children in someone else's care during her binge is almost seen as being responsible by those living on the fringe. This seems to depend on whether the supervision of the children is seen to be a burden or not for the part time carer. Single mothers also come under harsher criticism than mothers with partners.

(Aziz 1989: 25)

These observations are much more detailed and sensitive than the crude definitions of 'neglect' declared within much of the child protection literature, since they explore issues surrounding the context of what would normally be classified as neglectful actions.

Aziz's research paper came out with a series of recommendations to 'replace the Child Protection Service – *Guide to Case Practice*, when dealing with Aboriginal clientele'. Eleven criteria were introduced to enable practitioners to 'determine child abuse and neglect in Aboriginal Communities'. These criteria provide an excellent illustration of a child welfare agency's capacity to adapt to the realities of diverse child rearing practices as they are encountered by social workers.

1 The *context* in which it occurs, i.e. the community norms.
2 The *values* of the relevant community.
3 The *severity* of the act.
4 The *relationship* of the child to the person responsible for harm.
5 The *frequency* of the act.
6 The *degree of control* present when the act occurred in terms of:
   i) Individual control, e.g. emotional state, anger, etc.
   ii) Environmental control, e.g. transport availability, distance from hospital, presence of water supply.
   iii) Social/economic control, e.g. income, support structures.
7 *Presence or absence of understanding*, by the child and other observers.
8 Harm that occurs when the person responsible for the harm was *drunk*.
9 The *maturity* of the child.
10 The *survival skills* of the child.
11 The *intent or motive* of the person responsible for the harm or neglect.
(Aziz 1989: 3)

All these factors are detailed matters of context, a set of rules as it were to guide the situated moral reasoning of the investigator. In that sense they suggest that representing an act or actions as 'abuse' or 'neglect' is not of itself sufficient. Wholesale importation of 'child protection speak' and its unarticulated but taken-for-granted standards of European child rearing practices grossly distorts the judgements workers make about the children and families reported to child welfare agencies. This example of contextualized and ethnically sensitive practice is one to be emulated.

We have seen in this chapter how the importation of an ideology of child protection has had an impact on one conspicuous ethnic minority which might not originally have been intended by either the ideology's inventors in the 1960s or its international perpetrators in the 1980s. One manager of child welfare services in a remote area of Western Australia commented that, 'If they asked me to strictly apply these definitions [of child abuse] and act on them in this region, then we would be taking nearly all the Aboriginal children into care'. The effects of child protection practices on Aboriginal people are yet one more example of what happens when the well-intentioned purveyors of abstract welfare ideologies apply their ideas in contexts where they palpably do not fit. The modifications suggested by those faced with the practical realities of Aboriginal communities amount to a sound rebuttal to the perpetrators of the child 'abuse' moral panic, by means of the reintroduction of 'welfare' as opposed to 'protection'. These modifications also offer some clue as to how child protection might begin to be redefined.

10 Gender issues in child protection

Introduction

Gender perspectives have begun to play an increasingly important part in the analysis of social phenomena. The obvious reason for this is that social phenomena are made up of different types of social relations. 'Family' life for example can be understood in terms of the unwritten rules which determine the nature of the interactions and exchanges between children and caregivers. Gender analysis takes this a stage further by exploring the differences between the ways in which male children and caregivers relate to female children and caregivers.

Essentially, the issues explored by child protection researchers are those of specific types of social relations and the single most important relationship is considered to be that of caregiver and child, and the extent to which caregivers competently carry out those tasks which are assumed to be their sole responsibility. However, male and female caregivers do not necessarily do the same things for children. The role expectations of mothers are generally quite different from those of fathers. Accordingly, this chapter will explore gender perspectives in child protection from a number of different angles which will include those of responsibility for caring competently for children as well as the issue of offences against children. It is the latter which has been the subject of a good deal of intellectual debate amongst academics and child protection practitioners.

Much recent theorizing on child protection matters has come from women writers who have contributed a specifically feminist perspective to child welfare debates. This has been especially true of those aspects of child maltreatment which have involved 'domestic violence' and 'sexual abuse'. Inevitably however this has drawn feminist researchers into the contentious area of social control debates. If the state is required to intervene in those areas of private life in which women and children are victims of male violence and male oppression, then inevitably in the process some degree of female violence and maternal aggression will be uncovered. Feminist theoreticians are then forced to grapple with questions which are not easily answered or comfortably dealt with. This chapter will look at the issue of gender in child protection from both victim and offender perspectives as they emerge from the Western Australia study.

The nature of the dilemma for feminists is neatly summarized by Parton and Parton:

> Within feminism itself there is a debate about the role of the state in family life. While some feminists have viewed state welfare practices as oppressive to women, reinforcing their traditional responsibility for caring, others, particularly in relation to men's violence to women and children, have called for stronger state control of family relationships. Ironically, the current trends in child protection find support from not just the conservative, 'law and order' lobby but from some radical feminists. Lahey (1984), for example, argues strenuously for improvements in the surveillance of children, abuse reporting and enforcement laws and an extension of criminal prosecution of offenders. This apparent alliance ends with the agreement on the need for a strong authoritative response. The tensions and different perspectives of these two standpoints become highlighted in the area of child sexual abuse. For radical feminist analysis has argued that this form of sexual violence is an abuse, one which is widespread, of men's power and is rooted in the unequal sexual, economic and personal relationships between men, women and children.
>
> (Parton and Parton 1989: 40)

Gender analysis will take three perspectives in this chapter. First, the gender of the children included in the study will be looked at in terms of differences in numbers, types of substantiation, career type and the use of various legal powers by the agency. The emphasis here will be on the ways in which male and female children appear and are then dealt with by the child protection system. The second section in the chapter will look at those who committed sexual offences against children and it will report on police activity as a direct and overt form of state control in respect of those who commit criminal offences against children. The third and final section will look at gender within the context of caregiver family structure in order to ascertain how those responsible for the care of children were dealt with differentially by child protection workers.

Discussion of cases and gender

Table 10.1 looks at the gender and age distribution of 'at risk' and substantiated cases in the research. Fifty seven per cent of the children were female and 43 per cent male. There are however significant differences in the age distribution of male and female children. If the 11–14 year olds, 15–18 year olds and those over 19 are grouped together, there were 35 males (10.8 per cent of 'abused' or 'at risk' children) as opposed to 80 females (24.6 per cent of 'abused' or 'at risk' children). This finding suggests that there are more than twice the number of females than males of adolescent age.

Table 10.1   Age ranges of 'at risk' or 'abused' male and female children

Age range	Male	Female	Total	%
Under 1 year	14	12	26	8
1–4 years	39	47	86	26.5
5–10 years	52	46	98	30
11–14 years	24	54	78	24
15–18 years	11	24	35	10.8
Over 19 years	0	2	2	0.7
Total	140	185	325	100
%	43	57	100	

Table 10.2   Gender and substantiation

Substantiation	Male	Female	Total	%
'At risk'	54	55	109	33.5
Neglect	46	45	91	28
Emotional abuse	4	6	10	3.1
Physical abuse	25	25	50	15.4
Sexual abuse	11	54	65	20
Total	140	185	325	100
%	43	57	100	

Table 10.2 shows that there appears to be little difference in the 'at risk', 'neglect', 'emotional abuse' and 'physical abuse' categories between male and female children. However, in the 'sexual abuse' category there are nearly five times as many females as males. Overwhelmingly, the victims of sexual assaults are females.

Table 10.3   Gender and career type of 'at risk' and substantiated cases

Career type	Male	Female	Total	%
Begins care	25	39	64	19.7
Becomes care	26	14	40	12.3
Home-based services	61	78	139	42.8
No further action	28	54	82	25.2
Total	140	185	325	100
%	43	57	100	

Table 10.3 examines child protection careers and gender in respect of these 325 children. Twenty one per cent of the female children began their child protection careers in substitute care, while a slightly smaller proportion of males had similar experiences (17.8 per cent). However, the differences are much more marked with becomes care cases, with 18.5 per cent of the males falling into this category but only 7.5 per cent of the females. As far as home-based services are concerned there is little difference between the sexes, 43.6 per cent of males receiving this service and 42.1 per cent of females. Gender differences re-emerge in no further action cases with proportionately more females than males: 29.2 per cent as opposed to 20 per cent.

Gender differences in this table suggest that girls are more likely than boys to begin their careers with care, but less likely to enter care later. It may be therefore that girls are seen by workers as being *more* vulnerable during the investigation of allegations than are boys and that consequently they are more likely to receive a substitute care service. However significantly more boys than girls enter substitute care later because of crises encountered during the delivery of home-based services and, since girls enter care earlier, they are less likely to encounter such crises.

It is clear from Tables 10.1 and 10.2 that sexual assaults on children appear to be a reason why more female than male children are referred into the child protection system. One way of trying to see if this can be accounted for by other factors is to exclude victms of sexual assaults. Table 10.4 reproduces Table 10.3, but excludes cases where 'sexual abuse' was substantiated.

Table 10.4   Gender and career type of 'at risk' and substantiated cases excluding 'sexual abuse'

Career type	Male	Female	Total	%
Begins care	25	28	53	20.4
Becomes care	26	13	39	15
Home-based services	50	53	103	39.6
No further action	28	37	65	25
Total	129	131	260	100
%	49.6	50.4	100	

Once the 'sexual abuse' cases have been excluded, all the gender anomalies with the single exception of boys who enter care later disappear. 'Sexual abuse' accounts for overall total differences, since of the 260 cases shown in the table (which excludes children who are victims of sexual assaults) approximately half are males and half are females. The begins care difference between genders shown in Table 10.3 disappears in Table 10.4 (19.4 per cent of males and 21.4 per cent of females). The becomes care anomaly of Table 10.3 is retained and increases in Table 10.4 (20.1 per cent of the males and 9.9 per cent of the females follow this career). In Table 10.4 the proportion of male and female children receiving home-based services are almost exactly equal, but a difference is maintained with no further action cases (21.7 per cent of males as opposed to 28.2 per cent of females).

Table 10.5   Apprehension and gender

Apprehension	Male	Female	Total	%
Apprehended	21	26	47	14.5
Not apprehended	119	159	278	85.5
Total	140	185	325	100
%	43	57	100	

Table 10.5 examines gender differences in relation to the use of emergency legal powers of removal (apprehension). Twenty one (15 per cent) of the 140 male children found to be 'abused', neglected or 'at risk' were apprehended, as were 26 (14 per cent) of the 185 females. Despite the overrepresentation of girls in the begins care and sexual 'abuse' categories it is clear that boys stand an equal chance of being removed using emergency legal powers to secure their safety.

Table 10.6   'At risk' or 'abused' male children and care and protection applications

Care and protection application	'At risk'	Neglect	Emotional	Physical	Sexual	Total	%
Adjourned	0	4	0	0	0	4	17.4
Withdrawn	2	7	0	0	0	9	39.1
Granted	1	8	1	0	0	10	43.5
Total	3	19	1	0	0	23	100
%	13	82.6	4.4	0	0	100	

Tables 10.6 and 10.7 explore the results of care and protection applications to Children's Courts within the context of gender difference. Twenty three boys were subject to care and protection applications in Children's Courts. Nineteen of these were neglect applications (82.6 per cent). Wardship was granted by courts in less than half (43.5 per cent) of all these 23 cases and the agency withdrew applications in nine cases.

Twenty six girls appeared before Children's Courts when the agency submitted care and protection applications. As with the boys, the largest single group were neglect cases, but there were only ten such cases for the girls,

Table 10.7 'At risk' or 'abused' female children and care and protection applications

Care and protection application	'At risk'	Neglect	Emotional	Physical	Sexual	Total	%
Adjourned	1	3	0	0	1	5	19.2
Withdrawn	0	3	0	0	2	5	19.2
Granted	1	4	0	4	6	15	57.7
Dismissed	0	0	0	1	0	1	3.9
Total	2	10	0	5	9	26	100
%	7.7	38.5	–	19.2	34.6	100	

compared with with the boys' 19. Of these ten girls only four proceeded to wardship. In contrast, while no boys were subject to applications because of sexual 'abuse', such matters constituted over a third of the girls brought before Children's Courts and of these nine girls, six were made state wards. Overall, wardship was granted in 15 of the 26 applications (57.7 per cent) whereas with boys it was only granted in ten of the 23 applications (43.5 per cent).

Tables 10.1 to 10.7 suggest that female children in child protection systems are overrepresented primarily in terms of being victims of sexual assaults. This has a number of consequences which includes a larger proportion of female as opposed to male adolescents in the system as a whole, a higher likelihood of early admission to substitute care when they are victims and a higher likelihood of being subject to care and protection applications which result in wardship. For males, the anomaly is one of entering care later because of crises and the care and protection applications submitted for neglect. No explanation will be attempted in this book for the overrepresentation of males in becomes care and neglect care and protection applications, but this matter may be worth researching further. It is however clear from this research that in child protection system terms, girls are five times more likely to present as victims of sexual assaults than is the case with boys and as such they are more likely to enter substitute care and become state wards. In all other categories of substantiation, there is very little significant variation between genders.

Sexual offenders and police activity in cases

In exploring the issue of sexual assault further, the question of offenders inevitably arises. Table 10.8 crosstabulates the gender of victims against their relationship with offenders.

The largest single group responsible for sexual assaults on children were fathers of children (30.8 per cent), followed by family friends or neighbours (21.6 per cent). *De facto* fathers and stepfathers accounted for 13.9 per cent of the assaults, while 'unknown' assailants formed a similar proportion. The use of the

Table 10.8   Sexual 'abuse' cases, gender of victims and relationship with person believed responsible

Person believed responsible	Male victims	Female victims	Total	%
Father	3	17	20	30.8
De facto father	1	4	5	7.7
Stepfather	0	4	4	6.2
Sibling	0	3	3	4.6
Other relations	2	6	8	12.3
Friend/neighbour	4	10	14	21.6
Loco parentis	0	2	2	3
Unknown	1	8	9	13.8
Total	11	54	65	100
%	17	83	100	

category 'unknown' refers to two types of case – those where the identity of the person believed responsible was unknown to any official, and those where the identity was known but it was not recorded in the case file. In Table 10.8, all the assailants were male, varying in age from retired men over 65 years of age to young adolescents aged 12 years. This table overwhelmingly supports the view that those who commit sexual offences against children are already well known to their victims and are likely to be either members of the same family or living in the same household.

Tables 10.9 and 10.10 look at the nature of police activity with the 65 victims of sexual 'abuse' and compare it with similar activity with the 260 other children who were either 'at risk', neglected or victims of emotional or physical 'abuse'.

Table 10.9 shows a fairly even distribution across male and female children as far as child protection matters not involving sexual assaults are concerned. There

Table 10.9   Police activity and gender – 'at risk', neglect, emotional or physical abuse cases

Police activity	Male	Female	Total	%
Police involved	30	26	56	21.5
Police prosecution	1	0	1	0.4
Police not involved	98	105	203	78.1
Total	129	131	260	100
%	49.6	50.4	100	

was only one police prosecution recorded in this group in respect of an assault on a seven year old boy. In this instance, a 31 year old man had been

> temporarily caring for [three] children on Saturday night. [He] had been boarding with the family when [the child] would not eat his dinner. He was belted on the buttocks [bare hand] about a dozen times. [The man] has been charged with aggravated assault after the mother laid a complaint which had followed disappearance of 2 of the children on Sunday morning after 4 a.m. when the children were found at [the town's] bus depot. They indicated that their absence was due to the scolding and punishment received from [the boarder].
>
> (Case 505)

In sharp contrast to Table 10.9 (which showed police activity in just over a fifth of cases), Table 10.10 shows that as far as sexual assaults were concerned the police were active in a majority of cases, over two-thirds altogether. Levels of prosecution in this table continue to reflect the gender imbalance of sexual 'abuse' cases, since the police prosecuted males in respect of assaults on approximately half of the male children and half the female children. However, since there were five times more female victims than male victims, then five times more males were prosecuted for offences against females than was the case for offences against males.

Table 10.10   Police activity and gender – sexual 'abuse' cases

Police activity	Male	Female	Total	%
Police involved	2	12	14	21.5
Police prosecution	5	25	30	46.2
Police not involved	4	17	21	32.3
Total	11	54	65	100
%	17	83	100	

In total, 21 males were prosecuted for sexual offences against the 30 children shown in Table 10.10. Seven of these men were charged in respect of offences against two children each. One man was charged with offences against three children while the remaining 13 men were charged for offences against one child each.

Table 10.11 shows the frequency distribution of those offenders in respect of their relationships with the child victims. As in Table 10.8, fathers were the largest single group of sex offenders, so in Table 10.11 they are the single largest group to be prosecuted, followed by friends/neighbours of the families in which child victims were living. These two categories account for two-thirds of all prosecutions.

Table 10.11   Relationships of prosecuted males to child
victims of sexual 'abuse'

Relationship to children	Nos	%
Father	8	38
Friend/neighbour	6	28.6
Other relative	2	9.5
De facto father	2	9.5
Stepfather	1	4.8
Loco parentis	1	4.8
Unknown	1	4.8
Total	21	100

Child protection activity, especially in respect of females and sexual 'abuse'
involves criminal prosecutions by the police on a scale which is completely absent
from those cases which do not involve sexual offences. Female children were
overrepresented as victims of sexual assaults, all the offenders were males and
criminal prosecutions took place in respect of nearly half of the victims of these
assaults in the sample. With the exception of Case 505 mentioned earlier, only
one other person was prosecuted for an offence against a child. This was a
'second episode' case and will be dealt with in the last chapter.

Gender and caregiver family structure

In Chapter 4, the results of the preliminary analyses of the Western Australian
study were presented alongside those of a Welsh local authority where a virtually
identical research design was used to test the methodology developed in Western
Australia in a context of different legislation and a geographical distance of
thousands of miles. Tables 4.7 and 4.8 showed that the distribution of caregiver
family structures in child protection cases were very similar and that the largest
single category of caregiver family in both agencies was one in which children
were cared for by single female parents. These tables suggest an extensive gender
bias in respect of caregivers in child protection. This matter will now be explored
further.

Table 10.12 gives some idea of the *perceptions* of those who made allegations
about children to the Department for Community Services. Where percentages
are given in brackets within the table, they are approximate percentages of that
table. Neglect allegations were nearly half (47.3 per cent) of all allegations, but
over half of these were directed at single female parent families. Indeed this type
of allegation about such families was just over a quarter (26 per cent) of all
allegations made. So, a quarter of all child protection investigative activity is
aimed at single women caring for children without the support of a partner. It is
worth noting here that of the 45 allegations about the child rearing standards of

Table 10.12 Caregiver family structure and allegations of 'abuse' or neglect

Caregiver family structure	Physical 'abuse'	Emotional 'abuse'	Sexual 'abuse'	Neglect	Unknown	Total	%
Both biological parents	56 (9)	7 (1)	38 (6)	86 (13)	6 (1)	193	29.5
Reconstituting family	43 (7)	1	43 (7)	29 (4)	2	118	18
Single female parent	43 (7)	3	39 (6)	169 (26)	22 (3)	276	42.1
Single male parent	2	3	17 (3)	16 (2)	7 (1)	45	6.8
Substitute care	0	0	0	1	0	1	0.2
Unknown	3	0	6 (1)	8 (1)	5 (1)	22	3.4
Total	147	14	143	309	42	655	100
%	22.4	2.1	21.8	47.3	6.4	100	

single male parent families 17 were reports of sexual abuse and 16 reports of neglect. Single women were overrepresented in allegations and those over-representations were specifically about the neglect of children. While single men were underrepresented, proportionately they were overrepresented by sexual 'abuse' allegations particularly and to a lesser extent neglect.

Table 10.13 Caregiver family structure and substantiation

Family structure	'At risk'	Neglect	Emotional abuse	Physical abuse	Sexual abuse	Total	%
Both biological parents	30	18	4	20	23	95	29.2
Reconstituting family	14	10	3	14	15	56	17.2
Single female parent	52	56	3	16	16	143	44
Single male parent	13	5	0	0	6	24	7.4
Unknown	0	2	0	0	5	7	2.2
Total	109	91	10	50	65	325	100
%	33.5	28	3.1	15.4	20	100	

Table 10.13 examines those cases found to be 'at risk' or substantiated after investigations were complete. The overrepresentation of single women rises slightly, as does that of single men, after investigation – up to 44 per cent and 7.4 per cent of the sample respectively. Single women retain their place at the top of the league in the neglect column (61.5 per cent of all substantiated neglect cases), they are the highest in the 'at risk' category (47.7 per cent) and the second highest in the physical 'abuse' and sexual 'abuse' categories. However, since all those believed responsible for sexual assaults were males, the latter category indicates the extent to which the children of single female parents were vulnerable to sexual assaults from men who were not living with the family at the time of the assaults. While over half of the single male parent families were placed in the 'at

Table 10.14   Career types and substantiation – excluding children from single female parent families

Career type	'At risk'	Neglect	Emotional abuse	Physical abuse	Sexual abuse	Total	%
Begins care	7	9	1	7	8	32	17.6
Becomes care	8	15	0	1	1	25	13.7
Home-based services	26	5	5	12	24	72	39.6
No further action	16	6	1	14	16	53	29.1
Total	57	35	7	34	49	182	100
%	31.3	19.2	3.9	18.7	26.9	100	

risk' category, only six of the 17 allegations of sexual assault were substantiated along with five of the 16 neglect allegations.

Tables 10.14 and 10.15 are master tables which crosstabulate career type with substantiation. Table 10.14 however excludes the 143 children from single female parent families, while Table 10.15 deals solely with those children cared for by a women without a partner.

Table 10.15   Career types and substantiation – children from single female parent families

Career type	'At risk'	Neglect	Emotional abuse	Physical abuse	Sexual abuse	Total	%
Begins care	14	14	0	1	3	32	22.4
Becomes care	7	6	2	0	0	15	10.5
Home-based services	27	20	0	8	12	67	46.8
No further action	4	16	1	7	1	29	20.3
Total	52	56	3	16	16	143	100
%	36.4	39.2	2	11.2	11.2	100	

In both these tables, nearly one-third of children received a substitute care service. However, the children of single female parents were more likely to enter care at the time of the investigation than children from other types of family background (22.4 per cent as opposed to 17.6 per cent). The major difference in the reasons for entry can be seen in the substantiation columns. Twenty eight (87.5 per cent) of the single female parent family children were either 'at risk' or neglected. For other family types there was only 16 (50 per cent) in those categories. Of the 44 neglected and 'at risk' begins care cases, nearly two-thirds were from single female parent families. This situation is reversed in the physical and sexual 'abuse' columns where of the 19 begins care cases only four (21 per cent) came from such backgrounds. In the becomes care row, single female parent families are overrepresented in the neglect column. The anomaly of single female parenthood and neglect is carried into the use of substitute care measures.

Home-based services display marked differences between these two tables; 46.8 per cent of the single female parents received help of that nature compared with only 39.6 per cent of cases with other types of caregiver family structure. Once more, the differences lie between the 'at risk'/neglect and physical and sexual 'abuse' polarities, with single female parent families constituting nearly two-thirds of those in the former categories but only 35 per cent in the latter categories. They did however make up a third of the physical 'abuse'/home-based services sector.

The higher likelihood of single female parent families receiving home-based services than other family types appears to be caused by a relatively lower rate of case closure with no further action *especially* in the 'at risk' and neglect categories. Tables 10.14 and 10.15 suggest the following.

1 Single female parent families are more likely to receive services than families with other types of caregiver.
2 They are less likely to be closed with no further action.
3 Children from single female parent families who receive substitute care services cluster in the 'at risk' and neglect categories and are more likely to come into care during investigations than is the case for children from other types of family.
4 Home-based services for single female parent families are more focused on the 'at risk' and neglect categories than other 'abuse' categories.

Examination of case files reveals some of the difficulties which affect those women caring for children on their own. Table 10.15 indicates that there were 14 children in the neglect/begins care group being cared for by women on their own. These 14 children came from eight families, so there were eight women whose children were admitted into substitute care because of neglect shortly after investigations of allegations commenced. Of these eight women, the primary problem as perceived by investigators was the misuse of alcohol and between them they accounted for 12 of the 14 children in the neglect/begins care group.

For example, '[The child] stated she no longer wishes to live with her mother and cited her mother's frequent drinking and other alleged neglectful acts as the factors contributing to her decision' (Case 462). At the point when one child was admitted to care the worker was told by a relative that '[the mother] left [the child] at home, while she went drinking with her friends' (Case 387). Another mother 'dumps the child with [an aunt] and goes off drinking frequently, the child is left without food or clothing' (Case 381). Some of the effects of lack of attention, particularly towards small children, were on their health: 'Because of the child's delicate health and the past unsatisfactory history of [the mother] and her current drinking problem, we would request that the child be placed in the care and protection of the department' (Case 372). In yet another case, a mother confronted with the consequences of her drinking 'said she could not and did not at this time want to give up alcohol and wanted [a relative] to care for [the children]' (Cases 363 and 364). A final example was previously discussed in Chapter 5 (p. 70), Cases 1–3, in which three small children were left alone in a house while their mother went to a pub.

What is interesting about these cases is that none of the women concerned received any help whatsoever to deal with their alcohol problems. The focus of intervention was entirely on the children and that is where the services went. Only very recently has the question of alcohol misuse been placed on the social work agenda, since generally it has been perceived primarily as a problem which only men have. In other words, the gender bias of alcohol counselling and treatment services may in fact account for some of the overrepresentation of women in the child protection research.

Griffin (1990) surveyed 30 social workers in a UK social services department about women's misuse of alcohol. Her results are disquieting for child protection.

> 83 per cent of the sample felt that there was more stigma attached to women who misuse alcohol than to men. 60 per cent felt it was more difficult for women to seek help for their alcohol problems, and 60 per cent felt that women developed problems for different reasons than men.
>
> (Griffin 1990: 12)

Griffin raises a complex set of questions about alcohol counselling services, especially within the context of child protection programmes since she holds that 'women's needs from social workers are distorted by a primary concern for the protection of children'.

Conclusion

In this chapter we have seen that child protection is not unambiguously on the side of women and children. As far as criminal matters are concerned, specifically sexual offences, then it is clear that the prosecution of male offenders and the use of substitute care services to protect victims (who are primarily female) are all measures which are designed to control offenders in the interests of women and children. It is this which accounts for the overrepresentation of female children in the child protection system. However, the second type of overrepresentation – that of single female parents – suggests three things. First, that poor and disadvantaged people appear disproportionately in child protection programmes – and in this instance, single female parents are but one example of this phenomenon. Second, when families break up it would appear that women are the ones who overwhelmingly assume responsibility for the care of children. This is a matter of the role expectations of men and women within society, that it is the women who look after the children. Third, there is the issue of women as 'unfit' or incapacitated caregivers as exemplified by those who misuse alcohol and the attention paid to children rather than the problems of their mothers. The social construction of women and especially of mothers who misuse alcohol does not readily place them in a 'deserving' category (see for example Ettore 1989).

To return to the social control and feminism dilemma raised by Parton and Parton at the beginning of this chapter, it is worth noting that increased diligence in child protection emerges as a two-edged sword. On the one hand it does appear to go some way to redress the power which traditionally men have exerted over women and children, especially in respect of previously ignored sexual exploitation. On the other hand it has also exposed a different and very vulnerable group of women to state control activities by means of the 'at risk' and neglect definitions and the concerns of child protection programmes. This issue will not disappear, as Gordon (1986) concludes about these state programmes,

In wrestling with such bureaucracies one rarely gets what one really wants but rather another interpretation of one's needs. This is a contradiction that women, particularly, face and there is no easy resolution of it. There is no returning to an old or newly romanticised 'community control' when the remnants of community rest on a power structure hostile to women's aspirations. A feminist critique of social control must contain and wrestle with, not try to erase, this tension.

(Gordon 1986: 83)

11 Redefining child protection

In this final chapter, an attempt will be made to comment upon child protection activities as they have emerged in the Western Australian study. Three aspects of child protection are identified. The first is based closely on the quantitative data of the study and will look at the extent to which child protection services 'deliver the goods' within the context of very narrowly defined objectives. The second observation consists of a discussion about those results from the study which take a rather broader view of the operations of child welfare agencies and child protection activities. It will be situated within the more general contexts of society and government. The third and most abstract judgement will relate to the issues raised in the study about the child protection phenomenon itself, the nature of the discourse as it shows up empirically and the theoretical and moral issues raised by the new ideologies of child protection and their representation.

The performance of child protection

The question to be answered in this section is narrowly defined; it relates to the objectives of the child protection programme and the extent to which social workers' performances measurably meet those objectives. Essentially, this is an *effectiveness* question which can be reduced to an attempt to ascertain whether or not child protection activities actually protect children. It represents the narrowest and most simplistic interpretation of the Australian Welfare Administrators' desire that the national child protection database could be used to measure 'the degree of achievement of policy and programme objectives'. In doing this, an important range of other types of question will be excluded at this stage, since only two very limited (albeit important) outcome measures will be used. That is the main reason why this concluding chapter is split into three sections and in this first section no attempt will be made to ask the question 'What is it that children should be protected from?' One answer to that question could be that the intention is to protect children from 'abuse', but in turn, this begs yet another question – 'what is child abuse?' The second and third sections will focus more on the issues raised by these further questions. But for the time being, the intention is to examine hard, quantifiable outcome matters couched narrowly in terms of the further harm, injury or neglect of children. In Cheetham *et al.*'s terms,

> The challenge is to arrive at working definitions of effectiveness in specific situations, and hence of methods of studying it, which do not permanently lose sight of its conceptual context. One useful working definition, often adopted by researchers, managers and practitioners, is that social work is effective insofar as it achieves intended aims.
>
> (Cheetham *et al.* 1992: 10)

The aim of this last chapter is to move from the 'working definition' to the 'conceptual context'.

The two measures contained in this study which most immediately suggest themselves as being relevant to answering the performance questions are those which deal with further harm, injury or neglect in cases which were kept open after investigations and the analysis of 'second episode' cases. Accordingly, this section will begin by looking at those children who were further harmed, injured or neglected.

Table 11.1   Further harm, injury or neglect cases – family structure and ethnicity

Family structure	Aboriginal	Non-Aboriginal	Total	%
Both biological parents	4	6	10	19.6
Reconstituting family	0	10	10	19.6
Single female parent	12	14	26	51
Single male parent	3	1	4	7.8
Unknown	1	0	1	2
Total	20	31	51	100
%	39.2	60.8	100	

The case records revealed that of the 325 cases where 'abuse' was substantiated or risk factors identified, a total of 51 (15.7 per cent) children were harmed, injured or neglected during the time when the cases were open for service. Table 11.1 crosstabulates caregiver family structure against ethnicity for these cases. Thirty (58.8 per cent) of these cases were single parent families of which 15 were Aboriginal. This shows that disadvantaged families were a predominant feature of the further harm/injury or neglect cases.

Table 11.2 shows that 43 (84.3 per cent) of these 51 cases were originally assessed as being in the 'at risk' and neglect categories by investigating social workers. Not surprisingly, 22 (43 per cent) of these cases began with home-based services but entered care after a crisis. Indeed, the 22 cases shown in this table

Table 11.2 Further harm, injury or neglect cases, career types and substantiation

Career	'At risk'	Neglect	Emotional abuse	Physical abuse	Sexual abuse	Total	%
Begins care	1	2	0	1	3	7	14
Becomes care	7	13	2	0	0	22	43
Home-based services	9	11	1	1	0	22	43
Total	17	26	3	2	3	51	100
%	33	51	6	4	6	100	

constitute more than half of the 40 becomes care cases in the total sample of 325 (see Table 4.12). A further 22 cases however continued to receive home-based services despite being further harmed, injured or neglected after services had commenced. Only seven (14 per cent) fall into the begins care career category and five of these came from single parent families. Three children suffered emotional trauma, two as a consequence of placement breakdowns and one as a result of a three day court hearing. Two children were abandoned/deserted by their mother when they were returned to her care after six months in foster homes. The placement with their mother only lasted only five days. One child contracted a sexually transmitted disease during a period when both her mother and her aunt were in hospital and it was not clear who was caring for her. The seventh child (Case 434) was one of the two children originally admitted to care with unexplained fractures. After her return home, she lost weight and the suggestion was that feeding was being neglected.

It is interesting to see here that four of these seven children were harmed, injured or neglected *after* they had been in substitute care and were returned to the care of their families. However, with the possible exception of the child who contracted a sexually transmitted disease, child protection workers acted very quickly, within a matter of days, to secure their safety by bringing the children back into care. It is not easy to see from the records how these outcomes could have been avoided, since the restoration of these children to their mothers' care was in all cases carefully planned.

Table 11.3 looks at the nature of the further harms, injuries and neglect inflicted on these 51 children and the actions or inactions which caused them. Further trauma for 37 (72.5 per cent) of the 51 children shown in this table consisted of varying types of neglect ranging from abandonment (eight cases) to the temporary neglect of supervision (eight cases). All these children (with one exception) had originally been placed in the 'at risk' or neglect categories. Eighteen of these entered care during the crisis of neglect. Of the remaining 14 non-neglect cases, the one sexually abused child has already been discussed (Case 411, see p. 82) as have the three children traumatized by placement breakdown (Case 61, see p. 81 and Case 255, see p. 79) and a court appearance (Case 204, see p. 67). Of three children who were poisoned, two were in the

Table 11.3 Further harm, injury or neglect cases, nature of harm, injury or neglect and actions causing

Further harm/injury or neglect	Excess corporal punishment	Persistent caregiver hostility	Penetration	Other	Unknown	Inaction	Total	%
Neglect supervision	0	0	0	1	0	7	8	15.6
Neglect medical care	0	0	0	0	0	6	6	11.7
Neglect food	0	0	0	0	0	3	3	5.9
Neglect environment	0	0	0	0	0	11	11	21.6
Failure to thrive	0	0	0	0	1	0	1	2
Abandoned/deserted	0	0	0	0	0	8	8	15.6
Scalds/burns/fractures	0	0	0	1	0	0	1	2
Poison	0	0	0	3	0	0	3	5.9
Emotional trauma	0	4	0	3	0	0	7	13.7
Anal/vaginal trauma/disease	0	0	1	0	0	0	1	2
No identifiable injury	1	1	0	0	0	0	2	4
Total	1	5	1	8	1	35	51	100
%	2	9.8	2	15.6	2	68.6	100	

same family (Cases 218 and 219). One of the complaints in the original referral of these cases was that the mother put whisky and Coke in a feeding bottle. At the time, the mother denied this, but six months later one of the children was admitted to hospital and became unconscious. The mother claimed that one of her friends had put wine in her feeding bottle. Both these children were transferred to the care of their grandfather. Case 393, a one year old Aboriginal boy, was admitted to hospital after being given wine by his mother. He was removed to the care of his grandmother. One child (Case 688) appeared to have been accidentally burned and the injury was identified during a regular health check. No changes in regular visits by social workers were made. Case 505 was a child who had been assaulted by an adult male childminder although there were no identifiable injuries after medical examinations and Case 270 was a male infant whose mother suffered from a psychiatric disorder. This child was not 'bonding' with his mother, but he was being looked after by his father and grandparents in the same house.

Further harm/injury or neglect covers a variety of problems, but primarily they are ones of neglect in situations where families were already receiving services, but these services did not appear to be sufficient to ensure that children were cared for at a minimum standard of supervision, nutrition and health. As stated before, with the possible exception of the child who contracted a sexually transmitted disease and perhaps two of the children who were given alcohol, it is not easy to see how any of these matters could have been easily predicted or prevented. In the analysis of home-based services at the end of Chapter 6 it was made clear that workers found the physical and sexual 'abuse' much more straightforward.

During the 12 month period after the 655 child protection cases reported in this study were referred, 544 (83 per cent) were closed. These cases were eligible therefore for rereferral as second episode cases. In the event, 61 were in fact reported again to the department, giving a rereferral rate of 11 per cent. All these cases were investigated a second time.

Table 11.4 looks at the allegations and results of investigations. Over two thirds of second episode allegations concerned neglect, nearly a quarter alleged

Table 11.4 Second episode cases, allegations and results of investigations

Result of investigation	Physical abuse	Emotional abuse	Sexual abuse	Neglect	Total	%
Not substantiated	3	0	5	24	33	54
'At risk'	4	0	0	6	10	16.5
Neglect	0	0	1	8	9	14.8
Emotional abuse	0	0	0	1	1	1.6
Physical abuse	7	0	0	0	7	11.5
Sexual abuse	0	0	1	0	1	1.6
Total	14	1	7	39	61	100
%	23	2	11	64	100	

physical 'abuse' and only one-tenth were allegations of sexual assaults. As with first episode referrals, approximately one half were again not substantiated, leaving 28 'at risk' or substantiated cases for further career development. Of these 28 cases, 19 (67.8 per cent) were 'at risk' or neglected children. Rereferral appears, like other factors in career development, to accentuate the presence of disorderly families by means of 'at risk' and neglect classifications.

Table 11.5 is the second episode master table which crosstabulates career type with 'abuse' type for these 28 cases. The largest single group of cases in this table were the nine children who received home-based services and who were judged to be 'at risk'. In the first episode, allegations against four of these children had not been substantiated, while three children, previously judged to be 'at risk,' had received home-based services. The remaining two children had been admitted to care in the first episode because of their mother's psychiatric problems. Clearly this woman's difficulties had not been resolved, but in the second episode, admission to care was avoided. *All* these nine children lived in three single female parent families.

Table 11.5 Second episode cases, career types and substantiation

Career type	'At risk'	Neglect	Emotional abuse	Physical abuse	Sexual abuse	Total	%
Begins care	0	0	0	1	0	1	
Becomes care	0	0	0	3	0	3	
Home-based services	9	6	1	1	1	18	
No further action	1	3	0	2	0	6	
Total	10	9	1	7	1	28	100
%	37	29.5	3.8	25.9	3.8	100	

The second largest group of rereferred second episode cases were the six children in the neglect/home-based services cell in Table 11.5. These children came from two families of four children and two children respectively. Allegations in respect of the family of four had not been substantiated in the first episode, while the children in the family of two had originally been neglect/begins care cases. Both these families were parented by women without partners.

Table 11.5 shows that 15 (68 per cent) of the 22 second episode cases which received services of one kind or another were in the 'at risk' and neglect categories. All these children lived in five single female parent families. One of the five women had an extensive psychiatric history, while the remaining four were prone to frequent alcohol misuse.

[Mother] apparently drinks heavily (spirits) and phones [a friend] every night (she claims) – often very late. She complains that she cannot cope with all her problems.

(Cases 200–3)

[The doctor] believed a lot of the neglect and abuse of [the mother's] children occurred when [she] drank.

(Cases 427, 429 and 430)

[The mother's] lapse from her usually good standards of childcare resulted from an acute period of low spirits (due to a multitude of factors) in which she began drinking heavily.

(Cases 1 and 2)

[The mother] had been drinking during the day and was somewhat affected by alcohol.

(Cases 176–9)

The reason why some of these cases had not been substantiated on investigation during the first episode appears to have been because the women concerned were not drunk at the times when the investigators called to see them.

Nearly one-third (29.5 per cent) of second episode cases concerned physical 'abuse' and four of these seven children were admitted to care. The one begins care case (Case 428) was a four year old girl, a child in a family mentioned in the previous paragraph (Cases 427, 429 and 430) whose siblings were neglect/home-based services cases because of their mother's drinking. This girl was referred by the police via the hospital when she was admitted with 'multiple bruising to the left side of her face, throat and ear'. The mother had instigated the referral 'alleging that someone (person(s) unknown) had tried to strangle her daughter whilst she [the mother] was momentarily away from home . . . Later [the police] took a statement from [the mother] in which she admitted assaulting her daughter' (Case 428). Apparently the child had 'got into her mother's make-up box'. She was apprehended and detained in hospital for observation. After three days she was released to the care of her grandparents and a care and protection application lodged with the Children's Court. The police prosecuted the mother who was placed on a good behaviour bond for six months. She was the only female prosecuted for an offence against a child out of the 23 adults prosecuted. The girl stayed with her grandparents for only four weeks during which time she was made a state ward by the Children's Court. A very intensive programme was set up for the mother who was described in the following terms:

The degree of chaos and disorganisation in this family is high. Little seems organised and planned routines are few. [The mother] has little useful support from family and friends (neighbours) and makes no use of community resources. The interaction between this mother and her children is almost always negative, punitive and controlling.

(Case 428)

The mother participated in 'weekly parenting sessions which [focused] upon age appropriate behaviour, use of limit and boundary settings [the introduction] of control and management techniques [to] replace physical punishment'. Additionally a 'homebuilder' was contracted to be in the house every day.

The mitigation offered by investigating child protection workers specifically mentioned three factors. First, the mother had herself contacted the police after the assault on her daughter, second she was 'struggling to care for four children under the age of six years' and third she was 'co-operative as far as work and arrangements between herself and the Department for Community Services.' In the first episode, the children were identified as being 'at risk' but the mother 'refused to co-operate'. She 'refused any support of child care from 2–3 hours to days . . . she stated that she was coping with the children'. Even though in this first investigation the family doctor had mentioned a drinking problem, as had the anonymous source of the referral who 'claimed children neglected, mother on grog', it was not pursued and the doctor 'vouched for' the mother. He had examined the children 'and it was his opinion that there was little to be concerned about'. In this context it is difficult to see how this potentially fatal assault could have been predicted in the first episode. Problems were identified but the mother refused help – the doctor's comments went some way to allay anxieties. On the evidence of this one case, the notion that all children can be protected and fatalities avoided cannot be supported unless the public and professionals can accept intervention without supporting evidence on a massive scale.

Three other physical abuse second episode children entered care (Cases 431, 432 and 433). In the first episode it was alleged that these children were being 'inappropriately punished'. Concerns were expressed by both the school nurse and a neighbour. The family was visited and the mother denied the allegations. The school headteacher '[claimed] the children seem happy enough and although concerned believes mother cares for the children'. The case was closed. A month later the school health nurse complained again and 'intensive enquiries' got under way. This time all three children were interviewed. They claimed that 'their mother regularly hits them with whips and ropes, throws objects at them and that [a female child] was chained to her bed to prevent her wandering'. Simultaneously it was established that the children were in fact illegal immigrants to Australia, they had no legal guardian or legal status in the country. The parents refused to cooperate with child protection workers and threatened to use force against them if they returned to the house. The department, in consultation with the Immigration Department and the police, decided to forcibly enter the home by obtaining a warrant from the Children's Court. This they did and the children were apprehended. A police search of the house revealed 'a rope whip, chains and a lock, all identified by the children as being used for discipline or confinement'. A care and protection application was lodged with the Children's Court, but four weeks later, at an interim hearing, the court returned the children to their parent's care after their solicitor requested interim custody for four weeks. The children were duly returned home. A legal argument then took place in the courts as to the children's status. Since there was no evidence that they had been legally adopted in South America as the parents claimed, the issue was whether their legal guardian was the Federal Minister or the State Minister. The question was which laws took precedence, the Federal Immigration laws or the state's Child Welfare Act? In the midst of this argument, the children and their mother disappeared. Despite national and international efforts to trace them, they had not been found 12 months later. In this instance, it would appear that the parents' legal representative had skilfully exploited a contradiction between state and federal legislation. By the time the matter was being resolved, the mother had hastily departed the area with the children. Again, it is not easy to see how child protection workers could have done more, since it was the court's decision to release them from care even though the department made strenuous legal representations. This case provides an important clue as to how legal discourses can operate in child protection cases; it offers some idea about how the law thinks about children and simultaneously reminds us that there is no technology to monitor the legal discourse in addition to the social welfare discourse.

Case 264 was the only sexually abused child amongst the second episode cases. This was an eight year old girl living with a single female parent who had been assessed as an 'at risk' case in the first episode when the mother reported accommodation problems and difficulties in controlling the child. The department helped with these problems by contacting the Housing Department and introducing the mother to a parenting skills course. The case was closed, but opened again three months later when the mother again contacted a child protection worker and 'mentioned that [her daughter] had been "kidnapped" on Christmas Eve and sexually abused on Christmas Day'. The police had become involved but the person believed responsible had gone to another state. Interviews with the child revealed that an act of indecency had been committed against her. The mother then failed to keep a medical appointment after the case was transferred to a hospital for further assessment and possible help. The case record appears to peter out quietly.

This examination of the further harm and injury and second episode cases does not shed a great deal of light on the effectiveness of child protection practices in terms of inadequate techniques of investigation, treatment or professional and agency procedures. Two issues are revealed which reinforce the messages of previous chapters. First there is the matter of the continuing significant presence of poor, single female parent families usually with difficulties associated with alcohol misuse. Intervention in these cases is not focused in a genuine sense on resolving the problems of this group, but rather the social welfare discourse responds with a particular type of short term (punitive) remedy. Their problems appear to be complex and child protection training is much more suited to the straightforward 'rescue' interventions required of victims of assaults. Also, clearly this group is much more vulnerable to reporting than other groups.

Second, a much smaller number of children emerge who are victims of serious assaults in terms of potentially dangerous physical attacks, where legal action and substitute care measures come into play. Again, it is the latter group of cases which grab the headlines, come to the attention of 'rear end' specialists and reinforce the prevailing view that child protection is concerned primarily with these very serious matters. However, it is also clear that the child protection workers emerge quite well in their activities in respect of this latter group of cases, since there is no convincing evidence that either further harm or injury or second episodes could have been easily avoided. With regard to 'at risk' and neglect cases, a rather different judgement may be tentatively made. These cases maintain a continuing and problematic presence in the child protection system and the major characteristic of this group is that of social disadvantage of one kind or another. This observation leads us now to evaluate child protection operations within the broader context of society and government. The question posed is that of asking the price which is paid to achieve the relatively narrow and generally successful outcomes of protecting children who have already been harmed, injured or significantly neglected.

The price of child protection

This research has shown that allegations were made about 655 children and that after investigation only 216 (33 per cent) of these were substantiated, while 109 (17 per cent) were judged to be 'at risk'. A further group of cases were then closed with no further action by the agency, reducing the proportion of cases actually receiving a service to only 37 per cent of all those originally reported. A similar pattern holds with second episode cases, as is the situation with the Welsh local authority referred to in Chapter 4. This finding suggests that the majority of 'child protection' matters are dealt with by investigation and some degree of admonishment.

The text from case records demonstrates what amounts to an activity which can perhaps best be described as policing and investigation. What is being policed are the routine parenting practices of a substantial number of people. No norm is set for minimum standards, rather the onus is on the investigators to demonstrate that allegations have substance. In that sense, the bulk of child protection work can be said to consist of enquiries into parenting behaviours. These findings are not confined to Western Australia in 1987 and Wales in 1990. Besharov (1985) writes about a similar problem in the United States. Referring to those cases in the United States similar to the very small number of seriously harmed children in Western Australia, he notes that:

> Such horror stories make us eager to 'do something' about child abuse and child neglect. As a result, the last twenty years have witnessed a nationwide expansion of child protection programs. However, in the rush to deal with this long-ignored problem, the public, the policy makers, and the politicians have over-reacted. They have sought to protect children in possible danger of future maltreatment, as if this were even remotely possible. Through a combination of laws, agency policies, and public pronouncements, they have fostered the idea that all children coming to the attention of the authorities can be protected from future abuse and that, if a child is subsequently injured (or killed), someone must be at fault. Child protective professionals have taken this message to heart. They are now so fearful of 'letting a child die' that they intervene into private family matters far more than necessary, often with demonstrable harmful consequences for the children and families involved.
>
> Yet even this high level of unwarranted intervention does not prevent many obviously endangered children from being killed and injured, even

after their plight becomes known to the authorities; ironically, it makes matters worse. The system is so overburdened with cases of insubstantial or unproven risk to children that it does not respond forcefully to situations where children are in real danger.

(Besharov 1985: 539–40)

The Western Australian research goes some way to supporting Besharov's claims. Case 264 discussed earlier was only one of the 309 children about whom allegations of neglect were made in episode one, it was only one of the 109 cases considered to be 'at risk' and only one of the 53 such cases which received home-based services. The risk factors were identified as the mother's drinking, having to care for several small children on her own and her uncooperative attitude in episode one. Besharov points out that

more than sixty five percent of all reports of suspected child maltreatment – involving over 750,000 children per year – turn out to be 'unfounded' . . . Few of these reports are made maliciously; rather, most involve confusion over what types of situations should be reported. Approximately half involve situations of poor child care which, though of legitimate concern, are not sufficiently serious to be considered 'child maltreatment'.

(Besharov 1985: 556)

Besharov does not qualify what he means by 'poor child care' or the expression 'unfounded'. What emerges from the research in this book is a much clearer picture about 'poor child care'. In a later paper, Besharov again analysed the statistics on allegations of child 'abuse' and neglect and the results of investigations for the period 1976–87. He estimated that 'unfounded' reports were between 55 and 65 per cent of all allegations (Besharov 1990). His major judgements on child protection were that in interpreting complaints about the child rearing practices of particular parents, child protection workers became overstretched in investigations which successfully identified a very small number of 'serious' matters and that in the process, they lost sight of those 'serious' cases and failed to concentrate on them and protect children in danger.

Besharov however does not appear to be aware of the 'filtering' process revealed in the Western Australian research and which leads to patterns of different types of decisions. He somehow leaves one with the impression that nothing whatsoever happens in 65 per cent of cases when in fact a great deal happens in terms of the decision-making process. He also claims that these investigations which failed to produce a positive result (for the investigators) were intrusive and harmful.

Additionally he raised the question of the *underreporting* of child abuse and neglect and identified this as a problem which perhaps child welfare agencies should begin to address. In doing this he was repeating what criminologists have been saying about criminal statistics for many years, namely that these statistics primarily reflect police behaviour (see for example Cicourel 1968). Not all victims of crime report offences, many do not even know they are victims and that our knowledge of crime is confined to data collected by the police (see for example Home Office 1983). The naivety with which the child protection fraternity deals with 'incidence' reports is quite breathtaking to anyone with a criminological background. Finkelhor refutes Besharov's findings on several grounds. He concludes that:

> The goals of making the child protection system more efficient, effective and fair are laudable. The system has many problems and many faults. Besharov's criticisms point to some key issues. For example, many people inside and outside the system believe that reports could be better prioritized, so that investigators' time is spent on the most serious cases that are most likely to benefit from intervention. There is also broad support for the idea of defining child abuse more clearly, particularly in areas such as emotional abuse, so that workers can decide which reports warrant intervention . . . The system for collecting and analyzing statistics on child abuse needs to be refined; for example, the use of the term 'substantiation' does lead to confusion, as does the use of total number of reports – substantiated and unsubstantiated – as an indicator of the size of the child abuse problem.
>
> But two of the major needs of the child protection system run exactly counter to Besharov's analysis. First, the system needs more trained staff to respond to reports, conduct investigations and provide services to families. By almost everyone's analysis, the increase in serious child abuse cases coming to CPS attention has not been matched by commensurate increases in staff and budget to deal with these cases. This lack of staff has been one of the primary obstacles to effective action.
>
> Second, the system needs greater public and professional confidence and esteem. Child welfare workers need to be honoured and welcomed. The public clearly wants to combat child abuse. People need to be educated that this sometimes means accepting a modest level of outside scrutiny into the affairs of families. They also need to recognise that this sometimes entails difficult moral choices between family, neighbourhood, and professional loyalties, on the other hand, and the welfare of children on the other. Public and professional esteem for the child welfare system will certainly make it easier to identify and confirm child abuse.
>
> Unfortunately, critiques such as Besharov's are not helpful. They undermine political support for child protection, encourage public cynicism and fuel welfare bashing.
>
> (Finkelhor 1990: 29)

How do the competing claims of Besharov and Finkelhor look in the light of the Western Australian research? Substantiation rates, as has already been mentioned, support Besharov's view that services become overstretched and the evidence of the becomes care cases in Chapter 7 does suggest that more intensive services, especially those which deal with alcohol misuse rather than child '*abuse*', could potentially reduce rates of admission to substitute care. The issue of intrusiveness as identified by Besharov is more of a problem. The reason for that is that in this book, the 330 allegations which were not substantiated have not been analysed. There is however quite a lot of evidence to show that in many substantiated cases, child protection workers were not welcome – witness the high levels of 'drop out' and reluctance to participate in treatment programmes for sexual 'abuse' alone.

However, the evidence from Western Australia is that both Besharov and Finkelhor spectacularly miss the point. The main reason for that is that they remain locked into a 'child protection' frame which has at its core a vocabulary, a technology of intervention and a knowledge base which is constructed around 'child abuse'. The figures they deal with may represent something different. What emerges in Western Australia is the overrepresentation of poor and disadvantaged people – single female parent families and Aboriginal people. Neither Besharov nor Finkelhor pay any attention whatsoever to the social *contexts* in which allegations arise. They do not mention single female parents, ethnic minorities, the misuse of alcohol and drugs and conflicts between adolescents and caregivers. These contexts however appear to supply a new perspective on the phenomenon. Consider this. A total of *nine* children were admitted to substitute care because they were victims of sexual assaults in Western Australia. At the same time, *twelve* children were admitted to substitute care because they came from single female parent households where workers identified alcohol misuse as a problem. That figure of 12 is extracted from only one cell in Table 4.12 (p. 60) (neglect/begins care). Chapter 7 has already shown that of the 40 becomes care cases, 31 had no identifiable harm or injury and that in the majority of these 40 cases alcohol and drugs were important features. Of these impoverished and disadvantaged cases mentioned so far, the question must be asked, did 'child protection' do everything which was required, did it improve the lot of children who had come into the 'net' of the child protection system because of structural factors and alcohol misuse? The data suggests that the answer is 'no'. Rather, because of the epistemological frame created by the expression 'child abuse', it is parents who are pathologised, it is individuals who are blamed. The cumulative evidence from Chapters 6 and 7 and the beginning of this final chapter all point to the relatively poor performance of child protection measures when applied to 'at risk' and neglect cases.

Single parenthood and alcohol are familiar historical themes in child welfare work. In the first chapter of this book they feature extensively in Victorian and Edwardian accounts of child protection on both sides of the Atlantic. They reappear 100 years later in the text of Western Australian and Welsh child protection case records and they are specifically related to what Besharov vaguely describes as 'poor child care'. They also form the majority of cases which receive services.

A second matter emerges in the Western Australian research which does not feature in the Besharov/Finkelhor debate, and that is the way in which conventional child protection statistics fail to reveal what is perhaps the true nature of much child protection work – the observation of and categorization of parenting behaviours and the moral character of parents. This work can perhaps be best summed up by the term 'normalization' which conveys simultaneously the notions of observation, categorization and the use of technologies of intervention which aim to standardize child rearing practices. Case record texts show these activities in the context of the interactions between child protection workers, Aboriginal parents and 'disorganized' and disorderly parents. Parton describes the practice of 'normalization' in the following way:

> Disciplinary mechanisms which attempt to normalise, subject the individual to training and require a knowledge of the whole person in their social context and depend on medico-social expertise and judgement for their operation. They depend on direct supervision and surveillance and emphasize the need to effect change in characters, attitudes and behaviours in an individualised way. They are concerned with underlying causes and needs and attempt to contribute to the improvement of those being served as well as social defence. Because the 'psy' profession have an exclusive insight into the problems and the knowledge and techniques required, it is important they have wide discretion to diagnose and treat and thereby normalise.
>
> (Parton 1991: 6)

Investigations, judgements, assessments and interventions appear to fit more into an activity which could be described as the regulation of parenthood, the enforcement of standards and the imposition of norms rather than the protection of children. It is not entirely clear in many cases precisely what 'protection' actually consists of since the focus of the observation and interventions is on parents who are responsible for looking after children and in the case of the very vulnerable, minimizing as far as possible actual and potential environmental hazards. Why do the accounts of child protection workers dwell so readily on the moral character of parents which is used to qualify other observations about actual child rearing practices? It is probably because the category of competence 'parent' carries with it, indeed has embedded within it assumptions about moral character. It is one thing to speak of someone as being 'drunk' but quite another to speak of a 'drunken mother' or a 'drunken father'. Even if the drunkenness does not in any obvious way affect the care of children, 'drunken parents' are in some sense worse than 'drunks'.

The solutions offered by Besharov and Finkelhor amount to little more than technical fixes. Besharov argues for more sensitive 'screening' of allegations and better definitions of substantiation of 'abuse'. Finkelhor, in a more familiar vein, argues for better training, more resources and public and professional acceptance of greater intervention. However, like Boss (1980) and the *Guide to Case Practice* in Western Australia (DCS 1987), they do not mention moral character, non-standard child rearing practice, parenting and alcohol. Indeed the technical fixes they suggest all take place within the framework of the child protection discourse as it has emerged in the past 20 years and which Carter raised concerns about in her papers of the early 1980s.

The phenomenon of child protection

We come now to the final section of the last chapter in which the discussion will broaden out in an attempt to address the question of what child protection has become. At the heart of the question lies the issue of representation. The basic aim of the Western Australia research was an attempt to represent the phenomenon in ways which would enable more effective and efficient management of child protection work. In doing this, the researcher immediately encounters an apparently insurmountable problem, namely the use of the word 'abuse' as a means of representing the 'life world' as it is described in case records.

In the preceding section of this chapter which quotes Finkelhor's (1990) paper, the word 'abuse' is used seven times to describe the 'object' with which child protection purports to deal. All representations are of necessity abbreviations. Whatever the techniques and terminologies used to represent the people and events which fall within the ambit of child welfare programmes, they will be abbreviations, categories which attempt to condense complex and contradictory issues into 'one line' expressions. We have seen something of the variety of social events revealed by text, and how several important child welfare issues are concealed or perhaps even censored out by existing, conventional professional and agency representations. Indeed, insofar as much of this variety is obscured and made invisible by child protection statistics, it may be argued that existing categorizations serve to *misrepresent* this variety and hence some very crucial aspects of child protection work, particularly those related to the problems exhibited by those adults responsible for the care of children. What really appears to be required of child protection and its representation is a complete reconceptualization rather than sharper definitions. This reconceptualization would begin to distinguish between child *welfare* (those measures which promote the care and well-being of children) from child *protection* (those measures which act directly as a barrier between children and significant harm or injury).

The problem with the word 'abuse' as an abbreviated representation of the events dealt with by child protection programmes is that it serves to completely decontextualise those events. At best it appears to be a deeply flawed attempt to represent complexity and variety, at worst it can so misrepresent those events and mislead both the public and professionals that the very different types of problem and hence different potential solutions become lost in an atmosphere of panic and pressure. The specialist child protection workers in Western Australia for example believed that they needed more resources and more treatment skills. The response of the government was to fund a number of specialized sexual 'abuse' treatment programmes from 1988 onwards. The evidence of this research is that they were not priority requirements, rather it should have been training in alcohol and a substance misuse, full day care facilities for children and flexible home supports especially for isolated single parents. Resources were however directed instead into areas where the demand was obvious, but not high. Chapter 6 has shown that the chances of children receiving 'treatment' as a result of being a victim of a sexual assault, were much higher than the chances of adults with alcohol related problems receiving both treatment and child care support.

This then appears to be one of the end results of the new ideology of child protection, namely a distortion of the types of service required as well as the levels of servicing required. By presenting information (or misinformation) on allegations and using the word 'abuse' as a decontextualized and highly emotive signifier, the new ideology appears to have succeeded in changing the role of child welfare agencies from predominantly one of service provision, to one of policing and 'normalizing'. It can be construed as a switch from a view of the child in a context where caregivers are encouraged and supported by the state to look after and protect children, to one where the state 'intervenes' to 'protect'. It sees parents not as nurturing and supporting agents whose difficulties and structural disadvantages require compensation, but as potential threats from which children require protection.

Underpinning this shift has been the globalization of specific (Eurocentric, middle-class) norms on child rearing, achieved in part by a somewhat narrow interpretation of the 'rights of the child'. In the first chapter, reference was made to Carter's (1982) comment that the new child welfare legislation which began to appear in Australian states in the late 1970s and early 1980s reflected a 'revised image of childhood' and that the introduction to New South Wales' Community Welfare Bill of 1982 was extracted directly from Principle 2 of the United Nations Declaration on the Rights of the Child of 1959. There are two problems with the concept of 'Rights of the Child' as they are implemented in child protection practices. These problems are both caused by decontextualization. Wattam (1992) comments:

> The claim to a right is to enunciate a 'rule' which pertains to the status or treatment of a person. The claim could be that such a rule would apply to all persons in general, for example, the 18th century debates on natural rights, or to particular subgroups. The rule like character of 'rights' holds, however, irrespective of their authorisation in statute or more informally as a presumption underpinning case law, as in the UK. What rights in effect do is to propose a rule by, and through which, persons are treated. However, no rule dictates its own application, but needs to be applied in particular cases: a feature which applies to rules as diverse as those of games, to those of inachievable human rights. The right to life, liberty and the pursuit of happiness is, in practice, hedged around with qualifications, caveats, restrictions and so on, which make it less than universal. This does not mean that the right is of no relevance, for it is the qualifications which make it applicable as a moral principle relevant to the practical world. However, it is in the application of rules such as this, and legal rules need to be included here, that conflicts are likely to arise, not only between varying interpretations of the same rule, but between the competing claims of different rules.

> (Wattam 1992: 9)

This 'clash of rights' has been conveniently ignored by the new child protection ideology. It is possible to see how the conflict is dealt with in the context of child protection work in the practical activity of situated moral reasoning. Referring to a comment made by a teacher to a child protection worker investigating an allegation of 'physical abuse', the worker discovers that a single female parent is in conflict with her adolescent daughter. The conflict becomes a fight when the mother is drunk. The teacher says of the mother that 'She's a lovely woman when she's not drinking' (Case 303). The significance of this statement lies in its practical consequence, which was that the case was kept open for monitoring and surveillance. The woman in question is judged as socially competent, but the context of competence is also that of caring for an adolescent child on her own. It is in that context that alcohol becomes important as the competition between 'rights' comes to the fore. If a pure 'child rights' formulation was used, it could be said that the child in this case had a right to both a mother and a father who were also competent as providers and nurturers and whose competence should not be affected by alcohol. However, the reality of the situation was that the worker judged that the 'rights' of the child were best served by her remaining with her mother and maintaining a watching brief.

Seligman illustrates contemporary struggles in the institutional realms of health and welfare by examining the changing language of 'rights'. He argues that 'rights' are no longer framed in terms of 'citizen' or 'civil' rights – which can provide some measure of context – but in terms of 'human rights'. The consequences of this is that the realm of public space within which the 'citizen' is constituted, which is to say a real social, economic and political *place*, has disappeared. It has, he says, been replaced by 'the most abstract of generalities (instrumental reason) within which individuals exist in public only as generalised universals (humans etc.)' (Seligman 1990: 131).

It is precisely in these terms that we are now to understand the 'children's rights' sought after by the new ideology of child protection, the private invisible activities of child rearing and social work become projected into the public arena by means of representations such as 'abuse', 'maltreatment' and 'child protection'. Perhaps it was the intention originally of those who propagated the new ideology of child protection to bring these private 'life worlds' into the public domain. The decontextualization resulting from these abbreviated representations however then serves to abstract children from the practical realities of their day to day existence which more often than not are dictated by parental income, housing, and the cultural and social practices which are determined by class and ethnicity.

Early on in this book, reference was made to the construction of knowledge about 'child abuse' being dominated in the 1960s by medical practitioners who were exposed to seriously injured children. This theme was repeated in respect of Carter and Brazier (1969) who worked in a hospital, and those social workers in Western Australia who worked in the Child Sexual Abuse and Child Life Protection units and dealt with selected cases involving children who had been significantly harmed. It was their knowledge of these cases which in part determined the ideology of child protection and within the context of Australia as a whole, created the WELSTAT (1987) definitions which use the word 'maltreatment'. One of the Department for Community Services employees attached to the research discussed in this book had been a social worker in the disbanded Child Sexual Abuse Unit. Exposure to the 655 case records detailed in this book prompted from him the following spontaneous comment, 'It's like trying to use an atom bomb to sink a row boat!' What he was referring to was the way in which apparently vast child welfare resources were going into the child protection system and succeeding in filtering out a very small number of significantly harmed or threatened children. His knowledge of child protection cases had hitherto been confined almost entirely to that very small group of serious cases. Although he had very extensive experience as a practitioner in child protection, he had never before been aware of those cases which in reality constituted the bulk of work in child protection and which produced such comparatively problematic outcomes.

The reconceptualization of child protection can only be achieved by what amounts to a 'recontextualization'. In effect it requires not only a different vocabulary, but a different structure to the representation. There are a number of relatively easily identifiable and classifiable phenomena within these cases which are also linked together. The sequence of knowledge construction which occurs within case records and which to some extent reflect the 'work' in child protection takes the following form:

1 A caregiver (or caregivers) have specific – identified – problems.
2 A caregiver (or caregivers) have a particular moral character.
3 Services may or may not be made available to help the caregiver(s). These will have particular objectives.
4 The problems experienced by the caregiver(s) may or may not constitute a potential or actual threat to a child's well-being. This can be specified.
5 A child may or may not have sustained a specific harm or injury as a direct consequence of an identified caregiver problem.

In this formulation the work would begin with those responsible for the care of children and, reflecting the realities of investigative reasoning, make some assessment of their difficulties, their character and the services from which they could benefit. This is the context of child welfare practice. Since all caregivers have shortcomings, some attempt would be made to evaluate caregivers' strengths and weaknesses with regard to an articulated and contextualized minimum standard of child rearing. Finally, for those harmed or injured children a statement specifying the nature of the harm or injury would complete the representation. The words 'maltreatment' and 'abuse' would not be used and the word 'protection' would be confined entirely to those children receiving substitute care measures specifically because they require 'protection' not from a caregiver shortcoming as such, but from an identifiable real threat. Experimenting with this formulation alongside conventional statistical representations of child protection could potentially cause knowledge about these matters to be constructed in a different way and service development to take a different direction. Would it be a brave director of a child welfare agency who might consider such an experiment? Only the future can tell, but it's not easy to see where child protection can go in the future without a reconceptualization.

In accepting the new ideology of child protection and its representations of private social events, it seems that social work has bought another 'lemon'. In response to a moral panic it has obtained new resources, changed laws and agency procedures and introduced new technologies of intervention in order to secure the safety of a small number of children. The hidden agenda would appear to be one of changing the child rearing practices of millions of caregivers across the world, using decontextualized and abstract 'human rights' formulations as a justification. The narrow 'effectiveness' test of child protection stands up well, but the price which is paid considering the difficulties faced by many caregivers is excessive. Underlying some of these excesses is an attempt to use the state to enforce child rearing practices with which not everyone of every class, race or culture might be in agreement. There must be some other way of achieving the 'effectiveness' end without its unintended consequences. Child protection has become a 'Panoptical device', a means by which the private lives of those who struggle to bring up children in difficult conditions are made public and what is made public is more often than not a misrepresentation of what is required. That which does not conform to standard middle-class patriarchal child rearing norms is represented as 'at risk' of abuse, neglect or abuse.

There are children who are victims of serious neglect, physical or sexual assaults. They require protection and approximately 10 per cent of children drawn into the mouth of the child protection net will filter down into this category. The use of emotive words such as 'abuse', 'maltreatment' and 'perpetrator' should be confined to those cases.

The globalization of the child protection phenomenon has meant that there are hardly any child welfare agencies in the developed world untouched by its overt and hidden messages. This has been achieved by a limited number of people familiar only with tragic cases and confined largely to clinical settings. They have succeeded in painting emotive pictures without context. From Lancaster to Sydney the images signify urgency and pity, and they arouse deep concern in those who see them. In returning to these images at the end of the book I am bound to say that I cannot now accept them at face value, since without context they have no meaning other than one which creates alarm. They offer nothing to those who require help and sympathy in managing the contexts of poverty, deprivation and discrimination while managing their children's lives. The expectation of the new ideologies of child protection are that caregivers can manage these contexts *and* manage their children. Their representations make private events public, but lay the burden of blame back onto the shoulders of those who are not responsible for the material and social conditions which can make childhood for some, such an unhappy experience.

Appendix
Data items, data values and definitions

1 Case number

2 Date case opened

3 Date case closed

4 Length of time open
Less than 1 week
1–4 weeks
5–8 weeks
9–12 weeks
13–16 weeks
17–20 weeks
21–24 weeks
25–28 weeks
29–32 weeks
33–36 weeks
37–40 weeks
41–44 weeks
45–48 weeks
49–52 weeks

5 Age of child at referral
Less than 1 year to more than 19 years in yearly increments

6 Age range of child at referral
Less than 1 year
1–4 years
5–10 years

11–14 years
15–18 years
19 years or older

7 Source of referral

Child

Person believed responsible for maltreatment (if not parent)

Parent/guardian

Sibling

Other relative

Friend/neighbour

Medical practitioner (only registered medical practitioners)

Other medical personnel (persons engaged in supplementary, paramedical and/or ancillary medical services)

Hospital/health centre personnel (any person not elsewhere classified who is employed at a public or private hospital or health centre/clinic)

Social worker/welfare worker/psychologist/other trained welfare worker (any person engaged in providing a social or welfare work service in the community)

School personnel (any appropriately trained person involved in the instruction or of imparting knowledge to children or providing direct support for this education. This includes teachers, teachers' aides, school principals and counsellors who work in pre-school, kindergarten, primary, secondary, technical, sporting or art and craft education)

Family day care/day care personnel (any person engaged in providing occasional, part-time and/or full-time day care for children)

Police

Departmental officer (any person, not classified elsewhere, who is employed by a state welfare department)

Non-government organization (any non-government organization which provides services to the community on a non-profit making basis which is not classified above)

Anonymous (all those cases where the source of the allegation does not give his/her identity)

Other (all other persons not classified above)

Not stated (allegations received from unknown sources)

8 Context

Custody/access dispute (where a child, subject of an allegation, is involved in a familial dispute regarding custody and/or access as indicated by the referrer who is an interested party or a representative of an interested party in a custody/access dispute. Proceedings may or may not have started in a court of law)

Other conflict between family members (where there are disputes amongst family members on a range of matters which do not include custody or access, and where a child in that family has subsequently become the subject of an allegation of mistreatment)

Conflict between neighbours (where it is possible to identify conflict between groupings of people living within close geographical proximity)

Non-conflictual context (where it is clear that an allegation of child maltreatment has arisen in the context of concern for the child's well-being and a wish to see the child protected)

Other (where an allegation of child maltreatment has been made in the context of other situations, conditions or conflicts. For example, situations of conflict between non-family or non-neighbour groupings, or situations where the allegation of harm is secondary to some other involvement or investigation)

Unknown (this relates to situations where it is not possible to determine the context of maltreatment, e.g. in the cases of anonymous callers)

9 Allegation

Physical abuse (any non-accidental physical injury inflicted upon a child by a person having the care of a child)

Emotional abuse (any act by a person having the care of a child which results in the child suffering any kind of significant emotional deprivation and/or trauma)

Sexual abuse (any act by a person having the care of the child, exposing a child to or involving the child in sexual processes beyond his/her understanding or contrary to accepted community standards)

Neglect (any serious omissions or commissions by a person having the care of a child which, within the bounds of cultural tradition, constitute a failure to provide conditions which are essential for the healthy physical and emotional development of a child)

10 Previous case history

No previous case history, not known to the agency

Previous allegation, child classed 'at risk'

Previous allegation, not substantiated

Previous allegation, substantiated

Known to agency in juvenile justice programme

Known to agency in substitute care programme

Known to agency in family support service

Known to agency in a capacity other than those listed above

11 Order

None (child not currently subject to a Children's Court order)

Juvenile justice ward (child currently a state ward as a result of a criminal prosecution)

Child protection ward (child currently a state ward as a result of a care and protection application)

12 Gender

Female

Male

Unknown

13 Family Structure

Both biological parents (where the subject child is living in a family grouping which includes the biological mother and father, and the child recognizes these as its parents. The marital status of these parents is not of significance in choosing this category)

Reconstituted or reconstituting family (where the subject child is living in a family grouping with two caregivers, one of whom is not a biological parent, or relative, of the subject child. The marital status of the caregivers is not of significance in choosing this category)

Single female parent (where the subject child is living in a family structure where the child's mother or mother figure, is the only parent living in the home, and where the child recognizes that person as a parental figure)

Single male parent (where the subject child is living in a family structure where the child's father, or father figure, is the only parent living in the home, and where the child recognizes that person as a parental figure)

Aboriginal kinship (where the subject child is living within an Aboriginal kinship system where particular members beyond the immediate family have certain responsibilities for the child. This category does not include any family structure which is described in the other categories)

Substitute care (where the subject child is living in any type of care which is a substitute for the child's usual living circumstances, for example, foster or hostel care, emergency care or group living)

Adoptive parents (where the subject child is living in a family structure in which the parents have adopted the child and have been/are legally recognized as the child's guardians, and where the child recognizes these people as parents)

Other (where the subject child is (a) living in a situation which may be a combination of the above categories, e.g. adoptive parent, single female; or (b) in any other situation not included in other categories, e.g. independent living, homeless children, group living)

Unknown (where the child's family structure cannot be determined or is uncertain)

14 Ethnicity

Aboriginal (where the child belongs to, identifies with, or is accepted by the Australian Aboriginal culture)

Non-Aboriginal (where the subject child belongs to, or identifies with any culture which is not Australian Aboriginal, for example, Caucasian, Asian and European cultures)

Unknown (where the ethnicity or cultural identity of the subject child cannot be confirmed or is uncertain)

15 Division

There are 20 area offices in the Department for Community Services, Western Australia. Each was allocated a number from 1 to 20

16 Result of investigation

This item refers to the findings of investigations in response to allegations. In the case of multiple classifications, cases were allocated to a category which matched the type of 'abuse' considered to be the most serious in individual cases

Physical abuse (see 9 above)

Emotional abuse (see 9 above)

Sexual abuse (see 9 above)

Neglect (see 9 above)

'At risk' (where following an investigation of the circumstances surrounding the allegation by the relevant authority, no maltreatment can be substantiated but there are reasonable grounds to suspect the possibility of prior or future maltreatment and it is considered that continued departmental involvement is warranted)

Not substantiated (where an investigation of the circumstances surrounding an allegation by a relevant authority concluded that there is no reasonable cause to suspect prior, current or future maltreatment of the child)

No investigation possible (where for any reason it was not possible to investigate an allegation of child maltreatment)

Unknown (where the result of an investigation was not known)

17 Career type

Begins with substitute care (those cases in which a child enters substitute care within five days of the conclusion of an investigation into an allegation of maltreatment or neglect)

Becomes substitute care (those cases in which a child enters substitute care when home-based services prove insufficient to avert a crisis or it becomes necessary to remove a child from caregivers for its own protection. Usually this type of case is supplied initially with services other than those of substitute care)

Home-based services (those cases which remain open after an investigation and receive a range of services. They never use substitute care services)

Substantiated – no further action (those cases which are closed very shortly after an investigation is completed, but which are judged to be 'substantiated' by the investigator. Such cases may often have received minimal advice and guidance during the investigatory process. They do not however remain open beyond the investigatory phase)

Not substantiated or not neglected and not 'at risk' (those cases which are closed very shortly after an investigation is completed either because 'abuse' is not 'substantiated', or the subject child is not considered to be neglected or 'at risk', or it is not possible to complete investigation)

18 Action responsible for harm/injury

Excessive corporal punishment (action by the parent or caregiver in which: (a) physical punishment is administered to a child by the caregiver in an attempt to discipline a child and which results in either short or long-term physical harm to the child; or (b) it is apparent that the parent/caregiver did not control his/her reaction by stopping the punishment before it caused injury)

Throwing (the throwing of a child against a hard object, or solid surface, or with force or violence)

Shaking (the shaking of a child's body with force or violence)

Strangulation (choking with hands or other constriction around the throat which prevents the circulation of blood and/or oxygen)

Suffocation (the prevention of the air supply reaching the lungs, or the impeding of respiration)

Persistent caregiver hostility (constant or repeated hostility, coldness, or rejection by the caregiver to such an extent that the child's behaviour would be disturbed or suffer developmental impairment)

Indecent dealings/molestation (any intentional sexual contact between the person believed responsible and a child, for the purpose of arousal or gratification of the perpetrator of that contact. It includes the touching or handling of the child's sexual organ, anus or breast, or having the child fondle or stimulate parts of the body of the person believed responsible or self-masturbation in the child's presence or by the child where the intent is sexual arousal or gratification for the person believed responsible)

Penetration (any intrusion into the sexual organ or anus of a child by any part of the body of the person believed responsible or by an object)

Unknown (where it is unclear what the action has been committed upon a child but maltreatment has been substantiated or the child is considered to be 'at risk' of harm)

Other (any action which has been committed upon a child and which is not included in the above categories)

19 Resulting identifiable injury or harm

Neglect shelter (lack of shelter which is safe and which protects the child from harm from the elements. This definition concerns the minimum acceptable standard of housing for a child over and above which there may be variations due to differing cultural values, or climatic or socio-economic conditions)

Neglect supervision (lack of physical supervision which protects the child from environmental hazards)

Neglect medical care (lack of adequate medical or dental treatment for a health problem or condition which could become severe enough to constitute serious or long-term harm to the child)

Neglect food (a physical condition characterized by lack of food, inadequate or insufficient food, hunger or deficiency of essential vitamins and minerals)

Neglect environment (lack of adequate attention to potential or actual domestic hazards such as those of hygiene and dangerous substances or artifacts)

Neglect hygiene (lack of attention to the personal cleanliness of a child such as that which actually or potentially constitutes a health hazard)

Abandoned/deserted (the child is left destitute or without adequate support, protection or means of care)

Failure to thrive (a medical condition in which an infant's weight, height and motor development fall significantly below average growth weights. This failure may be due in some cases to an organic cause. It could also however, be due to non-organic causes such as disturbed parent–child relationship which results in a lack of physical or developmental growth of the child)

Cuts, bruises, welts, bites

Scalds, burns, fractures

Poisoning

Fractured skull/brain damage

Death

Identifiable emotional trauma

Non-physical sexual exploitation (this definition includes child pornography, a child being forced to watch sexual acts, solicitation of a child, or a child being procured for prostitution)

Anal or vagina trauma or disease

No identifiable injury

Other (any other injury or harm resulting from an action committed against a child which is not contained in the above categories)

20 Person believed responsible

Parent

De facto

Guardian

Foster parent

Sibling

Step-parent

Other relative

Friend/neighbour

Loco parentis (authorized child minder)

21 Reason case closed

Death due to maltreatment

Death by other causes

Permanent placement

Risk reduced

Case transferred

Case continues, not closed

Not known

22 Apprehension

Child apprehended

Child not apprehended

23 Care and protection application

No application made

Application made, adjourned

Application dismissed

Application made and withdrawn

Application made, wardship granted

24 Police activity

Police not involved

Police involved

Police prosecution

25 Action responsible for further harm or injury

(See 18 above)

26 Further resulting identifiable harm or injury

(See 19 above)

27 Intellectually handicapped child

Yes

No

28 Moved to friends/relatives

Yes

No

29 Monitoring and surveillance

Yes (where an extended period of assessment and supervision is undertaken within a family to assist in assessing harm or risk of harm to a subject child)

No

30 Financial assistance

Yes (where any form of financial payment, subsidy, concession or budgetary planning is offered or provided to the caregiver or family, subject child or person believed responsible)

No

31 Material/practical assistance

Yes (the provision of any goods, commodities, transport, home management services, child care services or holiday services to the caregiver or family, subject child or person believed responsible)

No

32 Advice/counselling

Yes (where any information is provided or counselling is undertaken for the caregiver or family, subject child or person believed reponsible)

No

33 Treatment

Treatment is where an identifiable therapeutic process is offered or provided. Treatment is defined as a process which has goals and includes primarily an acknowledgement of a need for change or resolution

For the child
For the family (includes subject child and caregiver)
For the caregiver
For the person believed responsible

34 Medical services

Examination only
In-patient treatment
Out-patient treatment

35 Substitute care

Foster care
Residential/hostel care
Placed with friends/relatives
Respite care
Independent living
Other
Unknown

36 Length of time in care

Less than 1 week
1–4 weeks
5–8 weeks
9–12 weeks
13–16 weeks
17–20 weeks
21–24 weeks
25–28 weeks
29–32 weeks
33–36 weeks
37–40 weeks
41–44 weeks
45–48 weeks
49–52 weeks
More than 52 weeks
Not known

Bibliography

Abercrombie, N., Hill, S. and Turner, B. (1984) *The Penguin Dictionary of Sociology*. London: Penguin.

Atkinson, E. *et al.* (1986) *Service Needs for Child Protection*. Perth: Department for Community Services.

Aziz, E. (1989) *Enhancing Child Welfare in Aboriginal Communities (Child Protection Issues)*. Perth: Department for Community Services.

Ball, M. (1972) *The Alice Mitchell Baby Farm Case of 1907 as a Major Cause for the Establishment of the State Children's Department of Western Australia*. Unpublished MA thesis. Perth: University of Western Australia.

Becker, H. S. (1963) *Outsiders: Studies in the Sociology of Deviance*. Glencoe: Free Press.

Berridge, D. and Cleaver, H. (1987) *Foster Home Breakdown*. Oxford: Blackwell.

Besharov, D. (1985) ' "Doing something" about child abuse: the need to narrow the grounds for state intervention', *Harvard Journal of Law and Public Policy*, 8, 539–89.

Besharov, D. (1990) 'Gaining control over child abuse reports', *Public Welfare*, 48, 34–9.

Bialestock, D. (1966) 'Neglected babies: a study of 289 babies admitted consecutively to a reception centre', *Medical Journal of Australia*, 2, 1129–33.

Bilson, A. and Thorpe, D. H. (1988) *Managing Child Care Careers*. Glenrothies: Fife Regional Council Social Work Department.

Birrell, R. and Birrell, J. (1966) 'Maltreatment Syndrome in children, a hospital survey', *Medical Journal of Australia*, 2, 10–28.

Boss, P. (1980) *On the Side of the Child*. Melbourne: Fontana.

Carter, J. (ed.) (1974) *The Maltreated Child*. London: Priory Press.

Carter, J. (1975) 'Co-ordination of health and social services for child abuse', *The Battered Child*. Proceedings of the First National Australian Conference, 65–69, Mt Lawley, Western Australia. Perth: Department for Community Welfare.

Carter, J. (1981) 'Current controversies in child abuse', *Second Australian Conference on Child Abuse*, Mt Gravatt, South Australia.

Carter, J. (1982) *Families Without Hope: A Report about Emotional Abuse*. Perth: Department for Community Welfare.

Carter, J. *et al.* (1984) *The Wellbeing of the People*. Perth: Department for Community Welfare.

Carter, J. and Brazier, J. (1969) 'Co-ordination of social work services for the maltreated child in Western Australia', *Australian Journal of Social Work*, 4, 14–21.

Cheetham, J. *et al.* (1992) *Evaluating Social Work Effectiveness*. Buckingham: Open University Press.

Choo, C. (1990) *Aboriginal Child Poverty*, Child Poverty Review 2. Melbourne: Brotherhood of St Lawrence.

Cicourel, A. (1968) *The Social Organization of Juvenile Justice*. New York: Wiley.

Denman, G. and Thorpe, D. (1993) *Family Participation and Patterns of Intervention in Child Protection in Gwent: a Research Report*. Lancaster: Lancaster University Department of Applied Social Science.

Department for Community Services (DCS) (1987) *Child Protective Services: A Guide to Case Practice*. Perth: Department for Community Services.

Department of Health (1991) *Working Together under the Children Act 1989: A Guide to Arrangements for Inter-Agency Co-operation for the Protection of Children from Abuse*. London: HMSO.

Department of Health and Social Security (DHSS) (1982) *Child Abuse: A Study of Social Inquiry Reports 1973–1981*. London: HMSO.

Dingwall, R. (1989) 'Some problems about predicting child abuse and neglect', in O. Stevenson (ed.) *Child Abuse and Public Policy and Professional Practice*. London: Harvester Wheatsheaf.

Dingwall, R., Eekelaar, J. and Murray, T. (1983) *The Protection of Children: State Intervention and Family Life*. Oxford: Blackwell.

Elkin, A. P. (1979) *The Australian Aborigines*. Sydney: Angus and Robertson.

Ettore, B. (1989) 'Women and substance use/abuse: towards a feminist perspective or how to make the dust fly', *Women's International Forum*, 12, 593–602.

Fanshel, D. and Shin, E. (1978) *Children in Foster Care: A Longitudinal investigation*. New York: Columbia University Press.

Finkelhor, D. (1990) 'Is child abuse over reported?', *Public Welfare*, 48, 23–29.

Franklin, B. and Parton, N. (eds) (1991) *Social Work, the Media and Public Relations*. Routledge: London.

Fuller, R. C. and Myers, R. D. (1941) 'The national history of social problem', *American Sociological Review*, 6, 318–29.

Garfinkel, H. (1974) ' "Good" organisational reasons for "bad" clinic records', in R. Turner (ed.) *Ethnomethodology*. Harmondsworth: Penguin.

Goffman, E. (1959) 'The moral career of the mental patient', *Psychiatry: Journal for the Study of Interpersonal Processes*, 22(2), 123–42.

Goffman, E. (1961) *Asylums*. Harmondsworth: Penguin.

Goldberg, E. M. and Fruin, D. (1976) 'Towards accountability in social work: a case review system for social workers', *British Journal of Social Work*, 6(1), 3–22.

Gordon, L. (1986) 'Feminism and social control: the case of child abuse and neglect', in J. Mitchell and A. Oakley (eds) *What is Feminism?* Oxford: Blackwell.

Gordon, L. (1989) *Heroes of Their Own Lives: The Politics and History of Family Violence*. London: Virago.

Griffin, L. (1990) 'More than a mother', *Alcohol Concern*, December, 12–13.

Griffiths, D. and Moynihan, F. (1963) 'Multiple epiphyseal injuries in babies ("battered baby syndrome")', *British Medical Journal*, 5372, 1558–61.

Guba, E. and Lincoln, Y. (1989) *Fourth Generation Evaluation*. Newbury Park: Sage.

Hallett, C. (1988) 'Research in child abuse: some observations on the knowledge base', *Journal of Reproductive and Infant Psychology*, 6 (3).

Hamory, J. and Jeffery, M. (1977) 'Flexibility and innovation in multi-disciplinary management of child abuse in Western Australia', *Child Abuse and Neglect*, 1, 217–39.

Harris, S. (1980) *Culture and Learning: Traditional Education in Northeast Arnhemland*. Northern Territory: Department of Education.

Healy, J., Hassan, R. and McKenna, R. (1985) 'Aboriginal families', in D. Storer (ed.) *Ethnic Family Values in Australia*. Australia: Prentice Hall.

Helfer, R. (1986) 'Looking at outcomes', *Child Abuse and Neglect*, 10, 277.

Heywood, J. (1970) *Children in Care*. London: Routledge and Kegan Paul.

Home Office (1983) *British Crime Survey*. London: HMSO.

Hornick, J. and Clarke, M. (1986) 'A cost/effectiveness evaluation of lay therapy treatment for child abusing and high-risk parents', *Child Abuse and Neglect*, 10, 309–17.

Hughes, E. C. (1937) 'Institutional office and the person', *American Journal of Sociology*, 43, 404–13.

Kempe, C., Silverman, F., Steele, B., Droegemueller, W. and Silver, H. (1962) 'The battered baby syndrome', *Journal of the American Medical Association*, 181, 17–24.

Lahey, K. (1984) 'Research on child abuse in liberal patriarchy', in *Taking Sex into Account*. Carlton University Press.

Lippman, L. (1981) *Generations of Resistance: The Aboriginal Struggle for Justice*. Melbourne: Longman Cheshire.

MacDonald, M. (1960) 'Social work research: a perspective', in N. Polanski (ed.) *Social Work Research*. Chicago: University of Chicago.

Millham, S. *et al.* (1978) *Locking up Children*. Guildford: Saxon House.

Millham, S. *et al.* (1986) *Lost in Care. The Problems of Maintaining Links between Children in Care and Their Families*. Aldershot: Gower.

Moseley, H. (1935) *Report of the Royal Commission appointed to Investigate, Report and Advise upon Matters in Relation to the Condition and Treatment of Aborigines*. Perth: Government of Western Australia.

Nelson, B. J. (1986) *Making an Issue of Child Abuse: Political Agenda for Social Problems*. Chicago: University of Chicago Press.

Packman, J. *et al.* (1986) *Who Needs Care? Social Work Decisions about Children*. Oxford: Blackwell.

Park, R. E. and Burgess, E. W. (1921) *Introduction to the Science of Sociology*. Chicago: University of Chicago Press.

Parr, J. (1980) *Labouring Children*. London: Croom Helm.

Parton, N. (1985) *The Politics of Child Abuse*. London: Macmillan.

Parton, N. (1989) 'Child Abuse' in B. Kahan (ed.) *Child Care Research, Policy and Practice*. London: Hodder and Stoughton.

Parton, N. (1991) *Governing the Family: Child Care, Child Protection and the State*. London: Macmillan.

Parton, C. and Parton, N. (1989) 'Women, the family and child protection', *Critical Social Policy*, 24, 38–49.

Parton, N. (1985) *The Politics of Child Abuse*. Basingstoke: Macmillan.

Parton, N. (1989) 'Child abuse' in B. Kahan (ed.) *Child Care Research, Policy and Practice*. London: Hodder and Stoughton.

Parton, N. (1991) *Governing the Family. Child Care, Child Protection and the State*. Basingstoke: Macmillan.

Pfohl, S. (1977) 'The "discovery" of child abuse', *Social Problems*, 24, 310–23.

Pithouse, A. (1987) *Social Work: The Social Organisation of an Invisible Trade*. Aldershot: Avebury.

Rowley, C. (1972) *The Destruction of Aboriginal Society*. Victoria: Penguin.

Rowley, C. (1978) *A Matter of Justice*. Canberra: ANU Press.

Seligman, A. (1990) 'Towards a reinterpretation of modernity in an age of postmodernity', in B. Turner (ed.) *Theories of Modernity and Postmodernity*. London: Sage.

Shaw, C. R. (1931) *The Natural History of a Delinquent Career*. Chicago: University of Chicago Press.

Standing Committee of Social Welfare Ministers and Administrators of Australia (1987) Minutes of Proceedings of the Spring Conference.

Steele, B. (1986) 'Notes on the lasting effects of early child abuse throughout the life cycle', *Child Abuse and Neglect*, 10, 283–91.

Stephenson, A. (1987) 'The media and the child abuse explosion', *Media Information Australia*. 46, 7–13.

Suchman, L. (1987) *Plans and Situated Actions. The Problem of Human Machine Communication*. Cambridge: Cambridge University Press.

Thorpe, D. H. (1982) 'Intermediate treatment: problems of theory and practice', in R. Bailey and P. Lee (eds] *Theory and Practice in Social Work*. Oxford: Blackwell.

Thorpe, D. H. (1988) 'Career patterns in child care – implications for service', *British Journal of Social Work*, 18(2), 137–53.

Thorpe, D. H. (1989) *Patterns of Child Protection and Service Delivery*. Report for the Standing Committee of Social Welfare Ministers and Administrators. Perth: Department for Community of Services, Western Australia.

Thorpe, D. (1991) *Patterns of Child Protection Intervention and Service Delivery: Report of a Pilot Project*. Research Report No 4, Crime Research Centre, Perth: University of Western Australia.

Thorpe, D. and Thorpe, S. (1992) *Monitoring and Evaluation in the Social Services*. Harlow: Longman.

Thorpe, D, et al. (1980) *Out of Care: The Community Support of Juvenile Offenders*. London: Allen and Unwin.

Tonkinson, R. (1991) *The Mardu Aborigines: Living the Dream in Australia's Desert*. Orlando: Rinehart Winston.

van Senden Theis, S. (1924) *How Foster Children Turn Out*. New York: State Charities Aid Association.

Vinson, A. (1987) 'Child Abuse and the Media', paper presented at Sydney University Institute of Criminology, April.

Wattam, C. (1992) *Making a Case in Child Protection*. Harlow: Longman.

WELSTAT (1987a) *Child Maltreatment Standards*. Sydney: Department of Family and Community Services, NSW.

WELSTAT (1987b) *Child Protection Systems in Australia*. Sydney: Department of Family and Community Services, NSW.

Williams, R. (1982) *A Report on the Child Life Protection Unit and the Development of a Unitary System of Child Protection by Integration with the Field*. Perth: Department for Community Welfare.

Wise, S. (1989) *Child Abuse Procedures and Social Work Practice: An Ethnographic Approach*. Unpublished PhD Thesis, University of Manchester.

Woolley, P. V. and Evans, W. A. (1955) 'Significance of skeletal lesions in infants resembling those of traumatic origin', *Journal of the American Medical Association*, 158, 539–43.

Wurfel, L. J. and Maxwell, G. M. (1965) 'The battered child syndrome in South Australia', *Australian Paediatric Journal*, 1, 127–30.

Zerk, G. (1975) 'Child abuse legislation to facilitate enquiry and treatment', *The Battered Child*. Proceedings of the First National Australian Conference, 37–40, Mt Lawley, Western Australia. Perth: Department for Community Welfare.

Index

CHILD ABUSE REVISITED
CHILDREN, SOCIETY AND SOCIAL WORK

David M. Cooper

Child abuse work has attracted an enormous amount of bad publicity in recent years which has increasingly brought serious disadvantages not only to the children and families involved, but also to social and other workers in the field. Social workers have been manoeuvred into a narrower form of state intervention that may be counter-productive at times, leaving them widely criticized and demoralized and thus less able to help children.

This book presents a major and possibly controversial re-assessment of child abuse work in Britain since the early 1970s. It draws on evidence from a wide range of areas: recent social and political history, changes in child care law, the theory base for much child abuse work, the professional development of social work and the national pressure group PAIN (Parents Against INjustice). These areas are explored before moving on to a proposed alternative approach to child abuse work where prevention and support are given priority over 'panic and rescue'. The legal, political and professional implications of this alternative approach are considered in detail, making the book a valuable resource for a wide range of students and professionals interested in child abuse and child care law.

Contents
Preface – Acknowledgements – Society – Law – Social work – Knowledge – Parents – Children – The future – Bibliography – Index.

128pp   0 335 15726 2 (Paperback)   0 335 15727 0 (Hardback)

WORKING WITH CHILD ABUSE
SOCIAL WORK PRACTICE AND THE CHILD ABUSE SYSTEM

Brian Corby

Child abuse, and the official response to it, is currently a highly emotive issue. Child abuse has been recognized as a major social problem in Britain since the early 1970s but recent much-publicized deaths and, in particular, the report of the inquiry into the death of Jasmine Beckford have added to the pressure to improve our methods of coping with child abuse. Most of this pressure is falling on the statutory social work departments.

Brian Corby draws on his four years research study (of the day-to-day practice of social workers with families suspected of abusing their children) to critically examine current practice and the overall system developed in the 1970s for dealing with the problem of child abuse. The questions he raises include:

- does the child abuse system work in a reactive rather than a positive fashion?
- are social workers denied autonomy, fearful of making mistakes and too concerned with covering themselves?
- are parents suspected of child abuse too easily deprived of their civil liberties or are children inadequately protected against them?
- is the case conference a venue for inter-professional rivalry rather than an effective forum for reaching decisions about child abuse cases?
- do social workers currently have the necessary specialist knowledge and training to deal with child abuse cases effectively?
- are crisis interventions successful – what are their longer term outcomes?

In the light of this research and analysis, Brian Corby goes on to suggest important policy changes in our handling of the complexities of child abuse. He provides essential reading for trainees and professionals in the field of child abuse and for students of social work and administration.

Contents
Introduction – Child abuse: the context – The research issues – The parents, their children and the social workers – Detecting and investigating child abuse – Official decision-making at case conferences – After the case conference: working with families – What happens to abuse cases: outcomes after two years – Present and future – Appendices – Index.

176pp   0 335 15395 X (Paperback)   0 335 15396 8 (Hardback)

THE EMOTIONAL AND PSYCHOLOGICAL ABUSE OF CHILDREN

Kieran O'Hagan

Recent public inquiries, research and new legislation have all compelled child care professionals to widen their focus beyond the narrow parameters of the physical health of the child. Emotional and psychological health are now rightly regarded as crucial. This book aims to enable practitioners to articulate precisely what is meant by the terms 'emotional' and 'psychological' abuse; to be able to identify it, and to formulate effective strategies for dealing with it. The author identifies certain categories of parent and parental circumstances which are conducive to the emotional and psychological abuse of children. He makes clear however, that parents are not the only carers who abuse children in this way. He explores such abuse within an historical, global and cultural context, and examines recent inquiry reports which have exposed the emotional and psychological abuse of children within the child care and child protection systems. Numerous case histories are provided, and one is explored in detail within the context of new child care legislation.

Contents

Court out – Knowing or feeling – Definitions of emotional and psychological abuse – Global, cultural and historical contexts – Case histories – Parents – Observation, communication and assessment – The emotional and psychological abuse of Michelle – Implications for management and training – Bibliography – Index.

176pp   0 335 09884 3 (Paperback)   0 335 09889 4 (Hardback)

SURVIVING SECRETS
THE EXPERIENCE OF ABUSE FOR THE CHILD, THE ADULT AND THE HELPER

Moira Walker

In recent years considerable attention has been paid to the subject of abuse in childhood. Less attention has been paid to what happens to the vast number of women and men who have reached adulthood with this experience haunting them. Moira Walker overviews the experience and its implications, dealing with physical, sexual and psychological abuse. An essential part of the content is based on interviews with survivors of child abuse, voicing their views on the effects of the experience and the effectiveness of the help offered. At the same time, *Surviving Secrets* seeks to understand the context in which abuse takes place, the society which itself contains and sustains abuse at various levels. It is a moving account of the experience and effects of childhood abuse, and a handbook for all those in the caring professions, in voluntary organizations and elsewhere who are helping survivors of abuse.

Contents
Introduction – A web of secrets: generations of abuse – Adults reflect: the child's experience – Childhood abuse: the adult's experience – Sharing secrets: the child's and the adult's experience – The development of Multiple Personality Disorder – Stages in the process of counselling and therapy – Particular issues in the process of therapy – Issues for the helper – References – Index.

224pp   0 335 09763 4 (Paperback)   0 335 09764 2 (Hardback)